The Way of the Psychonaut

Encyclopedia for Inner Journeys

Volume Two

Stanislav Grof, M.D., Ph.D.

The Way of the Psychonaut
Encyclopedia for Inner Journeys

Volume Two

MAPS
Multidisciplinary Association for Psychedelic Studies (MAPS)

100% of the profits from the sale of this book will be used to fund psychedelic and medical marijuana research and education. This MAPS-published book was made possible by the generous support of Dr. Bronner's.

The Way of the Psychonaut: Encyclopedia for Inner Journeys Volume Two
ISBN-13: 978-0-9982765-5-7
ISBN-10: 0-9982765-5-3
Copyright © 2019 by Stanislav Grof, M.D., Ph.D.
Multidisciplinary Association for Psychedelic Studies (MAPS)
P.O. Box 8423, Santa Cruz, CA 95061
Phone: 831.429.6362, Fax 831.429.6370
Email: askmaps@maps.org

Book and cover design: Sarah Jordan
Cover image: Brigitte Grof
Printed in the United States of America by McNaughton & Gunn, Saline, MI

About the cover image: "Shiva Nataraja appeared in my most important psychedelic sessions and I consider it to be my own personal Archetype. I also had many extraordinary experiences with Swami Muktananda around Shiva, described in *When the Impossible Happens*. This special image of Shiva was taken in my house in Big Sur by Brigitte, at the time when I lived for fourteen years at Esalen, a very important period in my life."—Stanislav Grof

Dedication

For Brigitte,
love of my life and my other half, who has brought light,
shakti, inspiration, enthusiasm, and unconditional love into my world,
wonderful wife and ideal companion on inner and outer journeys—with
deep gratitude and admiration for who you are and what you stand for.

"The expression…*psychonaut* is well chosen, because the inner space is equally endless and mysterious as outer space; and just as astronauts are not able to remain in outer space, similarly in the inner world, people must return to everyday reality. Also, both journeys require good preparation in order to be carried out with minimum danger and become truly beneficial."
—Albert Hofmann, *Memories of a Psychonaut* (2003)

In celebration of the seventy-fifth anniversary of Albert Hofmann's discovery of LSD-25.

"The scientific revolution that started 500 years ago and led to our current civilization and modern technologies has made tremendous progress in the last 100 years. Today we take for granted exploration of outer space, digital technologies, virtual reality, artificial intelligence, and communication at the speed of light. Despite all this progress the nature of fundamental reality eludes us. If you do an internet search on the open questions in science you will discover that the two most important questions regarding the nature of reality remain unanswered—What is the universe made of? What is the biological basis of consciousness? It is obvious that these questions are related. To know existence we must be aware of existence!

More than any person I can think of Stan Grof has pioneered our understanding of inner reality and its relationship to the experience of so called outer reality over the last sixty years. These volumes systematically explore his journey from personal to transpersonal to transcendent domains of existence. If anyone wanted to delve into the mysteries of existence and experience then ignoring this monumental work would be reckless.

What is the meaning of life and death? How does birth trauma influence our experience of life? Do other realms of experience beyond our waking "dream" exist? Why do we need to know them in order to alleviate our personal and collective suffering? How does humanity heal itself from its self-inflicted trauma? How do we overcome our fear of death? What is our true nature beyond the experience of mind body and universe?

Stan Grof is a giant amongst us and we are fortunate to stand on his shoulders. To call him the Einstein of consciousness would be an understatement. I am deeply personally indebted to him for leading the way. Future generations will forever acknowledge him for helping us wake up from our collective hypnosis that we call everyday reality.

I stayed up all night to read Stan Grof's magnificent magnum opus."

—Deepak Chopra, M.D.

Contents

Foreword
by Rick Doblin, Ph.D.

Dr. Stanislav Grof's first book, originally published in 1975, was *Realms of the Human Unconscious: Observations from LSD Research.* In 1972, I was given a pre-publication manuscript copy of that book by a guidance counselor at New College in Sarasota, Florida (now New College of Florida, the honors college of the State of Florida system). I'd gone to a guidance counselor in the middle of my freshman year at college, at age eighteen, seeking help to integrate a series of challenging LSD and mescaline experiences. At that time, despite the United States' criminalization of all psychedelics in 1970 and the withdrawal of permission for psychedelic research, some people still appreciated psychedelics as legitimate tools for catalyzing personal growth, to balance intellectual knowledge with emotional and spiritual development. At New College, I was able to speak honestly to my college guidance counselor, and he was able to hand me a copy of a book that was to completely change my life.

Realms of the Human Unconscious was my first introduction to psychedelic research. Before discovering it, I'd been unaware of how much psychedelic research had already been conducted around the world for several decades before the science was halted for political reasons. What so inspired me about Stan's book was the way in which he demonstrated that, in his words, "psychedelics would be to the study of the mind what the telescope is to astronomy and the microscope is to biology." Stan's cartography of the unconscious was a masterful work of scholarship that placed him in the company of Freud and Jung and other groundbreaking, historic pioneers in other fields.

Stan used the lens of science to rationally and profoundly investigate areas of human experience which are usually considered to be in the realm of religion. Stan's breadth of knowledge of science, medicine, culture, religion, mythology, art, and symbolism enabled him to turn the direct experience he gained from assisting and observing many thousands of LSD experiences into a new map of the human unconscious. Without dogma and with a fierce allegiance to the scientific method, Stan illuminated fundamental aspects of the human experience, including the unitive mystical experience—the feeling of existing in intimate connection with something much greater than ourselves .

For me, a politically-minded eighteen-year-old Vietnam War draft resister, indirectly traumatized by the Holocaust and by the threat of a globally devastating nuclear war, the new understanding I gained from Stan of the reality and validity of the unitive mystical experience provided me with new hope. I began to believe that if millions or billions of people could have such an experience—the essence of which was the recognition of our shared humanity and our unity with all life, nature, and matter—that the differences between us in religion, race, nationality, culture, gender, class, and on and on, could be celebrated rather than feared, and empathy and compassion for others would increase.

Yet what motivated me the most about Stan's first book, and indeed his whole life's work, was his focus on healing, on the importance of psychotherapy. The reality check for all the theories and cartographies that Stan created is whether they can be used effectively to help people live fuller and more loving lives in this world. All too often, spiritual and religious ideas are focused elsewhere than on this earth. Stan's psychiatric orientation grounded him in using his knowledge and experience to reduce human suffering, and to increase joy and love.

Reading Stan's work persuaded me of the tragic consequences of the political suppression of psychedelic research. It also moved me from despair to hope, from uncertainty about my path in life to certainty, to my decision to devote my life to bringing back psychedelic research, to continue to deepen my own psychedelic psychotherapy work, to become a psychedelic researcher, and to become a legal psychedelic therapist.

My life is just one of many that have been deeply influenced by Stanislav Grof's work. It's with a sense of life come full circle that the Multidisciplinary Association for Psychedelic Studies (MAPS)—the non-profit I founded in 1986—is now publishing *The Way of the Psychonaut: An Encyclopedia for Inner Journeys,* perhaps (though hopefully not) his final book. With this new book summarizing his life's work, forty-four years after the publication of his first book, Stan is inspiring new generations to continue the journey of exploration and healing that he helped to pioneer.

Stan's newest book is a gift of wisdom and guidance at a time of global crisis, of danger and opportunity. Humanity is in a race between catastrophe and consciousness. *The Way of the Psychonaut* is a priceless tool that has the potential to help consciousness triumph.

Rick Doblin, Ph.D.
May 2019

The Way of the Psychonaut

Encyclopedia for Inner Journeys

Volume Two

VII

Self-Exploration and Therapy with Psychedelics:
Importance of Set and Setting

The history of attempts to use LSD and other psychedelics as therapeutic agents has been filled with trial and error. Although psychedelics have been used in many different ways, these efforts were initially met with very little success. A decisive turning point in this history, however, was the discovery of how the success or failure of the therapeutic experiment critically depends on extra-pharmacological factors, which have been called the "set and setting." These include who administers the substance, the personality of the subject, the intention and purpose of the experiment, the interpersonal and physical environment, and even the collective astrological transits and individual transits of the persons involved.

Much of this confusion was caused by old-paradigm thinking about a substance which, properly understood and used, offers unprecedented and revolutionary alternatives to conventional methods and strategies of therapy. The first suggestion that LSD might have therapeutic potential can be found in Werner Stoll's historic paper "LSD-25: A Fantasticum from the Ergot Group" (Stoll 1947). In the context of Stoll's paper, the suggestion that this substance might be tried as a therapeutic agent appeared only as a fleeting comment, without any further specification.

The first actual therapeutic experiment was reported two years later by

Swiss psychiatrist and psychotherapist Gion Condrau. He explored the possibility that LSD might be an antidepressant and followed the formula for the treatment of depression by opium tincture: he administered increasing and then decreasing doses of this substance (Condrau 1949). The results were very disappointing. Condrau actually described occasional deepening rather than alleviation of symptoms. This is understandable since LSD, properly used, heals homeopathically—by temporary intensification of symptoms.

Equally disappointing were attempts of other researchers to follow this approach or use isolated, medium dosages of LSD, testing its effects as a chemical antidepressant. Two therapeutic experiments were based on the clinical observation that acute psychotic episodes respond better to therapy than slowly developing episodes with few symptoms. The idea here was to use LSD as an agent, activating the symptoms and then applying "real therapy." Thus, Jost and Vicari's failed attempt to use LSD seems, in retrospect, appalling and criminal to those of us who had personal experiences with this substance. These authors activated the symptoms of the patients with LSD and then applied electroshocks in the middle of their sessions (Jost 1957, Jost and Vicari 1958). Sandison, Spencer, and Whitelaw followed the same strategy but used the administration of Thorazine instead of electroshocks (Sandison, Spencer, and Whitelaw 1954).

Another extreme example of using LSD in the spirit of the old paradigm was to apply it as shock therapy, similar to electroconvulsive therapy and insulin comas—to administer it as a "single overwhelming dose" without any preparation or psychotherapy. The worst of these experiments was conducted in 1968 by Canadian psychiatrist Elliot Barker, Assistant Superintendent and Clinical Director at a maximum security hospital for the "dangerous mentally ill" in Ontario. Barker locked naked male offenders in a room for eleven days and gave them large amounts of LSD (2,000 mcg) in combination with antiepileptics. They had to suck food through straws in the wall and were encouraged to express by screaming their violent fantasies (Barker 19). Recidivism actually significantly increased after this "therapy." Barker was fired, but not because of his LSD experiments; it was in response to the inmates' rebellion against him. The increased recidivism of his experimental subjects also did not play a role in his firing; the follow-up was done at a later date.

One of the programs that started as shock therapy actually changed into the form of therapy referred to as "psychedelic," as used by many American and Canadian therapists. It consisted of a small number of sessions with large dosages of psychedelics and the goal was to induce a transcendental experience. European therapists preferred a different approach, which was called "psycholytic" (resolving tensions and conflicts in the psyche, from the Greek *lysis,* meaning dissolution). It consisted of a long series of psychedelic sessions with low to medium dosages and was strongly influenced by Freud's psychoanalysis.

The events that led to the development of true psychedelic therapy make a fascinating story. In 1959, Ditman and Whittlesey published an article in the Archives of General Psychiatry that showed some superficial similarities between the LSD experience and delirium tremens (Ditman and Whittlesey 1959). Canadian psychiatrists Abram Hoffer and Humphrey Osmond discussed this article while flying overnight on a "red eye express" and in a hypnagogic state of consciousness came up with the idea of using terrifying bad trips with LSD for the treatment of alcoholism. This was based on the clinical observation that the experience of delirium tremens is so horrible that it tends to deter alcoholics from further drinking and often represents a radical turning point in their lives.

Inspired by this discussion, Hoffer and Osmond started a program in their hospital in Saskatoon, Saskatchewan, which was designed to induce the worst possible experiences ("bad trips") in alcoholic patients by trying to mimic delirium tremens through the administration of LSD. Then the story became even more interesting when the legendary Al Hubbard, the most mysterious person in psychedelic history, unexpectedly appeared on the scene. It is very difficult to adequately describe Al Hubbard; his biography reads like a script for a Hollywood action movie.

In 1919, when he was not yet twenty years old, Hubbard—allegedly guided by otherworldly forces—invented the Hubbard Energy Transformer. It was a battery that allegedly drew energy directly from a radioactive ore; its technology could not be explained by the science of the day. The Seattle Post-Intelligencer reported that Hubbard's invention, hidden in a small box (11" x 14"), had powered a ferry-sized vessel around Seattle's Portico Bay nonstop for three days. Hubbard sold fifty percent of the patent to the Radium Corporation of Pittsburg for $75,000. The list of his affiliations and jobs is extraordinary. At various times he worked for the Canadian Special Services; the United States Justice Department; the United States Bureau of Alcohol, Tobacco, Firearms, and Explosives; the Office of Strategic Services; and allegedly also for the CIA.

During prohibition, he had a job as a Seattle taxi driver. With a sophisticated ship-to-shore communication system hidden in the trunk of his cab, he helped rum-runners successfully ferry booze past the U.S. and Canadian Coast Guards. He was proclaimed the "Bootleg King of the Northwest," then was caught by the FBI, and went to prison for eighteen months. For a short time, he also held a job as janitor at the Stanford Research Institute in California. In his early forties, Hubbard realized his lifelong ambition of becoming a millionaire. By 1950, he was the scientific director of the Uranium Corporation of Vancouver, owned his own fleet of aircraft, a 100-foot yacht, and Dayman Island in British Columbia.

His nickname "Captain Hubbard" came from his Master of Sea Vessels certification and a stint in the U.S. Merchant Marine Institute. He also had another nickname, "Johnny Appleseed of LSD," because he gave LSD to an estimated 6,000 people, including scientists, politicians, intelligence officials, diplomats, and church figures. According to his friends, he was able to hold naked wires from a 120 volt socket, encouraging them to do the same. When they got shocked, he gave them the advice: "You cannot fight electricity, you have to go with it." Hubbard kept appearing and disappearing at different places carrying a small black briefcase and had the reputation of being able to bilocate.

In 1953, Al Hubbard surprised Humphrey Osmond by inviting him for lunch at the Royal Vancouver Yacht Club. During their discussion, Hubbard expressed strong criticism of the therapeutic strategy that Osmond and Hoffer were using in their LSD treatment for alcoholics. He insisted that the approach should be the exact opposite; what these patients needed was a profound life-transforming transcendental experience. To achieve it, they should run sessions in a beautiful setting, decorated with flowers and universal spiritual symbols, and play spiritual music. Hoffer and Osmond followed his advice and the treatment results improved considerably (Hoffer 1970). This strategy became the standard for LSD treatment of alcoholics and addicts in Canada and the United States under the somewhat tautological name "psychedelic therapy."

Abram Hoffer (1917–2009), a Canadian psychiatrist and pioneer in psychedelic therapy known for his adrenochrome hypothesis of schizophrenia (top).

Humphry Osmond (1917–2004), a British-American psychiatrist, who coined the term "psychedelic" (bottom left).

Al Hubbard (1901–1982), a legendary mysterious figure in psychedelic history, known as the "Johnny Appleseed of LSD," who introduced LSD to over six thousand people (bottom right).

In the mid-1960s, the Czechoslovakian pharmaceutical company Spofa, the only producer of pure LSD besides the Swiss Sandoz, sent Al Hubbard to me to be interviewed. They wanted me to tell them if Hubbard was known in scientific circles, since he came to Prague to purchase 2g of LSD for the Hollywood Hospital in Vancouver. The fact that he had co-written a paper entitled "The Psychedelic Experience" (Stolaroff, Harman and Hubbard 1964) with Myron Stolaroff and Willis Harman turned out to be adequate proof of his legitimacy for the Czech authorities. His purchase of 2g of Czech LSD was a bargain; at that time, an ampoule with 100 mcg cost 10 U.S. cents.

During our discussion, Al opened his black briefcase and showed me authorized documents from both the U.S. and Canadian governments allowing him to transport any substances across the borders of these two countries. I also got the chance to ask him a question that had been on my mind since I heard about his advice on the use of LSD he had given to Osmond and Hoffer: how did he obtain that information? The answer was fascinating. He told me that ten years before Albert Hofmann discovered the psychedelic effects of LSD, he (Al Hubbard) had a vision of an archetypal angelic being who told him that a unique substance would be discovered in Switzerland and described the way it should be used.

In the summer of 1967, during my visit to Palo Alto, California, psychedelic pioneer Myron Stolaroff invited me to join him on a trip in his Cessna four-seater airplane to visit his close friend Al Hubbard. We flew

Myron Stolaroff (1920–2013), a psychedelic pioneer who researched the effects of LSD and mescaline on creativity.

over the Sierra Nevada mountain range and visited Al in his rocky retreat in Onion Valley. The three of us took an afternoon hiking trip in the mountains, during which Myron kept telling me fantastic stories about Al's life and abilities. At one point, to my surprise, he told me that he saw him as a great spiritual being who was on par with Jesus Christ.

The general conclusion from the early therapeutic experiments with LSD was that this substance is not *per se* a chemotherapeutic agent. To be effective, it has to be administered in combination with psychotherapy and in a specially structured environment. But even here, the history of trials and errors continued. When LSD was administered in small dosages as an adjunct to psychotherapy in a series of sessions, it did not noticeably enhance the therapeutic process. Instead, it significantly prolonged the sessions and occasionally actually intensified the symptoms. It was definitely better to reverse the emphasis—to increase the dose of LSD and use psychotherapy for processing and integration of the experience.

Another unsuccessful therapeutic attempt was hypnodelic therapy, a procedure developed by Levine and Ludwig for the treatment of alcoholics and drug addicts; it was a combination of LSD administration and hypnosis (Levine and Ludwig 1967). The patients were trained as hypnotic subjects and the latency period of the psychedelic effect was used for the induction of hypnosis. The idea was that at the time of the onset of the substance's effect, the patients would be in a hypnotic trance. Hypnotic suggestions could then be used to encourage them to let go, surrender to the experience, overcome feelings of fear, and direct them to specific aspects of their biography. The procedure was complex and time-consuming, requiring hypnotic training of both the clients and the experimenters, and it did not bring the expected favorable effects.

An ambitious, though poorly conceived, study testing the results of hypnodelic therapy brought devastating results. The authors assigned 176 patients to one of four groups:

1. "Psychedelic therapy" with LSD
2. Hypnodelic therapy
3. Administration of medium dosages of LSD alone
4. No specific therapy (just "milieu therapy")

In addition, half of each group received the medication Antabuse after the termination of treatment. The authors did not find any difference in therapeutic results between any of the groups and the overall remission rate was extremely low. In a six-month follow-up, between 70% and 80% of the patients were drinking and in the one-year follow-up, this number rose to 80%–90% (Ludwig, Levine and Stark 1970). Therapists in this study were mostly unmotivated residents, inadequately trained in any of the used modalities. An incisive critique of this study by Charles Savage can be found in my book *LSD Psychotherapy* (Grof 2001).

Some therapists, inspired by the early work of Sigmund Freud and Joseph Breuer (Freud and Breuer 1936), explored the possibility of using LSD as an abreactive agent, but this did not find acceptance as a specialized form of LSD therapy (Robinson 1963). Abreaction became very popular in WWII for the treatment of traumatic war neuroses but was declared ineffective in the therapy of psychoneuroses (Fenichel 1945). LSD brought abreaction back to therapy as an important therapeutic mechanism, but not as a prime goal or specific treatment modality.

London psychoanalysts Joyce Martin and Pauline McCririck developed a very interesting procedure which they called fusion therapy. It was designed for the treatment of patients who suffered childhood abandonment and emotional deprivation in their infancy. Joyce and Pauline administered medium dosages of LSD to their clients and had them lie on a couch in a semi-darkened room covered with a blanket. They then positioned their bodies parallel to the clients' bodies and held them in close embrace, like a good mother would do with her child.

Pauline and Joyce's 1965 presentation at the Amityville conference on LSD psychotherapy effectively dichotomized the therapists in the audience who were listening to their lecture and watching their video. Some of these therapists considered the fusion therapy as a very logical approach to a serious clinical problem that is beyond the reach of verbal therapy; others abhorred the danger that such close contact between the therapist and client would cause to the transference/countertransference relationship. Fusion therapy did not become a therapeutic trend and remained a unique experiment of two women, which was closely connected to their extraordinary personalities. Therapists, particularly men, did not feel comfortable venturing into this new risky territory behind the closed doors of their private offices.

I had the opportunity to spend a week in London with Pauline and Joyce in their clinic on Welbeck Street as well as a chance to experience two sessions of fusion therapy with Pauline, one in London, the other in Amsterdam. My own experiences and interviews with their patients convinced me that this was a very effective way of healing the trauma caused by anaclitic deprivation or what I call "trauma by omission." I introduced the fusion therapy into our work with psychedelics and also into the breathwork workshops and training and found it remarkably effective and helpful. My experiences and adventures with Pauline are described in the chapter "The Dying Queen" in my book *When the Impossible Happens* (Grof 2006).

The initial attempts to use LSD in group therapy were also unsuccessful. Small dosages given to patients in Eric Berne's type of transactional analysis did not seem to improve the group dynamics in any significant way. When the dosages were increased, the patients tended to focus on their own experiences, lost interest in focused group work, and many of them disappeared into their inner world. Eventually, group therapy with psychedelics developed in two directions:

1. Aggregate psychedelic therapy, in which a larger number of people took psychedelic substances together, but there was no effort during the sessions to work with the group as a whole. The main advantage of this approach is economical, considering the difference in the ratio between the number of the therapists or facilitators and the number of group participants. This approach is particularly useful in groups of experienced individuals who do not need much assistance and are capable of tolerating the noises made by other participants and can integrate them into their own experience. Under these circumstances, teams of two skilled facilitators have been able to work with groups of fourteen to sixteen people, particularly if these groups were meeting repeatedly and their members had developed a sense of community and mutual trust. The efficacy of this type of work can be enhanced if it is complemented with post-session group sharing and processing work.

An extreme example of aggregate psychedelic therapy was **psychosynthesis,** the marathon group psychotherapy process developed by Mexican psychiatrist Salvador Roquet (not to be confused with the psychospiritual system of the same name created by Italian psychotherapist Roberto Assagioli). Under Salvador's guidance, large groups of people (up to thirty) met in all-night sessions *("convivials")*. Participants were carefully selected with the explicit intention to make the group as heterogeneous as possible with regard to gender, age, clinical picture, length of previous treatment, and the psychedelic substance administered (Roquet 1971).

Some of the clients received medicinal plants, such as a variety of psilocybin-containing mushrooms, peyote, and *Datura ceratocaulum,* while others were given psychedelic substances such as LSD and ketamine. The purpose of the selection process was to provide a wide range of experiences and people for projection and imaginary roles—paternal figures, sibling substitutes, and sexual objects. During the sessions, Salvador subjected group participants to a sensory overload using disturbing, emotionally evocative films featuring images from Nazi Germany and sexual, aggressive, and sadomasochistic scenes.

Salvador's goal was to facilitate the experiences of ego death and rebirth. He had an eccentric personality and was a very controversial figure among

Mexican psychedelic pioneer Salvador Roquet (1920–1995) and Stanislav Grof at the 1976 Third International Transpersonal Conference held in Inari, Finland.

his colleagues. He invited a group of Mexican psychiatrists and psychologists to a party in this home and served, unbeknownst to them, sandwiches with psychedelic mushrooms. Salvador's therapeutic strategy was closely tied to his personality and remained a curiosity in psychedelic history.

Encouraging projection and using external stimuli for enforcing a specific type of experience tends to take the subjects' attention away from focused introspection and interferes with the spontaneous self-healing intelligence of the psyche. The unconscious certainly has the capacity to take us to the dark recesses of our unconscious, including the experience of annihilation, death and rebirth, if that is a natural trajectory of the healing process. Attempts to create a "bad trip" and facilitate disintegration can be a deterrent, however, and discourage patients from continuing therapy. This strategy might also interfere with the trajectory of a session that would otherwise take the person to a deeply ecstatic and healing mystical experience (a "Neptunian" rather than "Plutonic" type of transpersonal experience).

In 1974, Roquet was charged with drug trafficking and crimes against the health of his patients. The charges were dropped on April 10, 1975, after a Supreme Court trial during which he was declared not guilty. He also spent nine months in the infamous Black Palace, Palacio de Lecumberri, Mexico City's prison of no escape.

2. Psychedelic Rituals. The second way of utilizing psychedelic substances in groups is in the form of a ritual, which is the way they are used in many native cultures: the use of peyote in the Native American Church and by the Huichol Indians, of psilocybe mushrooms by the Mazatecs, of ayahuasca by ayahuasqueros, members of the Santo Daime religion and União do Vegetal in Brazil, or of iboga by natives in Central Africa. These ritual events are usually structured; they might require special attire, maintaining a certain position, prescribed forms of behavior, group dancing or chanting, etc.

British anthropologist Victor Turner, who dedicated his life to the study of native rituals, concluded that people who share participation in rituals involving holotropic states of consciousness tend to develop strong bonding, or a sense of *"communitas"* (Turner 1969). For this reason, this modality could be very important for industrial civilizations, since one of the most salient features of modern society is alienation.

We are alienated from our bodies, from each other, from nature, from the universe, and from the Divine. Rituals using psychedelics or other forms of holotropic states could become a powerful way of overcoming alienation. The holotropic state of consciousness experienced by the participants in a ritual also lifts the situation out of the everyday context. It dissolves the hierarchical structure of the society, at least for the time of the ritual, and creates a sense of equality. It is important to point out that native group rituals have profound social dynamics and are interesting from the anthropological point of view; however, because of their mostly extraverted orientation, they are usually not conducive to deeply focused self-exploration.

In the course of the complicated history described above, the use of LSD for self-exploration and psychotherapy for individuals developed into two main modalities: psycholytic therapy and psychedelic therapy.

1. Psycholytic therapy is a name that was coined by British psychiatrist and psychotherapist Ronald Sandison. It refers to releasing tensions and resolving conflicts in the psyche. It has been used mostly by European therapists (Hanscarl Leuner, Wilhelm Arendsen Hein, John Buckman and Thomas M. Ling, Milan Hausner, Juraj and Sonia Styk, Peter Bauman, Peter Gasser, and others). It is based on psychoanalytic theory, but without the principles and restrictions of Freudian praxis, such as the therapist's position, prohibition of acting out, not answering questions, strategic use of silence, not touching, etc.

Psycholytic treatment consists of a series of fifteen to a hundred sessions with medium dosages of LSD-25 in one- to two-week intervals. The type and extent of support provided for patients during the sessions varies. I myself stayed with my patients for five–six hours and then put them into the care of my nurses, who all had experienced training sessions with LSD, and of other patients in the ward, who were all participating in the research and had personal experiences with LSD.

Hanscarl Leuner's system was on the other side of the spectrum. His patients were generally left alone and could use a bell to call the nurses if they needed help. The rest of the therapists whom I knew personally were somewhere in between; they spent part of the sessions with the clients and used nurses and students as sitters.

Many of the psycholytic therapists kept verbal contact with the patients;

they expected a report from them about their experience and made occasional comments or even attempted to offer interpretations. The patients were allowed to keep their eyes open, make eye contact with the therapist and look around. They were encouraged to describe what they were seeing and how their perception of the world was being affected. Many therapists also asked the patients to bring photographs of their spouses, partners, and members of their family of origin to the sessions and look at them in the later stages of their experience.

The psycholytic strategy had its advantages and drawbacks. It was ideal for the exploration of the dynamics of the psyche. When I used it in the early stage of my research, it made it possible for me to explore sequentially different levels of the unconscious. It was a process that one of my patients called "chemoarcheology" and another the "onion peeling of the

Hanscarl Leuner (1919–1996), German psychiatrist and psychedelic pioneer, author of a psychotherapeutic method called Guided Affective Imagery (GAI).

unconscious." I was also able to study and understand the logic of the optical illusions that my patients were experiencing—why they saw me and the environment transformed in a particular way at different times of their sessions and stages of their therapy.

I collected literally hundreds of examples of this process, which showed the determination and overdetermination of LSD visions and optical illusions. They involved essentially the same mechanisms that Freud found when he was analyzing the dream work. I described and explained many of these transformations in my book *Realms of the Human Unconscious* (Grof 1975). The most important and valuable yield from this research strategy was the discovery of the self-healing intelligence of the psyche, which guided the therapeutic process to the most important unconscious memories underlying the symptoms. The gradual unfolding of the psyche in sequential sessions provided a unique opportunity for charting a new map of the psyche and discovering its dynamic governing principles: COEX systems, Basic Perinatal Matrices (BPMs), and archetypal templates in the collective unconscious.

However, the use of lower dosages, the fact that the patients spent significant parts of the sessions with their eyes open, and frequent talking were not the most effective way to achieve positive and fast therapeutic results. I realized that the price which I paid for my curiosity and for these fascinating insights was the slowing down of therapeutic progress. This strategy diverted the process of focused vertical exploration, which is the most effective method for finding the causes of emotional problems, to horizontal probing. This was intellectually interesting for me as well as my patients, but also unfortunately served the patients' resistance and avoidance of deeper painful issues.

When I realized that, I changed the strategy of therapy—I increased the dosages and internalized the sessions by introducing eyeshades, limiting the verbal exchange, and using music to deepen the experience. This modification brought the strategy close to the "psychedelic therapy" developed in Canada that I described earlier.

2. Psychedelic therapy is the other popular way of conducting treatment with psychedelic substances. It consists of a small number of sessions with large doses of LSD: 400-600 mcg (a "single overwhelming dose"). The experiences are strictly internalized by the use of eyeshades and headphones. The treatment rooms are decorated with beautiful paintings and flowers and high-fidelity spiritual music is played throughout the sessions. Supervision is usually provided by two facilitators, preferably a male and female team.

Preparation for the sessions consists of several hours of drug-free interviews. The purpose of these sessions is getting to know the patients' life histories and their symptoms, developing a good therapeutic relationship, and explaining to them the effects of the psychedelic substance they will receive. After the sessions, the therapists schedule drug-free interviews to discuss the patients' experiences and help them with the integration. This approach has been practiced mostly by Canadian and American therapists: Abram Hoffer, Humphry Osmond, Ross MacLean, Duncan Blewett, Ralph Metzner, Richard Alpert, Timothy Leary, Myron Stolaroff, James Fadiman, Robert Mogar, Willis Harman, and others. We also used this strategy in our projects at the Maryland Psychiatric Research Center (MPRC) in the treatment of neurotics, alcoholics, narcotic drug addicts and cancer patients, as well as in LSD training sessions of mental health professionals (Pahnke et al. 1970, Grof 2001).

Using this approach brings very impressive therapeutic results; the life of many patients can be dramatically changed by one to three psychedelic sessions, but the mechanisms of this change remain obscure. This situation resembles the changes that David Rosen found in survivors of suicidal jumps from the Golden Gate Bridge and the San Francisco-Oakland Bay Bridge (Rosen 1975). However, using the observations from serial psycholytic sessions, it becomes possible to imagine that the mechanisms underlying these changes might be accelerated and intensified by the high-dose psychedelic therapy and therefore produce these results.

Representatives of the two approaches of using psychedelic substances expressed criticisms of the opposing camp. Psycholytic therapists argued that psychedelic therapists avoid important biographical issues and cause "spiritual bypass." Psychedelic therapists criticized psycholytic therapists for "nitpicking," dwelling unnecessarily on unimportant biographical issues, and wasting the opportunity for a life-transforming psychedelic peak experience.

After this brief historical review of the therapeutic experiments with LSD, we can now discuss the basic principles that increase the benefits and reduce the potential risks of using LSD. Many of these principles apply to other psychedelics as well.

Microdosing with LSD

We can start with microdosing, a strategy which has been recommended and researched by James Fadiman. Jim is currently conducting a study on microdosing with LSD in order to improve normal functioning (Fadiman 2017). Microdosing (or sub-perceptual dosing) means taking a sub-threshold dose, which for LSD is 10–20 micrograms. The purpose of microdosing is not to experience a non-ordinary state of consciousness, but to enhance normal cognitive and executive functionality *(nootropic effect).*

In this study, the volunteers self-administer the drug approximately every third day. They then self-report perceived effects on their daily duties and relationships. Volunteers participating in the study include a wide variety of scientific and artistic professionals and students. So far, the reports suggest that, in general, the subjects experience normal functioning but with increased focus, creativity and emotional clarity, as well as slightly enhanced physical performance. Albert Hofmann was aware of microdosing and called it "the most under-researched area of psychedelics."

James Fadiman, a psychedelic pioneer specializing in the effects of psychedelics on creativity and the effects of microdosing.

Recreational Use of LSD and Other Psychedelics

People who know their reaction to LSD can take small doses (25–75 mcg) to enhance their perception in natural settings, as long as they know the quality and dose of the substance they are taking and their reaction to it. For most people, this dosage range does not interfere with ordinary everyday functioning (with the exception of driving). It can greatly enhance the experience of hiking, swimming in a river, lake or ocean, and bring a new dimension to lovemaking. Sharing this experience with like-minded friends—listening to music, enjoying good food, and talking about philosophical and spiritual matters—can create very special social events.

The model for such parties was set by the *Club des Hashischins* or *Club of the Hashish Eaters,* a Parisian group dedicated to the exploration of drug-induced experiences. It counted among its members the French intellectual elite, including Victor Hugo, Alexandre Dumas, Charles Baudelaire, Gérard de Nerval, Eugène Delacroix, Théophile Gautier, and Honoré de Balzac. Before we embark on the recreational use of psychedelics, it is essential that we test our response to the psychedelic substance of choice in private. The individual response to psychedelics varies greatly and for some people, even the moderate dosages mentioned above can trigger an unexpectedly strong reaction.

Psychotherapy and Self-Exploration with Psychedelics

Once we move to higher dosages, which can activate deep levels of the unconscious, the most productive and safest sessions seem to be those that are internalized, involving minimum contact with the external world with the exception of music. It is important to be in a secluded place where one is not disturbed by external noises and has the freedom to express anything that needs to be expressed. To have a safe and healing session, it is also essential to have a sitter, a person who has had personal experiences with psychedelics and feels comfortable with the process.

Although I am aware that many readers take psychedelics under various conditions for self-exploration or spiritual quest, I will describe here how we conducted sessions with people who had significant emotional problems and came to us for therapy. Some of these precautions would be useful even for sessions run outside of the therapeutic context. A necessary prerequisite for any work with psychedelics or other methods involving holotropic states of consciousness is a good medical examination.

Above all, we need to know if the person is in good cardiovascular condition. It is difficult to predict how intense the emotions that the psychedelic substance will elicit may be. High uncontrolled blood pressure, cardiac arrhythmia, history of strokes or heart attacks, or presence of an aneurysm could be a serious risk. While LSD is biologically a very safe substance, the use of entheogens related to amphetamine, such as MDA, MMDA, MDMA, etc. significantly increases the danger of a cardiovascular episode. The doses should stay in a reasonable range and people with cardiovascular problems should never take substances belonging to this group. There have been reports of fatalities in cases where these precautions were not respected.

Another consideration is the overall physical condition of the person who is taking a psychedelic substance. The sessions, particularly with high dosages, can be emotionally and physically demanding. Current debilitating disease or exhaustion after a disease, recent operations, or injuries can represent a contraindication; such situations have to be individually evaluated. In our Maryland program of LSD therapy for terminal cancer patients, we only screened out patients who had serious cardiovascular problems. Out of more than 200 patients, none died in the session or experienced any physical emergency. And yet, one of these patients died four days after the session. He had skin cancer that had metastasized all through his body, but he had a paralyzing fear of death and seemed to be desperately hanging onto life. In the session, he had a powerful experience of psychospiritual death and rebirth that liberated him from this fear. He died peacefully four days later. After some initial attempts, we decided not to run sessions with patients who had brain tumors. Their experiences seemed to be disjointed and confused and they had difficulties with the conceptual integration of the content.

Pregnancy, particularly when advanced, represents a relative contraindication. Women who experience the reliving of their own birth also often experience themselves as delivering. This actually involves the strong contraction of the uterus; I have worked with women who in a session combining birth and delivery started menstruating in the middle of their cycle. Such contractions could possibly cause premature delivery. Over the years, I have allowed many pregnant women to do Holotropic Breathwork, but we had the agreement that they would not continue if the process began to take the form of birth/delivery. In psychedelic therapy, one cannot make such an agreement and it is wise not to work with women while they are pregnant. However, the postpartum period is an excellent time for psychedelic sessions, since pregnancy and delivery activate the perinatal memories and make them more available.

A good completion of the session often requires bodywork. There are conditions that might require limitation or modification of physical interventions, including post-fracture or post-operation, vertebral disk prolapse, whiplash, osteoporosis, diaphragmatic or umbilical hernia, colostomy, etc. Blockages or pains near the genital area cannot be released by direct bodywork; however, they can be reached indirectly by working with the legs the way it was described in the chapter on Holotropic Breathwork (pp. 365, Volume I).

Another important consideration is the emotional condition of the person who is coming to a psychedelic session or Holotropic Breathwork. If this person has a history of psychiatric hospitalization, particularly a longer one, it is necessary to find out what was the nature of this disorder, what form it took, and the circumstances that led to it. This evaluation has to be done by a person who is familiar with traditional psychiatry and also with transpersonal psychology. In many instances, the condition that was diagnosed as a psychotic episode was a misdiagnosed spiritual emergency. In that case, we did not hesitate to accept such a person into a Holotropic Breathwork workshop or into psychedelic therapy and they usually did not cause any special problems.

Ideally, the therapists or sitters should know the history of the person whom they will accompany in the session—the nature of their prenatal life and birth (if the information is available), the quality of the care they received in their infancy and childhood, main events in their lives, the traumas they remember, and the conflicts of which they are aware. It is very useful to find out if there are any repetitive patterns in their lives concerning relationships with certain categories of people, such as authorities, peers, men or women (interpersonal COEX systems). These tend to be activated and replicated in the sessions and can create problems.

An important function of the pre-session interviews is to establish a good working relationship and trust. If the candidate for the session does not already have information about the effect of the substance they are about to take and about the nature of the experience, we have to briefly provide it. This involves the length of the session, the need to keep the session interiorized, agreement on how we will communicate, and the main categories of experiences they might encounter. Even if the intellectual information about perinatal and transpersonal experiences cannot adequately convey their power and impact, it is extremely important and useful to know about their existence and the form they take.

We have to correct the misconceptions of Western civilization and mainstream psychiatry concerning what is normal and what is "crazy." People need to know that such experiences as reliving one's birth or episodes of prenatal life, ancestral, phylogenetic, and past life memories, or encounters with archetypal beings and visits to archetypal realms are perfectly normal aspects of the experiential spectrum of holotropic states of consciousness. Experiencing them can expand our worldview and be important components in the process of spiritual opening and inner transformation.

Naturally, a critically important element in psychonautics with psychedelics is the nature of the substance we are using and its quality, as well as its dosage. Under current circumstances, unless a reliable source of pure chemicals is available, the best choice might be plant medicines. In some states and countries, one is allowed to grow one's own marijuana, psilocybe mushrooms, peyote, or ayahuasca. The parotid and skin secretions of the toad *Bufo alvarius* can be obtained from experienced and honest healers. Street samples of substances purchased on the black market represent a gamble and can be dangerous. One can never be sure about the nature of the substance, its dose, and quality.

In the 1970s, Stanley Krippner analyzed street samples of alleged LSD and reported the results. The analysis showed the presence of eighteen contaminants, including amphetamines, angel dust, small amounts of strychnine, and even urine. Unfortunately, various degrees of uncertainty will continue to plague psychonauts until psychedelics are decriminalized and available in pure form. In spite of the current renaissance of interest in psychedelics, people who would like to have a legal psychedelic session have to fit in one of the research categories, such as patients with cancer, PTSD, migraine headaches, anxiety states, etc.

Unless testing or comparing various dosages is our intention or is required by our research design, it is preferable to use higher dosages of LSD, around 250–500 mcg. It might mean a somewhat more demanding management of the sessions, but it brings faster and better results and it is safer. Lower dosages tend to activate the symptoms and not bring the experience to a good resolution, because they make it easier to use defense mechanisms. Higher dosages thus usually bring a cleaner resolution.

In the higher dosage range, it is important to keep the session internalized; this makes it possible to see and understand what is emerging from the unconscious and what we are dealing with. Leaving the eyes open and interacting with the environment in high-dose LSD sessions is dangerous and unproductive. It confuses and mixes the inner and outer and makes self-exploration impossible.

I have met people who have taken LSD hundreds of times and had not discovered that the experience had anything to do with their own unconscious. For them, it was like going to a strange movie, where they saw colors and patterns, everything was moving, people's faces and the environment were strangely distorted, and they experienced intense but incomprehensible waves of emotion. Such use of LSD is dangerous and is conducive to poorly resolved experiences, prolonged reactions, and flashbacks, or worse. Safe psychonautics requires undivided attention to one's unconscious material as it is emerging, the full experience of emotions, and the processing of the content.

The ideal situation for therapeutic sessions is a protected environment which allows the client to make noises if necessary and includes the presence of a male-female duo of facilitators or sitters. We keep the experience internalized by using eyeshades and keep the verbal interaction and interventions at a minimum, unless the client initiates or asks for it. If the person interrupts the experience and opens their eyes, we try to do what it takes to gently persuade them to return to introspection.

Playing music through the session can help the client stay in the flow of the experience and move through possible impasses; it can also activate and bring deep emotions to the surface. The choice and use of music is similar to how it was described in the chapter on Holotropic Breathwork. The general principle is to closely support what is happening in the session, rather than trying to program the experience in a specific way. We can get the necessary clues from observing the facial expressions, occasional verbal comments, and body language, which may include sensual movement of the pelvis, clenched fists and jaws, a relaxed position and blissful smile, uttering the name of the country in which the experience unfolds, etc.

We also follow the general course or trajectory of the LSD session: the intensity of the music gradually increases, reaches a climax around three hours into the experience, and then becomes more emotional, comforting, and feminine. In the final stage of the session, the music becomes timeless, flowing, meditative, and quiet. We tend to avoid pieces of music which are well known and would guide the experience in a specific way, as well as vocal performances in languages that the client knows. If we use recordings of human voices, they should be perceived just as sounds of musical instruments and not convey any specific verbal message.

About five hours into the session, it is useful to take a break and get a brief verbal report about the client's experience. This might also be a good time to move outside. Ideally, the psychedelic sessions would be held in a beautiful environment—in the mountains, near a park, meadow, forest, river, lake or ocean. In the termination period of a psychedelic session, taking a shower or bath, or swimming in water can be an ecstatic and healing experience.

This period can facilitate regression to a prenatal state or even take our experience to the beginning of life in the primeval ocean. Depending on the place and the time of day, we might want to take the client to a place where we can watch the sunset, the moon, or the night sky. If we do not have the luxury of any of the above, we try to find as much of a natural setting as we can. Psychedelic experiences tend to connect us with nature and make us realize how deeply we are connected and embedded within it, as well as how much the industrial civilization has obscured this and alienated us.

If the session does not reach a good closure, it is essential to use bodywork to release any residual emotions or physical tensions and blockages. However, I have been able to find very few psychedelic therapists who are actually using this. The principles are the same as was described in the chapter on Holotropic Breathwork (pp. 365, Volume I). We do not use any preconceived techniques but let ourselves be guided by the healing intelligence of the client's own psyche. We find the best possible ways to accentuate the existing symptoms and encourage him or her to fully express whatever this brings.

In our therapeutic and training programs at the Maryland Psychiatric Research Center, we organized family reunions in the later hours of psychedelic sessions. The patients would invite partners, spouses, family members, or friends of their choice for these events. We would order meals from a nearby Chinese or Japanese restaurant, which had interesting tastes, textures, and colors, and we all shared a dinner listening to quiet music. At this time, the clients were still in holotropic states of consciousness, which can remarkably enhance the quality of sensory perception. By directing this "opening of the doors of perception"—to use Aldous Huxley's term—to objects and activities of everyday life, they learned new ways to experience nature, watch sunsets, taste food, listen to music, and interact with people.

In spite of its complicated history, psychedelic-assisted psychotherapy has shown its great potential in the treatment of phobias, depression, psychosomatic disorders and physical pain. Using LSD as a catalyst, it became possible to extend the range of applicability of psychotherapy to categories of patients that previously had been difficult to reach: alcoholics, narcotic drug addicts, sexual deviants, and criminal recidivists. The current extraordinary renaissance of interest in psychedelics will hopefully make it possible to use all the clinical experiences that have lain dormant for forty years, avoid the mistakes of the past, and have a fresh new start. I have no doubt that the new research will confirm that psychedelics are unique therapeutic agents of an entirely new kind, unparalleled in the history of psychiatry.

Literature

Condrau, G. 1949. "Klinische Erfahrungen an Geisteskranken mit LSD-25" (Clinical Experiences in Psychiatric Patients with LSD-25). *Act. Psychiat. Neurol. Scand.* 24:9.

Ditman, K. S. and Whittlesey, J. R. B. 1959. "Comparison of the LSD Experience and Delirium Tremens." *Arch.gen. Psychiat.* 1:47.

Fadiman, F. 2017. "A Researcher Wants to Test the Effects on Microdosing on Cognitive Ability and Productivity." *Futurism* August 10.

Fenichel, O. 1945. *A Psychoanalytic Theory of Neurosis.* New York: W. W. Norton.

Freud, S. and Breuer, J. 1936. *Studies in Hysteria.* New York: Nervous and Mental Diseases Publication Company.

Grof, S. 1975. *Realms of the Human Unconscious: Observations from LSD Research.* New York: Viking Press. Republished in 2009 as *LSD: Gateway to the Numinous.* Rochester, VT: Inner Traditions.

Grof, S. 2001. *LSD Psychotherapy.* Santa Cruz, CA: MAPS Publications.

Grof, S. 2006. *When the Impossible Happens: Adventures in Non-Ordinary Realities.* Louisville, CO: Sounds True.

Jost, F. 1957. "Zur therapeutischen Verwendung des LSD-25 in der klinischen Praxis der Psychiatrie" (Apropos of the Therapeutic Use of LSD-25 in the Clinical Practice of Psychiatry). *Wien. klin. Wschr.* 69:647.

Jost, F. and Vicari, R. 1958. "Zu den Provokationsverfahren in der Meedizin: LSD als Provokationsmittel" (Apropos of the Provocation Processes in Medicine: LSD As A Provocation Agent). *Medizinsche Nr.* 8:319.

Krippner, S. 1970. Letter. Drug deceptions. *Science* 168, 654-655.

Levine, J. and Ludwig, A. M. 1967. "The Hypnodelic Treatment Technique." In: H. A. Abramson (editor): *The Use of LSD in Psychotherapy and Alcoholism.* New York: The Bobbs-Merrill Co. Inc.

Ludwig, A. M., Levine, J., and Stark, L. H. 1970. *LSD and Alcoholism: Clinical Study of Efficacy.* Springfield, IL: Charles C. Thomas.

Martin, A. J. 1957. "LSD Treatment of Chronic Psychoneurotic Patients Under Day-Hospital Conditions." *Internat. J. soc. Psychiat.* 3188.

McCririck, P. 1965. "The Importance of Fusion in Therapy and Maturation." Unpublished mimeographed paper.

Hoffer, A. 1970. "Treatment of Alcoholism with Psychedelic Therapy." In: Aaronson, B. S And Osmond, H.: *Psychedelics: The Uses and Implications of Psychedelic Drugs.* New York: Anchor Books.

Pahnke, W. A. 1970. "The Experimental Use of Psychedelic (LSD) Therapy." *J. Amer. Med. Assoc. (JAMA)* 212:856.

Robinson, J. T. et al. 1963. "A Controlled Trial of Abreaction with LSD-25." *British J. Psychiat.* 109:46.

Roquet, S. 1971. *Operación Mazateca: Estudio de hongos y otras plantas hallucinogenas Mexicanas, tratamiento psicoterapeutico psicosintesis (Mazatec Operation: Study of the Mushrooms and Other Mexican Hallucinogenic Plants, Psychotherapeutic Treatment Psychosynthesis).* Mexico City: Associatión Albert Schweizer,.

Rosen, D. 1975. "Suicide Survivors; A Follow-Up Study of Persons Who Survived Jumping from the Golden Gate and San Francisco-Oakland Bay Bridges." *West. J. Med.* 122: 289.

Sandison, R. A., Spencer, A. M. and Whitelaw, J. D. A. 1954. "The Therapeutic Value of LSD in Mental Illness." *J. Ment. Science* 1900:491.

Stoll, W. A. 1947. "LSD-25: Ein Fantastikum aus der Mutterkorngruppe" (LSD-25: A Fantasticum from the Ergot Group). *Schweiz. Arch. Neurol. Psychiat.* 60:279.

Turner, V. 1969: *The Ritual Process: Structure and Antistructure.* New York: PAJ Publications.

VIII

Synchronicity:
C. G. Jung's "Acausal Connecting Principle"

Many of us have experienced situations in which the seemingly predictable fabric of everyday reality, woven from complex chains of causes and effects, seems to tear apart, and we experience stunning and highly implausible coincidences. During episodes of holotropic states of consciousness, though, striking coincidences that seem meaningful tend to happen with great frequency. The accumulation of extraordinary coincidences can bring the elements of magic, numinosity, and cosmic artistry into everyday reality and play an important role in the process of spiritual opening.

However, experiencing chains of coincidences can also create serious problems in life and become a dangerous pitfall. Sometimes, these coincidences can be very ingratiating, promising and empowering, and convince the individual that he or she is special and has been chosen for an important role in the world: a saint, prophet, savior, leader or spiritual teacher. This situation—dangerous ego inflation—can cause irrational behavior and lead to psychiatric hospitalization. Other times, the content of these coincidences is ominous and they seem to portend danger or disaster. The individual has the sense of a rapidly closing circle of threatening circumstances and becomes terrified and paranoid.

Mainstream psychiatry does not recognize the concept of personally meaningful coincidences and labels any patients who talk about them as suffering from *"delusions of reference."* According to materialistic science, there is no inherent meaning in the universe and, in a world that is random and disenchanted, any semblance of a deeper personal meaning of events has to be an illusion introduced into it by human projection. However, anyone who is open-minded and is willing to listen and learn about these occurrences has to admit that the probability of these just being happenstances is astronomically low.

Such violations of linear causality can occur so frequently that they raise serious questions about the nature of reality and the worldview in which we have all grown up. This can be very disturbing for people who draw a great sense of comfort and safety from the belief that they live in a lawful and predictable world; any experiences that challenge it can trigger a fear of insanity. Understanding the phenomenon of meaningful coincidences is therefore essential for safe navigation through non-ordinary realities and is a *sine qua non* for psychonauts experimenting with psychedelic substances or experiencing spiritual emergency. Indiscriminate sharing of such experiences with the wrong people and acting under their influence can become the reason for psychiatric diagnosis and hospitalization.

The Swiss psychiatrist C. G. Jung was the scientist who brought the problem of meaningful coincidences defying rational explanation to the attention of academic circles. Aware of the fact that the staunch and unswerving belief in rigid determinism represents the cornerstone of the Western scientific worldview, he hesitated for more than twenty years before he felt that he had collected enough supportive evidence to make his discovery public. Expecting strong disbelief and harsh criticism from his colleagues, he wanted to be sure that he could back his heretic claims with hundreds of examples.

He finally described his groundbreaking observations in his famous essay "Synchronicity: An Acausal Connecting Principle" and presented it at the Eranos meeting of 1951. Eranos meetings were conferences of stellar European and American thinkers in which Jung was the principal initiator and participant. It included the intellectual elite of the world, including people like Joseph Campbell, Heinrich Zimmer, Karl Kerenyi, Erich Neumann, Olga Froebe-Kapteyn, Erwin Schrödinger, Wolfgang Pauli, Daisetz Teitaro Suzuki, Paul Tillich, Marie-Louise von Franz, Rudolf Otto, Richard Wilhelm, Mircea Eliade, and Gershom Scholem.

Jung began his essay with examples of extraordinary coincidences occurring in everyday life (Jung 1960). He acknowledged the Austrian Lamarckian biologist Paul Kammerer, whose tragic life was popularized in Arthur Koestler's book *The Case of the Midwife Toad* (Koestler 1971), as one of the first people to be interested in this phenomenon and its scientific implications. Kammerer studied and described a type of striking coincidence which he called *seriality*. One of the remarkable examples Kammerer had reported was a sequence of three encounters with the same number on the same day—his streetcar ticket bore the same number as the theater ticket he bought immediately afterward. Then later that evening, he asked for a telephone number and was given the same sequence of digits.

Kammerer was fascinated by this phenomenon; he spent many hours

Carl Gustav Jung (1875–1961), Swiss psychiatrist and pioneer of depth psychology.

in parks and other public places watching how many people passed by, how many had umbrellas, hats, dogs, and so on. In his book *Law of the Series,* he described one hundred anecdotes of remarkable coincidences (Kammerer 1919). His biographer, Arthur Koestler, reported that when he was writing Kammerer's biography *The Case of the Midwife Toad,* he experienced a "meteor shower of coincidences," as if Kammerer's ghost was grinning down at him and saying, "I told you so!" (Koestler 1971).

Jung was also interested in seriality and described his own examples of it. One morning he saw an inscription with a figure which was half man and half fish. The same day, he was served fish for lunch and someone made "an April fish" of another person (Swiss equivalent of the American making an "April fool" of someone). In the afternoon, a former patient showed him an impressive picture of a fish. That evening, Jung saw an embroidery with sea monsters and fishes on it. The next morning a patient reported a dream of a large fish. A few months later, when Jung was writing about this extraordinary series of events, he went for a walk and saw a foot-long fish lying on the wall by the lake. He pointed out that earlier that day, he had walked by that spot several times and did not see the fish, and nobody was around. Jung was aware that this phenomenon could be accounted for by using statistics but emphasized that "the large number of the repetitions made it highly unlikely."

In the same essay on synchronicity, Jung also related the amusing story told by famous astronomer Camille Flammarion about the French writer Émile Deschamps and a special kind of plum pudding. As a boy, Deschamps was given a piece of this rare pudding by a Monsieur de Fontgibu. For the ten years that followed, he had no opportunity to taste this delicacy until he saw the same pudding on the menu at a Parisian restaurant. He called the waiter and ordered it, but the waiter came back with the message that they had already served the last portion of it to another guest. He pointed across the room and there sat Monsieur de Fontgibu, enjoying the last bites of the dessert.

Many years later, Monsieur Deschamps was invited to a party where this pudding was served as a special treat. While he was eating it, he remarked that the only thing lacking was Monsieur de Fontgibu, who had introduced him to this delicacy and had also been present during his second encounter with it in the Paris restaurant. At that moment, the doorbell rang, and an old man walked in looking very confused. It was Monsieur de Fontgibu, who had burst in on the party by mistake because he had been given the wrong address.

The existence of such extraordinary coincidences is difficult to reconcile with the understanding of the universe that has been developed by materialistic science, which describes the world in terms of chains of causes and effects. And the probability that something like this would happen by chance is so infinitesimal that it cannot be seriously considered as an explanation. It is certainly easier to imagine that these occurrences have some deeper meaning and that they may be playful creations of cosmic intelligence. This explanation is particularly plausible when they contain

Paul Kammerer (1880–1926), Austrian biologist who studied and advocated Lamarckism, the theory that organisms may pass to their offspring characteristics acquired in their lifetime.

an element of humor, which is often the case. Although coincidences of this kind are extremely interesting in and of themselves, the work of C. G. Jung added another fascinating dimension to these challenging, anomalous phenomena.

The situations described by Kammerer and by Flammarion involved highly implausible coincidences, and the story about the plum pudding certainly has an element of humor. However, both stories described happenings in the world of matter. Jung's observations added another astonishing element to this already baffling phenomenon. He described numerous instances of what he called "synchronicity"—remarkable coincidences in which various events in reality were meaningfully linked to intrapsychic experiences, such as dreams or visions. He defined synchronicity as "a simultaneous occurrence of a certain psychic state with one or more external events which appear as meaningful parallels to the momentary subjective state."

Situations of this kind show that our psyche can enter into playful interaction with what appears to be the world of matter. The fact that some-

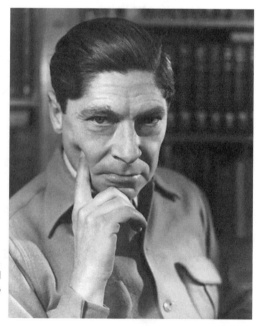

Arthur Koestler (1905–1983), Hungarian/British journalist and writer, author of *The Case of the Midwife Toad* (top).

thing like this is possible effectively blurs the boundaries between subjective and objective reality. Struggling with this phenomenon, Jung became very interested in the developments in quantum-relativistic physics and in the radically new worldview to which they were pointing. He had many intellectual exchanges with Wolfgang Pauli, one of the founders of quantum physics, who was initially his client and later his personal friend.

Pauli came to Jung with bizarre dreams, which featured combinations of numbers and archetypal figures reaching back into the Middle Ages, such as the Wild Man, Veiled Woman, Ouroboros, World Clock, Quadrature of the Circle, and Perpetuum Mobile. Later, when they became friends, they explored various problems involving the interface between mathematics, physics, and psychology. Arthur Miller wrote a remarkable book about the extraordinary relationship between Jung and Pauli, especially their fascination with the number 137 (Miller 2009). Under Pauli's guidance, Jung became familiar with the revolutionary concepts in modern physics, including the challenges to deterministic thinking and linear causality that had been introduced into science.

Wolfgang Pauli (1900–1958), Austrian-born, Nobel Prize-winning Swiss and American physicist and one of the pioneers of quantum physics.

Synchronicity is of great theoretical significance in quantum relativistic physics due to important experiments that seem to indicate that the universe might be "radically nonlocal." This deserves a brief detour into the history of this discipline. Throughout his life, Albert Einstein, whose work had initiated the development of quantum physics, showed great resistance to the idea of the fundamental role of probability in nature. He expressed it in his famous statement: *"God does not play dice."* In order to show that Niels Bohr's interpretation of quantum theory was wrong, Einstein devised a thought experiment, which later became known as the Einstein-Podolsky-Rosen (EPR) experiment. Ironically, several decades later, this experiment served as the basis for John Bell's theorem that proves that the Cartesian concept of reality is incompatible with quantum theory (Bell 1966, Capra 1975).

The simplified version of the EPR experiment involves two electrons spinning in opposite directions so that their total spin is zero. They are made to move apart until the distance between them becomes macroscopic; their respective spins can then be measured by two independent observers. Quantum theory predicts that, in a system of two particles with a total spin of zero, the spins along any axis will always be correlated, which is to say, opposite. Before the actual measurement, one can only talk about tendencies to spin. Once the measurement is made, though, this potential is transformed into certainty.

The observer is free to choose any axis of measurement, which instantly determines the spin of the other particle that might be thousands of miles away. According to the theory of relativity, no signal can travel faster than light, and therefore this situation should, in principle, be impossible. The instantaneous, nonlocal connection between these particles cannot thus be mediated by signals in the Einsteinian sense; communication of this kind transcends the conventional concept of information transfer. Initially, Einstein's thought experiment was designed to disprove quantum theory, but a number of experiments have since confirmed that the particles remain entangled. Bell's theorem leaves the physicists with an uncomfortable dilemma; it suggests that either the world is radically nonlocal, connected by supraluminal links, or not objectively real.

Jung published his essay on synchronicity in the 1951 Eranos volume; Wolfgang Pauli's article on a related subject was in the same issue. Jung's essay on synchronicity and Pauli's study of the influence of the archetype of the Sun on the work of Johannes Kepler has often been published in one volume. It is interesting that Pauli's life involved an ongoing incidence of synchronicities. Physical instruments, for example, broke down with great frequency whenever he was in the building. Astronomer George Gamow called it the *Pauli effect*. It was humorously called the *second Pauli exclusion principle,* according to which "a functioning device and Wolfgang Pauli may not occupy the same room." Pauli himself was convinced that the effect named after him was real. He corresponded about it with German parapsychologist Hans Bender and saw this effect as an example of synchronicity.

Jung was aware that his own observations appeared much more plausible and acceptable in the context of the emerging new understanding of reality. Additional support for Jung's ideas came from no less than Albert Einstein who, during a personal visit, encouraged Jung to pursue his idea of synchronicity, because it was fully compatible with the new discoveries in physics. Since the publication of Jung's essay on synchronicity, this concept has become increasingly important in science and has been the subject of many articles and books. On the other side of the spectrum, the existence of synchronicity aids in the understanding of esoteric systems of divination, such as Tarot, work with cowry shells, and the I Ching.

As Marie-Louise von Franz pointed out in her book *On Divination and Synchronicity: The Psychology of Meaningful Chance,* synchronistic thinking was the classic way of thinking in ancient China and was developed and differentiated there much more than in any other civilization (von Franz 2015). This involved thinking in terms of fields, rather than in terms of linear causality. The question is not why something has come about, or what caused a specific effect, but what happens together in a meaningful way in the same moment? The Chinese philosopher always asks: "What tends to happen together in time?" So the center of their field concept would be the moment of time in which certain events assemble in clusters.

In the Chinese way of thinking, one does not ask whether material processes caused psychological events or if the psychological processes caused events in the material world. Only in later thinking did we find a differentiation between the material and psychological aspects of existence. Therefore, when we inquire what tends to occur together, we can bring in both inner and outer facts. For the synchronistic way of thinking, it is essential to watch both areas of reality, the physical and the psychic, and to notice that at the moment when one had certain thoughts or certain dreams, there were certain physical and psychological events. It is a certain moment in time which is the uniting fact, the focal point for the observation of this complex of events.

The concept of synchronicity could only have originated in a civilization that has a materialistic worldview and sees the world as an assembly of separate objects interacting in a way that is governed by the principle of linear causality. The universe is portrayed as an infinitely complex system of chains of causes and effects. In the primal worldview, where everything is interconnected in a *participation mystique,* synchronicity is seen as a universal principle. The entire natural world is so pervaded by meaning and replete with signs and symbols that synchronicity is not a separate concept.

To describe the universe, ancient humanity used words like sympathy, harmony, and unity. In the fourth century BC, the Pre-Socratic Greek philosopher Heraclitus of Ephesus viewed all things as being interrelated. Similarly, the legendary Greek physician Hippocrates said: "There is one common flow, one common breathing, all things are in sympathy." And

Marie-Louise von Franz (1915–1998), Swiss analytical psychologist and follower of C. G. Jung.

38

Roman philosopher Plotinus, the founder of neo-Platonism and author of the Enneads, wrote: "The stars are like letters that inscribe themselves at every moment in the sky. Everything in the world is full of signs. All events are coordinated. All things depend on each other. Everything breathes together." These are examples of the classic idea that separateness is an illusion (Plotinus 1950).

The native, ancient, classical and medieval worldviews also postulated the existence of a principal alternative to linear causality in the form of a higher force. Even for Wilhelm Gottfried Leibniz, nineteenth-century German philosopher, causality was neither the only view, nor the principal one. One example of an alternative to linear causality are the processes of movie-making and movie-watching, in which the causality that we observe only seems to be true; it is in fact only a method to communicate a story. The people who created the movies arranged the sequences of scenes and images in such a way that we perceive them as causally connected.

The Hindus, who understand the universe as *lila,* a divine play created by a cosmic consciousness who is orchestrating experiences, apply the same type of thinking to the world of matter. All the magical and mantic procedures of earlier ages were based on a similar understanding of the world. With the rise of physical sciences, the correspondence theory vanished completely, and the magical world of earlier ages disappeared. It was replaced by thinking in terms of linear causality, which became the cornerstone of materialistic science.

Synchronistic thinking is also essential for an adequate understanding of archetypal astrology. Jung used astrology in his essay to demonstrate the multiple synchronistic interconnections involving the material world and the human psyche. In the later years of his life, he routinely looked at the astrological charts of his patients before he began working with them. His daughter, Gret Baumann-Jung, specifically studied astrology to cast the horoscopes of Jung's patients for him and to present a paper on her father's chart for the Psychological Club in Zürich in 1974. Toward the end of his life, Jung became so convinced of the importance of synchronicity in the natural order of things that he used it as a guiding principle in his everyday life.

The most famous case of synchronicity in Jung's own life occurred during a therapy session with one of his clients. This patient was very resistant to psychotherapy, to Jung's interpretations, and to the notion of transpersonal realities. During the analysis of one of her dreams featuring a golden scarab, when the therapy had reached a major impasse, Jung heard something hit the windowpane. He went to check what had happened and found a shiny rose-chafer beetle *(Cetonia aurata)* on the windowsill trying to get inside. It was a very rare specimen, the nearest analogy to a golden scarab that can be found in that latitude. Nothing like that had ever happened to Jung before or afterwards. He opened the window, brought the beetle inside, and showed it to his client. This extraordinary synchronicity became an important turning point in this woman's therapy.

The observations of synchronicities had a profound impact on Jung's thinking and his work, particularly on his understanding of archetypes, primordial governing, and organizing principles of the collective unconscious. The discovery of archetypes and their role in the human psyche represent Jung's most important contribution to psychology. For much of his professional career, Jung was very strongly influenced by the Cartesian-Kantian perspective dominating Western science, with its strict division between subjective and objective, inner and outer. Under its influence, he initially saw the archetypes as transindividual, but essentially intrapsychic

Cetonia aureata, the "scarab" from C. G. Jung's synchronicity story.

principles, comparable to biological instincts. He presumed that the basic matrix for them was hard-wired into the brain and was inherited from generation to generation.

The existence of synchronistic events made Jung realize that archetypes transcend both the psyche and the material world. He believed that they are autonomous patterns of meaning that inform both the psyche and matter. He saw that they provide a bridge between inner and outer and suggested the existence of a twilight zone between matter and consciousness. For this reason, Jung started referring to archetypes as having a *"psychoid"* (psyche-like) quality, using the term coined by Hans Driesch, the founder of vitalism (Driesch 1914). Stephan Hoeller described Jung's advanced understanding of the archetypes in a succinct way, using poetic language: "The archetype then, when manifesting in a synchronistic phenomenon, is truly awesome if not outright miraculous—an uncanny dweller on the threshold. At once psychical and physical, it might be likened to the two-faced Roman god Janus. The two faces of the archetype are joined in the common head of meaning" (Hoeller 1982).

Psychiatrists often hear from their patients about "fantastic coincidences;" however, the remarkable phenomenon of synchronicity has not been recognized by mainstream psychology and psychiatry. References to "unbelievable coincidences" are dismissed and seen as pathological distortions of perception and judgment, or "delusions of reference." However, anyone who takes the time to check the facts has to admit that the probability of many of these coincidences being accidental is infinitesimally low.

During the sixty years I have been involved in consciousness research, I have observed many extraordinary synchronicities in my patients, particularly in those undergoing psychedelic therapy and experiencing spiritual emergencies, as well as in participants in Holotropic Breathwork workshops and training. I have also heard many stories about them from my fellow researchers and therapists, and personally experienced hundreds of them myself. I would like to illustrate this discussion of synchronicity with several examples. Interested readers can find more examples of remarkable synchronicities in my book *When the Impossible Happens* (Grof 2006).

The first of these examples is an extraordinary story involving my late friend and teacher, the famous mythologist Joseph Campbell. It bears some similarity to Jung's encounter with the golden beetle in that it involves the appearance of an insect in a highly unlikely time and place. During one of his many workshops at the Esalen Institute in Big Sur, California, Joe gave a long talk on his favorite subject: the work of C. G. Jung and his revolutionary contributions to the understanding of mythology and psychology. During this lecture, he made a fleeting reference to the phenomenon of synchronicity. One of the participants, who was not familiar with this term, interrupted Joe and asked him to explain it.

After giving Jung's brief, general definition and description of this concept, Joe decided to share with the audience an example of a remarkable synchronicity from his own life. Before moving to Hawaii later in life, Joe and his wife, Jean Erdman, had lived in New York City's Greenwich Village. Their apartment was on the fourteenth floor of a high-rise building on Waverly Place and Sixth Avenue. Joe's study had two pairs of windows, one facing the Hudson River, and the other up Sixth Avenue. The first set of windows offered a beautiful view of the river, and during nice weather they were always open. The view from the other two windows was uninteresting, and the Campbells very seldom opened them. According to Joe, they might not have opened them more than two or three times during their forty-odd years living there, except for cleaning.

Christina and Stanislav Grof with Jean Erdman and Joseph Campbell at a seminar in Honolulu, Hawaii.

One day in the early 1980s, Joe was in his study working on his magnum opus, *The Way of the Animal Powers,* a comprehensive encyclopedia of shamanic mythologies of the world (Campbell 1984). At that time, he was writing the chapter on mythology of the African !Kung Bushmen, a tribe living in the Kalahari Desert. One of the most important deities in the Bushman pantheon is Mantis, who combines the characteristics of a Trickster figure and the Creator God.

Joe was deeply immersed in this work, surrounded by articles, books and pictures on the subject. He was particularly impressed by the story Laurens van der Post wrote about his half-Bushman nanny, Klara, who had taken care of him since the moment of his birth. Van der Post vividly remembered instances from his childhood when Klara was able to communicate with a praying mantis *(Mantis religiosa).* When she talked to the member of this species, asking specific questions, the insect seemed to respond by moving its legs and body.

In the middle of this work, Joe suddenly felt an irresistible and completely irrational impulse to get up and open one of the windows facing Sixth Avenue (windows with a boring view that normally remained closed all the time). After he opened it, he immediately looked to the right without understanding why he was doing it. The last thing one would expect to encounter in Manhattan is a praying mantis. And yet, there it was, a large specimen of its kind, on the fourteenth floor of a high-rise building in lower Manhattan, climbing slowly upward. According to Joe, it turned its head and gave him a meaningful look.

Although this encounter lasted only a few seconds, it had an uncanny quality and left a powerful impression on Joe. He said that he could confirm what he had read just minutes earlier in Laurens van der Post's story: there was something curiously human about the face of the mantis; its "heart-shape pointed chin, high cheek bones, and yellow skin made it look just like a Bushman's." The appearance of a praying mantis in the middle of Manhattan is a very unusual occurrence in and of itself, to say the least. If one considers the timing of its appearance, though, and coinciding with Joe's intense immersion in the mythology of Kalahari Bushmen and his unexplainable irrational impulse to open the window, the statistical improbability of this event is truly astronomical. And the fact that Bushmen see Mantis as a Cosmic Trickster seems very appropriate for this situation.

Only a hardcore materialist committed to his or her worldview with a quasi-religious fervor could believe that something like this might have happened by pure chance.

The events described in the next story happened during one of our month-long seminars at Esalen, at a time when Christina was experiencing her spiritual emergency. Her spontaneous experiences were very intense and rich and combined elements from various levels of the personal and collective unconscious. One day she had particularly intense and significant visions involving a white swan. Our guest faculty for the following day was Michael Harner, a well-known anthropologist and dear friend. Michael belonged to a group often referred to as "visionary anthropologists." In contrast to traditional mainstream anthropologists, they actively participated in the ceremonies of the cultures they studied, whether these involved consciousness-expanding substances such as peyote, magic mushrooms, ayahuasca, or datura, or all-night trance dances and other non-pharmacological "technologies of the sacred."

Michael's discovery of the way of the shamans' work and their incredible inner world began in 1960, when the American Museum of Natural History invited him to make a year-long expedition to the Peruvian Amazon to study the culture of the Conibo Indians of the Ucayali River

Praying mantis (Mantis religiosa), the insect in Joseph Campbell's synchronicity story.

region. His guides told him that if he really wished to learn, he had to take the shaman's sacred drink. Following their advice, he ingested *ayahuasca*, a brew containing a decoction of the jungle liana *Banisteriopsis caapi* and the *cawa plant*, which the Indians called "soul vine" or "little death." He undertook an astonishing visionary journey through ordinarily invisible dimensions of existence, during which he experienced his own death and obtained extraordinary insights and revelations about the nature of reality.

When he later found out that a Conibo elder, a master shaman, was quite familiar with everything he himself had seen and that his ayahuasca experiences paralleled certain passages from the *Book of Revelation*, Michael became convinced that there was indeed a hidden world to be explored. He decided to learn everything that he could about shamanism. Three years later, Michael returned to South America to do field work with the Jivaro, an Ecuadorian head-hunting tribe, who Michael had lived with and studied in 1956 and 1957. Here he experienced another important initiatory experience, which was key to his discovery of the way of the shaman. Akachu, a famous Jivaro shaman, and his son-in-law took him to a sacred waterfall deep in the Amazonian jungle and gave him a drink of *maikua,* the juice of a *Brugmansia* species of datura, a plant with powerful psychoactive properties.

Michael Harner (1929–2018), famous American anthropologist and practicing shaman.

As a result of these and other experiences, Michael—an anthropologist with good academic credentials—became an accomplished practitioner and teacher of shamanism. He and his wife Sandra also started the Foundation for Shamanic Studies, an institution dedicated to teaching shamanic methods to interested students and to offering shamanic workshops for the public. Michael had written a book entitled *The Way of the Shaman,* in which he gathered various methods of shamanic work from all over the world and adapted them for use in experiential workshops and in shamanic training for Westerners (Harner 1980).

During our Esalen month-long workshop, Michael led us on a healing journey using the method of the Spirit Canoe as practiced by the Salish Indian tribe in the American Northwest. He began the session by beating his drum and invited participants to move and dance until they identified with a specific animal. It did not take long, and soon people were crouching, crawling on all fours, and jumping around, emulating many climbing, digging, clawing, swimming, and flying movements. The main room in Esalen's Big House was filled with various recognizable and unrecognizable voices of animals and birds.

When everybody had made the connection with a specific animal, Michael asked the group members to sit down on the floor in a spindle-like formation, creating an imaginary "Spirit Canoe." He then asked if there was a person who needed healing, and Christina volunteered. Michael stepped into the "boat" holding his drum, beckoned Christina to join him, and instructed her to lie down. With the scene for the healing voyage all set, Michael asked us to imagine that we were an animal crew undertaking a journey on a canoe into the underworld to retrieve Christina's spirit animal. The specific location that Michael chose for this imaginary expedition was the system of interconnected underground caverns filled with hot water that allegedly stretches under much of California. The entry into it was easy to find, since this system feeds the Esalen hot springs.

As the captain of this spirit boat, Michael explained, he would indicate the pace of the paddling by the beat of his drum. During the journey, he would look for spirit animals. When a particular spirit animal appeared three times, this would be the sign that he found the one he was looking for. At that point, he would seize it and would signal to the crew of the boat by the rapid beat of the drum that it was time for a hasty return. We had done the Salish Spirit Canoe with Michael several times before. The first time we did it, we did not go into it with great expectations. The whole thing sounded like innocent fun—a great idea for children's play, but a somewhat silly activity for mature adults.

The very first thing that happened in this initial experience, however, made us change our minds. In the group was a young woman who behaved in a way that had antagonized the entire group. She was very unhappy about it, since the same thing had happened earlier in her life in just about every group in which she had been involved, and she decided to volunteer for the spirit canoe journey to be healed. As the imaginary boat was traveling through the "underworld," she had a very violent reaction at the exact moment when Michael signaled that he had identified and seized her spirit animal. She suddenly sat up and, as Michael was giving the signal for return by rapid beats of his drum, she went through several spastic episodes of projectile vomiting.

As she was throwing up, she lifted the front part of her skirt, trying to contain what was coming out, and completely filled it with her vomit. This episode, lasting no more than twenty-five minutes, had a profound effect on her personality. The change in her behavior was so dramatic that before the month-long workshop ended, she became one of the most loved and popular people in the group. This, along with similar episodes later on, made us approach this process with respect.

Michael began drumming, and the journey into the underworld began. We all paddled and made sounds of the animals with which we had identified. Christina went into intense convulsions that were shaking her entire body. In and of itself, this was not unusual, since she was in the middle of Kundalini awakening, during which experiences of powerful energies and tremors (kriyas) are very common. After about ten minutes, Michael greatly accelerated the rhythm of his drumming, letting us know that he had succeeded in finding Christina's spirit animal. Everybody began paddling quickly, imagining a rapid return to the Middle World. Michael stopped drumming, indicating that the journey had ended.

He put down the drum, pressed his mouth on Christina's sternum, and blew with all the force he could muster, making a loud sound. He then whispered into her ear: "Your spirit animal is a white swan." Following this, he asked her to perform in front of the group a dance, expressing her swan energy. It is important to mention that Michael had no prior knowledge of Christina's inner process and that this bird had figured importantly in her experiences the day before. He also had no idea that the swan had been a very important personal symbol for Christina. She was an ardent devotee of Swami Muktananda and a student of Siddha Yoga, where the swan played an important role as a symbol of Brahma.

The story continued the next morning, when Christina and I walked to our mailbox on Highway 1 to get our mail. Christina received a letter from a person who had attended a workshop we had given several months earlier. Inside was a photograph of Christina's spiritual teacher, Swami Muktananda, which this person thought Christina might like to have. It showed him sitting on a garden swing with a mischievous expression near a large flowerpot shaped like a white swan. The index finger of his left hand was pointing at the swan; the tips of his right thumb and index finger were joined, forming the universal sign indicating hitting the bull's eye and excitement. Although there were no causal connections between Christina's inner experiences, Michael's choice of the white swan as her power animal, and Muktananda's photograph, they clearly formed a meaningful psychological pattern. This met the criteria for synchronicity, or an "acausal connecting principle," as defined by C. G. Jung.

Even more remarkable events happened in connection with one of our training modules. It took place in a beautiful retreat center called Pocket Ranch near Healdsburg, California, which is north of San Francisco. The center was located in the mountains, in a natural setting abounding with wildlife—deer, rabbits, rattlesnakes, raccoons, skunks, and a wide range of birds. One of the participants had a very powerful and meaningful session with many shamanic motifs. An important part of it was an encounter with a horned owl; she felt that the owl had become her personal power animal.

After the session, she went for a walk into the forest and came back with remnants (bones and feathers) of a horned owl. Two days later, when she was driving home from the training, she noticed something moving in the trench on the side of the road. She stopped and found a large wounded horned owl. The owl allowed her to pick him/her up, drive home, and nurse it back to health. This was an extremely rare occurrence, but in combination with her moving and important experience of receiving a horned owl as a spirit animal, this certainly makes it an extraordinary synchronicity.

As I mentioned earlier, Jung had such trust in the authenticity and reliability of synchronicity that he used it as a guiding principle in his life. I have also learned over the years to honor synchronicities in my life but more cautiously, tempering their compelling effect with discerning intellectual judgment. I found that it is particularly important not to act under their influence when I am in a holotropic state of consciousness and I advise the same to my friends, trainees, and patients. I described how I learned the hard way to deal with synchronicities and archetypal experiences in my book *When the Impossible Happens,* in the chapter "The Rainbow Bridge of the Gods: In the Realm of the Nordic Sagas" (Grof 2006).

The first five weeks of my relationship with Florida anthropologist Joan Halifax, which culminated in our wedding in Iceland, was replete with extraordinary and glorious synchronicities which seemed to indicate that our union would be a "marriage made in heaven." The wedding ceremony took place during the First International Transpersonal Conference with seventy-four enthusiastic participants sharing our excitement. Our joiner was renowned philosopher and religious scholar Huston Smith, author of *The World's Religions* (Smith 1991). Joseph Campbell and Icelandic my-

Joan Halifax and Stanislav Grof celebrating their Viking wedding in Bifrost, Iceland, in 1972.

thologist Einar Pálsson recreated an ancient Viking ritual for us that had not been performed in Iceland since the arrival of Christians on the island.

The central archetypal symbol for this wedding ritual was the rainbow, which the Vikings saw as the union of Father Sky and Mother Earth. It was June beyond the Arctic Circle, the time of the amazing White Nights. During the dinner banquet preceding the wedding ritual, a glorious double rainbow appeared and disappeared three times. We also found out that Bifrost, the name of the place where the wedding took place, meant the Rainbow Bridge of the Gods. To our disappointment, the glorious marriage that this "meteor shower of synchronicities" (to use Arthur Koestler's expression) seemed to predict did not materialize. After three years of a difficult and challenging marriage, we came to the conclusion that our personalities were too different and decided to dissolve our union.

On the opposite side of the spectrum was a remarkable synchronicity that brought very positive results, which was also connected with an International Transpersonal Conference. I founded the International Transpersonal Association (ITA) as an organization designed to bridge the gap between modern science and the spiritual traditions of the world and between Western pragmatism and ancient wisdom. Since the ultimate goal of the ITA was to create a global network of mutual understanding and cooperation, during our international conferences we very much missed participants from the countries beyond the Iron Curtain, who at that time were not allowed to travel abroad and did not have the financial means to join us.

When the situation in the Soviet Union changed and Mikhail Gorbachev declared the era of "glasnost" and "perestroika," it suddenly seemed plausible that the next ITA meeting could be held in Russia. When Christina and I were invited to Moscow as official guests of the Soviet Ministry of Health in order to conduct Holotropic Breathwork workshops, we used our visit to explore the possibility of holding such a conference in Russia. We tried very hard, but without success; the situation seemed too unstable and volatile to take the chance. Our efforts to bring our conference to Russia felt like walking through molasses.

In November 1989, I was traveling when I received a telephone call from Christina, who asked me if I knew what was happening in my native country. Our training was very intense and featured three sessions a day.

We were deeply immersed in the process, and none of us had the time or interest to watch television or follow the news. Christina informed me that the Prague Velvet Revolution was underway and that the Czechoslovakian Communist regime would very likely fall. This meant that we might be able to hold the next ITA conference in Prague, the city where I was born.

A few weeks later, Czechoslovakia was a free country, and the ITA board decided to hold its next meeting in Czechoslovakia. Since I was born in Prague, it seemed only logical to send me to Czechoslovakia as an envoy to find the site and prepare the ground for this conference. However, the years I had spent in my native country turned out to be much less of an advantage than the Board expected. I had left Czechoslovakia at the time of a major liberalization movement aimed at creating "socialism with a human face."

In 1968, when the Prague Spring was brutally suppressed by the invasion of Czechoslovakia by Soviet tanks, I was in the United States on a scholarship at the Johns Hopkins University in Baltimore, Maryland. After the invasion, I was ordered by Czech authorities to return immediately, but decided to disobey and stay in the United States. As a result, I was not able to visit my native country for more than twenty years. During this time, I could not maintain open contact with my friends and colleagues in Czechoslovakia. It would have been politically dangerous for them to exchange letters or telephone calls with an illegal emigrant.

Due to my long absence, I had lost all my connections except for my close relatives, was not familiar with the new situation, and did not have any idea where to begin. My mother met me at the Prague airport, and we took a taxi to her apartment. After we had spent some time together, she left the apartment to visit a neighbor and run a few errands. Alone in the apartment, I sat down in an armchair, had a cup of tea, and reflected on my mission. I contemplated the situation for about ten minutes but was not getting very far.

Suddenly, my train of thought was interrupted by a loud ringing of the doorbell. I answered the door and recognized Tomáš Dostál, a younger psychiatrist colleague of mine who, in the old days, used to be my close friend. Before my departure for the United States, we had shared some explorations of holotropic states of consciousness by sitting for each other in our LSD sessions. Tomáš had heard from an acquaintance of his about my visit to Prague and came to welcome me.

I then learned, to my astonishment, that just as Tomáš was leaving his apartment, his home telephone rang. It was Ivan Havel, a prominent researcher in artificial intelligence and the brother of the Czech president Václav Havel. He was also the leader of a group of progressive scientists who had held secret underground meetings during the Communist era, exploring various new avenues in Western science. They were particularly interested in the new paradigm thinking, consciousness research, and transpersonal psychology. Ivan Havel and Tomáš had been classmates in the gymnasium (the Czech equivalent of high school) and had remained close friends ever since.

Tomáš had been a frequent guest in the Havel household and also knew Ivan's brother Václav. Ivan Havel's group had heard about my work through the lecture of Vasily Nalimov, whom they had invited to Prague as guest lecturer. Vasily was a brilliant Russian scientist, mathematician and philosopher; as a former Soviet dissident he had spent eighteen years in a Siberian labor camp. By strange coincidence, the title of his most famous book was *Realms of the Unconscious* (Nalimov 1982), which is very close to the title of my first book, *Realms of the Human Unconscious* (Grof 1975).

Vasily had included an extensive report about my psychedelic research in his book and discussed my work at length in his lecture for the Prague group. As a result of Vasily's talk, the Prague group became interested in having me as a guest lecturer. Ivan Havel knew that Tomáš and I were old friends and called him to inquire whether he had my address or telephone number and would be able to mediate contact between the Prague group and myself. He was astonished when Tomáš told him that I happened to be visiting Prague and that he was about to walk out of his apartment to pay me a visit.

This very unlikely concatenation of synchronistic events made us feel that we were "surfing a powerful wave," rather than "paddling against the rapids," the way it had felt when we were in Moscow. This spectacular set of coincidences greatly facilitated my role as envoy for the ITA conference. It took me only ten minutes in unfamiliar circumstances to find the ideal contact and support for our future meeting: a group of highly competent academics connected to the university system, who were vitally interested in bringing to Prague a stellar cast of foreign scientists whom they had admired for years. By the same token, I had also found access to the president of the country, who happened to be an enlightened and deeply spiritually oriented person, open to the transpersonal perspective. In view of these circumstances, we felt that we were hired to do the conference rather than striving to organize it.

The conference was held in 1993 in Prague's Smetana Concert Hall and the Municipal House under the aegis of President Václav Havel. President Havel was an ideal guest of honor for an ITA conference. He was not a run-of-the-mill politician, but somebody who was much more appropriately referred to as a "statesman," the head of state with a broad, spiritually based global vision. A well-known playwright, he did not become president as a result of years of struggle for political power. He very reluctantly accepted the nomination, responding to an urgent plea of the Czech people, who loved him as a courageous dissident of the Communist regime and who had spent many years in Communist prison. One of the first things he did after his inauguration was to acknowledge His Holiness the Dalai Lama as the head of Tibet and invite him for a three-day state

Václav Havel (1936–2011), writer, playwright, dissident against Communism, and Czechoslovakian president.

visit. Wherever he went, he impressed his audiences with his eloquent call for spiritually based democracy and global solidarity.

The Prague ITA conference, which was the first opportunity for Eastern and Western representatives of the transpersonal movement to meet and exchange information, was a great success. The highlight of the program was the performance of Babatunde Olatunji, a Yoruba singer, with ten African drummers and dancers. After receiving an enthusiastic standing ovation for their stunning act, the performers decided not to recede behind the curtain, but continued dancing through the center of the hall and out through the front entrance of the building into the streets of Prague. Followed by a significant part of the audience, they sang, drummed, and danced down Celetná ulice, a small street in the historical part of Prague, to Old Town Square. On the way they were joined by a large number of Prague citizens from the neighboring houses, attracted by the bacchanalian spectacle. The jubilant crowd filled the square and continued to dance to the sound of African drums and songs until the wee hours of the morning. After forty years of Communist oppression, when even the twist was considered an unacceptable indulgence, this event was an apt symbol of freshly regained freedom.

The incidence of synchronicities seems to increase around events involving transpersonal psychology; they occur with great frequency to participants in our workshops and training. The most remarkable synchronicity I have ever experienced occurred during my first visit to China. Our small group included several Holotropic Breathwork facilitators, my brother with his partner Mary, camerawoman Sally Li, myself, and Bill Melton and Mei Xu, who inspired and supported the expedition. The purpose of this trip was to introduce transpersonal psychology and Holotropic Breathwork to China.

Before telling this story, I have to mention an important piece of information. In 1978, my wife Christina and myself founded the International Transpersonal Association (ITA). We had spent some time trying to choose the best logo for this organization and finally decided to use a stylized design of the chambered nautilus shell, a perfect example of sacred geometry. We used this logo over several decades on the brochures of all our conferences (there have been twenty of them to this day), on advertising, and on our stationery.

Our first Holotropic Breathwork workshop took place in Jinan, the birthplace of the Chinese spiritual teacher and philosopher Confucius. During the dinner break, one of the participants, Mrs. Meng (meaning "dream"), came to me holding a small beautiful blue velvet bag. She told me that her great-grandmother had appeared in her dream and told her that they had kept a very special stone in their family for several generations and that she should take it to "Dr. Grof." She then handed the object to me. It was a fossil nautilus shell, a marine mollusk; but it had been found and collected at the top of Mt. Everest.

I had never heard about fossil marine forms of life being found on the top of Mt. Everest. I decided to study the geological history of the Himalayas and found out that the age of this famous mountain range was estimated to be about fifty million years, when large tectonic plates collided, starting a series of volcanic explosions, and lifted up the bottom of the ocean. The top of Mt. Everest therefore contains layers of various provenance, including those that originated at the bottom of the ocean. The fossil nautilus thus had to have been at the bottom of the sea before the Himalayas had been created and therefore be at least fifty million years old.

ITA
International
Transpersonal
Association

The Nautilus logo of the International Transpersonal Association (top).

A fossilized Nautilus (Ammonite) collected at the top of Mount Everest.

The purpose of our expedition was to bring transpersonal psychology to China. The fact that Mrs. Meng's great grandmother appeared in her dream and asked her to bring me the symbol of the International Transpersonal Association, a nautilus shell, fossilized and lifted from the bottom of the ocean to the top of the highest mountain of the world tens of millions years ago, was truly a miraculous synchronicity. I mentioned it briefly in my presentation at the Beijing University and in the Chinese press it received more attention than anything else in my talk. However, this was not the only remarkable synchronicity that we encountered during this trip; it seemed that we had entered a magic world where linear causality no longer applied.

I will mention just two more of these memorable coincidences. We found out that the organizers of the Chinese trip scheduled an appearance at Beijing University for my close and dear friend Jack Kornfield, a Vipassana Buddhist teacher, on the same evening that the organizers of our trip quite independently tried to schedule me. When this was discovered, the

Jack Kornfield (1945–), Vipassana Buddhist teacher, transpersonal psychologist, and founder of Spirit Rock Insight Meditation Center in Woodacre, California, visiting with Stan Grof in the Forbidden City in Beijing, China.

organizers decided to create a joint evening for us called "Grof in discussion with Kornfield." Jack and I had led and co-led many events over the last forty years but had never met anywhere unless we had jointly planned it. The second of these synchronicities involved one of our translators and a breathwork facilitator, who were scheduled to join us on a train from Jinan to Beijing. Although they purchased their tickets independently, one from Northern China and the other from the South, they ended up sitting not only in the same wagon and compartment as our group, but in seats adjacent to each other.

As I was witnessing how the series of synchronicities brought an element of magic into our group, I had to think about the quote from the Czech-French writer, Milan Kundera, the author of *The Unbearable Lightness of Being:* "It is wrong to chide the novel for being fascinated by mysterious coincidences…But it is right to chide man for being blind to such coincidences in his daily life. For he thereby deprives his life of a dimension of beauty."

The knowledge of the phenomenon of synchronicity is essential not only for psychonauts and archetypal astrologers, but also for scientists who still subscribe to the materialistic worldview. It is one of the most obvious and critical challenges to monistic materialistic philosophy. A statement that Jung made in 1955 in a letter to R. F. C. Hull made it clear that he was well aware of this fact: "The latest comment about 'Synchronicity' is that it cannot be accepted because it shakes the security of our scientific foundations, as if this were not exactly the goal I am aiming at." On the same day he wrote to Michael Fordham about "the impact of synchronicity upon the fanatical one-sidedness of scientific philosophy."

Marie-Louise von Franz, aware of the paradigm-breaking potential of synchronicity, said in an interview late in her life: "The work which has now to be done is to work out the concept of synchronicity. I don't know the people who will continue it. They must exist, but I don't know where they are." Fortunately, the literature on synchronicity and its pivotal importance for a number of disciplines has since grown exponentially and this concept has become an integral part of the emerging new paradigm in science.

Literature

Bell, J. S. 1966. "On the Problem of Hidden Variables in Quantum Physics." *Review of Modern Physics* 38:447.

Campbell, J. 1984. *The Way of the Animal Powers: The Historical Atlas of World Mythology.* New York: Harper and Row.

Capra, F. 1975. *The Tao of Physics.* Berkeley: Shambala Publications.

Driesch, H. 1914. *The History and Theory of Vitalism* (translated by C. K. Ogden). London: Macmillan.

Franz, M. von. 2015. *On Divination and Synchronicity: The Psychology of Meaningful Chance.* Toronto, Ontario: Inner City Books.

Grof, S. 1975. *Realms of the Human Unconscious: Observations from LSD Research.* New York: Viking Press.

Grof, S. 2006. *When the Impossible Happens: Adventures in Non-Ordinary Realities.* Louisville, CO: Sounds True.

Harner, M. 1980. *The Way of the Shaman: A Guide to Power and Healing.* New York: Harper & Row.

Holler, S. 1982. *The Gnostic Jung and the Seven Sermons for the Dead.* Athens, Greece: Quest Publications.

Jung, C. G. 1959. *The Archetypes and the Collective Unconscious.* Collected Works, vol. 9,1. Bollingen Series XX, Princeton, NJ: Princeton University Press.

Jung, C. G. 1960. *Synchronicity: An Acausal Connecting Principle.* Collected Works, vol. 8, Bollingen Series XX. Princeton, NJ: Princeton University Press.

Kammerer, P. 1919. *Das Gesetz der Serie (Law of the Series).* Stuttgart/Berlin: Deutsche Verlags-Anstalt.

Koestler, A. 1971. *The Case of the Midwife Toad.* New York: Random House.

Main, R. (ed.) 1998. *Jung on Synchronicity and the Paranormal.* Princeton, NJ: Princeton University Press.

Miller, A. 2009. *Deciphering the Cosmic Number: The Strange Friendship of Wolfgang Pauli and Carl Jung.* New York: W.W.Norton & Co.

Nalimov, V. V. 1982. *Realms of the Unconscious: The Enchanted Frontier.* Philadelphia, PA: ISI Press.

Plotinus. 1950. *The Philosophy of Plotinus: Representative Books from the Enneads.* Appelton, WI: Century-Crofts.

Smith, H. 1991. *The World's Religions: Our Great Wisdom Traditions.* San Francisco, CA: Harper One.

IX

Holotropic States of Consciousness and the Understanding of Art

The work and research into psychedelics and other forms of holotropic states of consciousness have brought revolutionary insights into the understanding of art and artists. Sigmund Freud did pioneering work in this regard and his followers attempted to apply the observations from their clinical work to the creative process.

There are limitations, however, to the approaches that use models of the psyche which are confined to postnatal biography and Freud's individual unconscious. The explanatory power of depth psychology only increases when the cartography of the psyche is expanded to include the perinatal and transpersonal domains.

In our classes at the California Institute of Integral Studies (CIIS) in San Francisco, seminars at Esalen and in Europe, and our joint telecourses, Rick Tarnas and I have tried to demonstrate that combining the extended model of the psyche with archetypal astrology raises the understanding of art to a completely new level. It brings a depth and clarity that was previously unimaginable. Unfortunately, I do not have time in the context of this encyclopedia to explore this fascinating avenue of research. Interested readers will find more information in our writings dedicated to this topic (Tarnas 2006, Grof 2009, 2012). A more complete treatment of this subject will have to wait for a future publication.

Sigmund Freud

The dawn of the twentieth century saw the discovery of the unconscious and the birth of depth psychology. This new field was inspired and spearheaded by Sigmund Freud, who practically single-handedly laid its foundations. Initially, Freud's interest in the human psyche was primarily clinical—to explain the etiology of psychoneuroses and to find the way to treat them. However, in the course of his explorations, his horizons expanded enormously to include many cultural phenomena, including art.

Freud's work opened up a new original approach to the understanding of art and artists and had a profound influence on artistic circles. He attempted to apply the observations from the patients' analyses to understanding the artist's personality, the motives for artistic creation, and the nature of art. According to him, an artist is a person who has withdrawn from reality into his fantasies. The primary sources of these fantasies are Oedipal wishes associated with strong feelings of guilt. The artist finds his way back to the world and society by representing these forbidden wishes in his work.

The public, having Oedipal wishes of its own, admires the artist for the courage to express what they have repressed and for relieving them of their guilt. For the artist, the acceptance of his work means that the public shares his guilt, which relieves him of his own guilty feelings. According to Freud, art offers substitutive satisfaction for the oldest and still most deeply felt cultural renunciations of basic biological drives and, for that reason, it serves to reconcile humans with the sacrifice they have made on behalf of civilization (Freud 1911).

Freud also discovered that it was possible to use psychoanalysis to understand the content of the works of art in the same way that it is possible to understand dreams. Freud's most famous attempt to interpret works of art is his analysis of the ancient Greek tragedy *Oedipus Rex* by the Athenian playwright Sophocles. In this play, the protagonist Oedipus unwittingly kills his father Laius and marries his mother Jocasta, thus fulfilling the prophecy of the Delphic oracle.

Freud's insights into this work were the main source of his famous Oedipus complex. In Freud's own words, Oedipus' "destiny moves us only because it might have been ours—because the oracle laid the same curse upon us before our birth as upon him. It is the fate of all of us, perhaps, to direct our first sexual impulse towards our mother and our first hatred and our first murderous wish against our father. Our dreams convince us that that is so" (Freud 1953).

Freud also made an interesting attempt to understand Shakespeare's *Hamlet*. He wanted to be remembered as the psychological detective who found the solution to "The Problem"—the reason for Hamlet's procrastination to kill Claudius. This mystery has been called the "Sphinx of modern literature." According to a widely accepted explanation by Goethe, Hamlet represented the type of man whose power of direct action is paralyzed by an excessive development of his intellect. Freud offered a radically different interpretation: Claudius acted out Hamlet's own repressed

Sigmund Freud (1856–1939), Austrian neurologist, founder of depth psychology, and discoverer of psychoanalysis.

Oedipal fantasies, and to kill him would be to murder a part of himself (Freud 1953).

Another one of Freud's famous attempts to understand artists is his analysis of Leonardo da Vinci based on Leonardo's earliest childhood memory, which he described in mirror-writing in one of his notebooks in the *Codex Atlanticus*. Explaining his obsession with devising a flying machine, Leonardo wrote that when he was a baby, a kite *(nibbio,* a small kind of hawk) landed on him and stuck its tail into his mouth, repeatedly hitting his lips with its feathers.

Freud concluded that this was a fantasy involving fellation by a phallic mother and also being nursed by her. The idea that the mother has a penis is, according to Freud, a common fantasy of small children. For Freud, this fantasy indicated that Leonardo did not spend his early childhood with his father, as was commonly believed, but with his mother (Freud 1957b).

According to Freud, this had far-reaching consequences for Leonardo's personality, his scientific interests, and his artistic activity. Leonardo's enormous curiosity, which drove him to avid exploration of so many areas, from human and animal anatomy, botany, and paleontology to the laws of mechanics and hydraulics, was the sublimation of a great interest in sexuality that this situation had evoked in him as a child. According to Freud, this insatiable curiosity also interfered with Leonardo's artistic activity and creativity.

He painted slowly and it took him a long time to complete his works; for example, painting the *Mona Lisa* took him four years. This difficulty was responsible for the enormous damage that his famous painting the *Last Supper,* which is in the refectory of the Convent of Santa Maria delle Grazie in Milan, has suffered over the course of the centuries. Leonardo chose the slow process of painting with oil colors, rather than the more durable *al fresco* technique that required much faster activity.

According to Freud, the excessive sublimation of the sexual drive also inhibited Leonardo's sexual life. Leonardo was very shy, and sexually withdrawn and blocked. He was repulsed by the sexual act and, with a few exceptions—several drawings of the anatomy of pregnancy and a strange drawing of sexual intercourse—avoided sexual topics. He did not seem to have a relationship with a woman and liked beautiful young men as his models and students. During his apprenticeship with Verocchio, he was accused of homosexual relationships. Freud attributed Leonardo's homosexual tendencies to the disappointment that he experienced as a child when he discovered that his mother did not have a penis.

Freud also pointed out Leonardo's conflicts in relation to aggression. He was a vegetarian and was known for buying captured birds in the market and letting them go. However, as an engineer for Lodovico Sforza, he designed a large number of war machines, some of them truly diabolical. All through his study, Freud put great emphasis on the fact that the bird in Leonardo's childhood experience was a vulture. He pointed out that ancient Egyptians believed that there were only female vultures and that they were inseminated by the wind while flying. This belief was used by Christian Church Fathers as an argument for the possibility of immaculate conception.

Freud found surprising support for his thesis in the work of Oskar Pfister, a Lutheran minister and lay analyst, who suggested that Leonardo's painting *The Virgin and Child with St. Anne* contained a hidden figure of a vulture with its tail near the mouth of the child (Pfister 1913). This discovery is extremely puzzling, because Freud's references to a vulture were based on a linguistic error. The term *"nibbio"* used in Leonardo's description of his childhood memory actually means a kite *(Milvus milvus)* and not a vulture *(Gyps fulvus)*. When Freud discovered this error, he was deeply disappointed because, as he confessed to Lou Andreas-Salomé in a letter of February 9, 1919, he regarded the Leonardo essay to be "the only beautiful thing I have ever written."

According to Freud, the complexity of Leonardo's relationship with his mother found its expression in the mysterious, ambiguous "Leonardesque smile" on Leonardo's *Mona Lisa*—simultaneously cold and sensual, seductive and reserved. To paint her took Leonardo an extremely long time; the painting was considered unfinished when he took it with him to France after four years of working on it. This smile also figures prominently in some of his other paintings, including *St. John the Baptist* and *Bacchus,* as well as others.

It is important to mention Freud's concession that psychoanalysis only has relevance for understanding the content of works of art but has nothing to contribute to the phenomenon of genius. Freud's attempt to analyze artists and works of art was a pioneering venture into a new field, but essentially a major failure. Erich Neumann's Jungian essay, entitled "Art and the Creative Unconscious: Leonardo da Vinci and the Mother Archetype" offered a strong criticism of Freud's interpretations, pointing out some major factual errors that made Freud's argument and his essay irrelevant (Neumann 1974). It also shows how the understanding of art changes when we introduce the transpersonal perspective of the Jungian collective unconscious and the archetypal dynamics.

Neumann presented evidence that Leonardo lived with his father and stepmother in his grandfather's house and was brought up by his grandmother, not by his mother. These facts disqualified Freud's speculations about Leonardo's relationship with his mother and its effect on his curiosity, sexual orientation, and art, which was the cornerstone of his essay. Neumann also demonstrated that Freud's far-reaching speculations considering the "vulture" in Leonardo's childhood memory involved Freud's serious linguistic error.

However, for Neumann, Freud's linguistic error was of relatively little significance. He not only corrected the factual errors in Freud's study, but he also shifted the focus of Leonardo's analysis to the archetypal level, bringing in the element of "higher creativity." For Jungians, the inspiration of a genius comes from the archetypal domain, not from the biographical domain (see also James Hillman's *The Soul's Code,* Hillman 1996).

For Neumann, Leonardo's bird was the uroboric symbol of the Great Mother, who is both male and female. It is the archetypal Feminine, the all-generative power of nature and creative source of the unconscious. The nursing mother is uroboric; her breasts are often represented as being phallic; she is nourishing and fecundating the male, as well as the female child. It was Leonardo's connection with the archetypal Great Mother that, according to Neumann, was the source of his immense creativity. Leonardo's driving force was of a spiritual, not sexual nature.

> *"Thus the Great Mother is uroboric: terrible and devouring, beneficent and creative; a helper, but also alluring and destructive; a maddening enchantress, yet a bringer of wisdom; bestial and divine, voluptuous harlot and inviolable virgin, immemorially old and eternally young."*

Mona Lisa, with her enormous richness, ambiguity, and mysteriousness, did not reflect Leonardo's strongly ambivalent relationship with his biological mother. Instead, she clearly represents an Anima figure, Sophia. As far as the image of the vulture hidden in Leonardo's painting is concerned, it might have been a joke. Leonardo, known for his playfulness and for his strong opposition to all secular and religious authority, might have used it to ridicule the attempt of the Church Fathers to use the allegedly unisex vulture to support the possibility of immaculate conception.

Freud's attempt to apply psychoanalysis to the understanding of Fyodor Mikhailovich Dostoevsky in his article "Dostoevsky and Parricide," was equally unsuccessful. In this essay, Freud concluded that Dostoevsky did not suffer from epilepsy, an organic neurological disease, but hysteria, a psychoneurosis caused by emotional trauma. He attributed great significance to the rumor that Dostoevsky's father was murdered by his serfs and asserted that this was the cause of Dostoevsky's alleged "epilepsy" (Freud 1957a).

According to Freud, the ecstasy that Dostoevsky experienced at the beginning of his seizures *(aura)* reflected his joy at the news of his hated father's death and his own ensuing liberation. The ecstasy was followed by a fall, a loud scream, convulsions, and unconsciousness (typical manifestations of *grand mal epilepsy).* The slow and confused recovery was associated with depression and a profound feeling of guilt, as if he had committed a great crime.

Freud interpreted these symptoms as a punishment imposed on him by his superego—his father's authority introjected into his unconscious. "Dostoevsky's whole life," Freud wrote "is dominated by his twofold attitude to the father-czar-authority, by voluptuous masochistic submission on the one hand, and by outraged rebellion against it on the other." Freud's conclusions were seriously criticized by neurologists as well as historians; Dostoevsky's disease was epilepsy, not hysteria, and his father was not murdered.

Freud's interpretation of Goethe's *Poetry and Truth,* and Wilhelm Jensen's *Gradiva,* as well as Shakespeare's *Merchant of Venice* and *King Lear* did not bring any major revelations. In *Poetry and Truth,* Freud introduced the concept of "sibling rivalry" and used it to explain little Goethe's destruction of a doll house by attributing it to his anger about the birth of his sister; however, he was not able to bring any evidence that these two events actually coincided in time (Freud 1917). In *Gradiva,* Freud used the image of Pompeii covered by volcanic ashes as a dramatic illustration of a childhood memory buried in the unconscious (Freud 2003). His analysis of the two Shakespeare plays is also complex, convoluted, and unconvincing (Freud 1913).

Marie Bonaparte

The most interesting attempt to apply psychoanalysis to art is the trilogy on the *Life and Works of Edgar Allan Poe,* written by Greek princess Marie Bonaparte, an enthusiastic follower of Freud who arranged his safe escape from Nazi Germany. Like her teacher and idol, she used the Oedipus complex as the basic explanatory principle and source of artistic inspiration (Bonaparte 1949). This is reflected in the basic structure of her three-volume opus.

The first volume is an extremely detailed reconstruction of Poe's biography. The second one, *Tales of the Mother,* focuses on the stories that, according to Bonaparte, were inspired by Poe's relationship with his mother, Elizabeth Arnold. She was a frail actress dying of tuberculosis, to which she succumbed before little Edgar was three years old. These stories describe seriously ill and dying female lovers and wives who suffer from mysterious afflictions, including Berenice, Morella, Ligeia, Rowena, Eleonora, Lady Madeline, and others. Some other stories in this volume feature the murder of a female figure, portray the mother as a landscape, or represent a confession of impotence.

The third volume, *Tales of the Father,* presents an analysis of the stories that reflected his relationship with male authority: these involved either a revolt against the father figure, patricide, masochistic surrender to the father, or a struggle with conscience (Superego). The male figures in Poe's life were as equally problematic as the female ones. His father David was an erratic and intractable alcoholic who also suffered from tuberculosis. He disappeared in New York City when Poe was eighteen months old. After his mother's death, little Edgar was taken into the home of Frances Allan and adopted by the couple more or less against the will of her husband, John Allan, a Scotch merchant, who was a strict disciplinarian and became Poe's second father figure.

Marie Bonaparte's basic tenet is that works of art reveal the creator's psychology, particularly the dynamics of the unconscious. She described Poe's unconscious as "extremely active and full of horrors and torments" and mentioned explicitly that without his literary genius, he would have spent his life in prison or in a mental institution. She attributed the blood appearing in several of Poe's stories to his observation of *hemoptysis*, coughing of blood, a frequent symptom of tuberculosis. She also attributed great significance to the fact that in the restricted quarters in which his poor parents lived, little Edgar very likely experienced the famous Freudian "primal scene"—observed their sexual activities and interpreted them as sadistic acts.

Marie Bonaparte (1882–1962), Greek princess and ardent student of Sigmund Freud.

Bonaparte's conceptual framework is limited to postnatal biography and to the Freudian individual unconscious. Although Poe's early life was difficult, it is not a convincing source of the kind of horrors found in his stories. Bonaparte makes several references to birth and the maternal womb, but—as is common with most psychoanalysts—her language shifts at this point from "memories" to "fantasies." Like Freud, she refuses to accept the possibility that prenatal life and birth could be recorded in the unconscious as actual memories.

However, many of Poe's stories, particularly the most macabre and emotionally powerful ones, have unmistakable perinatal features. For example, Poe's story "A Descent into the Maelstrom," a hair-raising adventure of

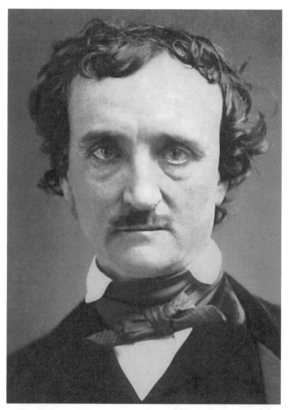

Edgar Allan Poe (1809–1849), American writer, who invented the modern detective story and created tales of horror and the macabre.

three Norwegian brothers, shows a deep resemblance to the experience of the engulfing whirlpool, which typically accompanies the reliving of the onset of birth (BPM II). The boat the brothers are using during their fishing expedition is entrapped by the monstrous Maelstrom and drawn relentlessly toward its center. Two of the brothers lose their lives in a hopeless fight with this raging force of nature. The third one, using an ingenious strategy, makes a fortuitous escape after a close encounter with death and survives to tell the story.

The prison of the Inquisition described in Poe's story "The Pit and the Pendulum," with its diabolical torments and its contracting and eventually fiery walls, from which the hero is rescued at the last moment, has many characteristics of the delivering uterus. Similarly, the escape of the dwarf Hop-Frog from the torturous ambience of the royal court, described in Poe's novel of the same name, resembles rebirth experiences (BPM III-IV) from Holotropic Breathwork and psychedelic sessions.

In this book, when the clever court jester is asked to devise a special form of entertainment for a masked ball, he camouflages the cruel king and his ministers as orangutans by using tar and flax, and then sets them ablaze. In the ensuing mayhem, he climbs up a rope to a hole in the ceiling to unite with his female companion Trippetta. The experience of being buried alive, Poe's favorite theme that appears in many of his stories, including "Premature Burial," "The Cask of Amontillado," "Loss of Breath," "The Fall of the House of Usher," and others, is a frequent motif in perinatal sessions. Many perinatal motifs are also found in Poe's longest, strange, and mystifying novel entitled *The Narrative of Arthur Gordon Pym of Nantucket.*

Marie Bonaparte's interpretive approach, which was limited to the Freudian model, proves most inadequate when she uses it in the analysis of Poe's *Eureka.* This magnificent vision of cosmic creation is very different from anything that Poe had ever written. The reaction to its publication ranged from critical to highly positive, including praise from scientists. Albert Einstein made the following comment in a letter written in 1934: *Eureka* is "Eine sehr schöne Leistung eines ungewöhnlich selbständigen Geistes" (a very beautiful achievement of an unusually independent mind).

In his introduction, Poe promises to speak about the Material and Spiritual Universe, about its Essence, its Origin, Creation, its Present Condition, and its Destiny. When writing about these things, he capitalizes the first letters of nouns and adjectives in a way that psychiatric patients often do. Marie Bonaparte sees this as a sign of psychopathology, but it is clearly an indication that Poe was tapping deep transpersonal sources. For this reason, his experience—like the experiences of the mystics—could not be adequately conveyed in ordinary language.

Poe's cosmological vision has a deep resemblance to the worldviews of the great spiritual philosophies of the East, particularly their tantric branches (Mookerjee and Khanna 1989). He describes the creation of the universe as a process that begins in a singularity and involves a series of countless divisions and differentiations. This then creates a counter-reaction—the tendency to return to the original unity. The continued existence of the universe also requires a third force, which is repulsion, preventing the coalition of the separated parts.

The parallels between Poe's singularity and Mahabindu—the source of the creation of the universe described in Tantric scriptures—is remarkable. The same is true for Poe's three cosmic forces, which have the characteristics of the Tantric gunas: *tamas, sattva,* and *rajas,* which are feminine powers of creation. The final aim which the completed universe strives toward, then, is the ultimate reunion with God; the sole function of the repulsive force would be to delay that reunion. In my book *The Cosmic Game: Explorations of the Frontiers of Human Consciousness,* I have described a similar cosmology that emerged from the psychedelic and Holotropic Breathwork sessions of the people participating in my research (Grof 1998).

Like my clients' insights, Poe's cosmological vision has a strong resemblance not only to the scriptures of the spiritual systems that Aldous Huxley called perennial philosophy (Huxley 1945), but also to theories of modern science, in this case to cosmological speculations of famous physicists based on astronomical observations. Poe himself believed that his *Eureka* would revolutionize astronomy, and his ideas have actually been seriously discussed in scientific circles.

One of Poe's major hypotheses, that the universe filled with matter after a single, high-energy particle exploded, is the rough equivalent of the cosmogenetic theory developed in the twentieth century by Lemaitre, Gamov, and Alpher. Its opponent, Fred Hoyle, referred to it facetiously as the "Big Bang" theory and it has been known by this name ever since. It has remained one of the leading cosmogenetic theories to this day (Alpher and Herman 2001).

Poe theorized that the universe must be expanding, since the energy of the explosion is pushing matter outward. He also concluded that eventually gravity would pull all particles back together and the process would start all over again; this idea appeared in Alexander Friedman's theory of the pulsating universe (Friedman 1922).

In *Eureka,* Poe also offered a reasonable solution to Olbers' "paradox of the dark sky" that plagued astronomers: a static universe with an infinite number of stars could not be dark, unless some of the stars are so far that the light would not reach us. Modern consciousness research has shown that visionary states have a remarkable potential to provide not only extraordinary religious illumination and artistic inspiration, but also brilliant scientific insights that open new fields and facilitate scientific problem-solving.

Numerous examples of this kind can be found in the excellent book by Willis Harman, entitled *Higher Creativity: Liberating the Unconscious for Breakthrough Insights* (Harman 1984). We will return to this important subject in the next chapter. Considering Poe's brilliant insights that matched those of professional scientists, Bonaparte was most blatantly reductionistic in her analysis of *Eureka.*

For her, Poe's God was his physical father and the creation of the cosmos referred to the biological creative act. Poe's original particle from which the cosmos evolved was allegedly the spermatozoon. In his fantasy, the universe was purportedly created by a Father figure without female participation. Yearning for the original unity was a return to the Father and reflected Poe's detachment from the feminine. Poe's cosmic fantasy about multiple universes reflected the fact that there were other siblings in his family.

According to Bonaparte, *Eureka* revealed Poe's avoidance of Mother and Woman; he thus ended his literary career with a cosmic homosexual fantasy. I hope that this brief excursion into Marie Bonaparte's Freudian interpretation of art showed that the expanded cartography of the psyche, including the perinatal and transpersonal domains, provides a much deeper, richer, and convincing conceptual framework for a psychological analysis of the content of works of art.

Otto Rank

Otto Rank disagreed with Freud's insistence on the primacy of the Oedipus complex as the source of artistic inspiration. According to him, the artists' creativity is driven by a profound need to come to terms with the primordial anxiety associated with the trauma of birth *(Urangst)* and to return to the safety of the maternal womb (Rank 1989).

Rank's general thesis concerned the paramount importance of the memory of birth as a powerful motivating force in the psyche, which was convincingly supported by modern work with holotropic states of consciousness. Instead of emphasizing the desire to return to the womb, though, it shifted the focus to the drive to relive the trauma of the passage through the birth canal and to experience psychospiritual death and rebirth. As we saw earlier, it was actually possible to identify specific experiential patterns related to the four consecutive stages of birth, Basic Perinatal Matrices (BPMs), and describe the specific psychodynamic significance of each of them.

This research has also shown that the mythological figures and realms of the psyche are not derived from the trauma of birth, as Rank believed, but are expressions of archetypes, autonomous organizing principles of the collective unconscious. Instead of being products of birth memories, they are instrumental in forming and informing the experiences in the different stages of birth. Thus Rank saw the Sphinx and other demonic female figures, such as Hekate, Gorgo, the Sirens, and the Harpies as representations of the anxiety-laden mother of childbirth rather than figures belonging to a superordinated archetypal domain.

Carl Gustav Jung

As we will see in the following section, this is the perspective that emerged from the therapeutic work of another renegade from the psychoanalytic movement, C. G. Jung. Jung strongly disagreed with Freud's idea that the motivation for artistic creation is to share forbidden Oedipal fantasies. According to him, the secret of artistic creation and the effectiveness of art is to be found in the return to the state of "participation mystique"—to that level of experience at which it is the collective Man who lives, and not the individual. It was not Goethe who created Faust, it was the archetype of Faust that created Goethe (Jung 1975).

Another major point of dissent between Jung and Freud was the concept of libido. For Jung, libido was not a biological drive, but a universal force comparable to Aristotle's entelechy or Henri Bergson's *élan vital*. This understanding of art answers the problem of genius that Freud was not able to account for by using the explanatory principles of his psychoanalysis.

The phenomenon of genius cannot be understood in terms of individual psychology. According to Jung, the genius functions as a channel for cosmic creative energy of the World Soul *(Anima mundi)*. Jung also rejected Freud's model of the psyche because it was limited to postnatal biography and the individual unconscious. He extended it to include the collective unconscious with its historical and mythological domains (Jung 1990). The concept of the collective unconscious and its organizing principles, the archetypes, brought the depth that Freudian psychology could not provide to artistic analysis.

Jung's first major attempt to analyze art was his extensive analysis of the partly poetic, partly prosaic book of an American woman, Miss Frank Miller, which was published in Geneva by Theodore Flournoy and became known as the *Miller Fantasies* (Miller 1906). Jung's analysis of this book, entitled *Symbols of Transformation* (Jung 1956), was a work of major historical importance, because its publication marked the beginning of a break between Jung and Freud.

The method of "amplification" that Jung used in the analysis of Miss Miller's book became the model for the Jungian approach to the analysis of dreams, psychotic experiences, art, and other manifestations of the psyche. This technique consists of finding parallels between the motifs and figures of analyzed work in folklore, history, literature, art, and mythology of other cultures and revealing their archetypal sources.

Jung had a profound influence on modern writers and filmmakers. Like Freud's famous concepts (the Oedipus complex, castration complex, vagina dentata, the Id, and the Superego), Jung's descriptions of the principal Archetypes (the Shadow, Anima, Animus, Trickster, Terrible Mother, Wise Old Man, and others) not only provided insights into already existing works of art, but also inspiration for generations of new artists.

Contribution of Psychedelic Research
to the Understanding of Art

The serendipitous discovery of the powerful psychedelic effect of LSD by Albert Hofmann and the experimentation with this extraordinary substance brought revolutionary discoveries concerning consciousness, the human psyche, and the creative process. For historians and critics of art, the LSD experiments provided extraordinary new insights into the psychology and psychopathology of art.

They saw a deep similarity between the paintings of "normal" subjects depicting their LSD visions and the Outsider Art (Art brut) and the art of psychiatric patients, as was documented in Hans Prinzhorn's classic *Artistry of the Mentally Ill* (Prinzhorn 1995), Walter Morgenthaler's book *Madness and Art* (Morgenthaler 1992), and Roger Cardinal's *Outsider Art* (Cardinal 1972). Other psychedelic paintings bore a deep resemblance to artifacts of native cultures, such as African masks and fetishes, the sculptures of the New Guinea tribes of the Sepik River, bark paintings of the Australian Aborigines, yarn paintings of the Mexican Huichol Indians, Chumash cave paintings in Southern California, and others.

There was also an unmistakable similarity between the art of LSD subjects and that of representatives of various modern movements: abstractionism, expressionism, impressionism, cubism, dadaism, surrealism, and fantastic realism. For professional painters who participated in LSD research, psychedelic sessions often marked a radical change in their artistic expression. Their imagination became much richer, their colors more vivid, and their style considerably freer. On occasion, people who had never painted before were able to produce extraordinary drawings and paintings. It seemed that the power of the deep unconscious material that had surfaced in their sessions somehow took over the process and used the subject as a channel for artistic expression.

However, the impact of LSD and other psychedelic substances on art went much further than influencing the style of the artists who volunteered as experimental subjects. An entire generation of avant-garde young artists embraced them as tools for finding deep inspiration in the perinatal domain and in the archetypal realm of the collective unconscious. They portrayed, with extraordinary artistic power, a rich array of experiences that originated in these deep and ordinarily hidden recesses of the human psyche (Grof 2015).

Their self-experimentation also led to serious interest in areas closely related to their psychedelic experiences—study of the great Eastern spiritual philosophies, intense meditation practice, participation in shamanic rituals, worship of the Goddess and of the Sacred Feminine, nature mysticism, and various esoteric teachings. Many of them documented their own spiritual and philosophical quests in their art.

Psychedelic therapy and self-experimentation with psychedelics by psychiatrists and psychologists also contributed to interpretations of art and to art criticism. It revealed the inadequacy of the mainstream model of the psyche and the need for its radical extension and revision. In an earlier chapter, I described my own proposal for such a new model based on the experiences and observations from the research of holotropic states.

I would like to close this chapter with a brief review of one of the first attempts to use my extended cartography of the psyche in the analysis of art. It is a brilliant study of the great French writer and philosopher Jean Paul Sartre, entitled *Sartre's Rite of Passage*. It was written thirty-five years

J. P. Sartre (1905–1980), French writer, novelist, playwright, and existential philosopher, with his wife Simone de Beauvoir (1908–1986), French writer, philosopher, and political activist.

ago by Tom Riedlinger and published in the *Journal of Transpersonal Psychology* (Riedlinger 1982). It brought convincing evidence that significant aspects of Jean Paul Sartre's writings and his existential philosophy can be understood through his poorly managed and unresolved psychedelic session that focused on the perinatal level.

In February 1935, Sartre was given an intramuscular injection of mescaline at Sainte-Anne's Hospital in Le Havre, France. He was twenty-nine years old, unpublished and unknown, and worked as a college philosophy teacher. He was writing a book on imagination and hoped that the drug would induce visions and give him some insights into the dynamics of the psyche. His wish was fulfilled, but he got more than he bargained for.

When his partner Simone de Beauvoir called him in the afternoon of his session, he told her that her call had rescued him from a desperate battle with octopuses. As we saw earlier, the octopus is a frequent symbol of BPM II, representing the termination of freedom experienced in the aquatic setting of the womb. Sartre also experienced massive optical illusions. The objects in the environment were grotesquely changing their shape, becoming symbols of death: umbrellas were transforming into vultures and shoes into skeletons, and human faces looked monstrous. He was afraid that he was losing his mind. All these are typical manifestations of BPM II.

He saw frightful apparitions for the rest of the evening. The next morning, he seemed to be completely recovered, but several days later, he began suffering recurrent attacks of depression and anxiety and felt pursued by various aquatic monsters (such as giant lobsters and crabs), houses had leering faces, eyes and jaws, and every clock face seemed to turn into an owl. These states continued until summer. Sartre made his own diagnosis: "I am suffering from a chronic hallucinatory psychosis."

He blamed the psychiatrist Lagache, who gave him the mescaline, for his "bad trip"; he was "rather saturnine" and told him during the preparation for the session: "What it does to you is terrible!" Sartre himself insisted that the drug was not primarily responsible for what was happening to him. He called its effect "incidental" and thought that the primary "profound" cause of his reaction was his pervasive identity crisis resulting from his passage to adulthood. He was unwilling to accept the social responsibilities imposed on the individual by bourgeois society.

However, Sartre's visions clearly had much deeper and earlier roots than his identity crisis and his fear of being swallowed by bourgeois society. Similar confrontation with deep-dwelling oceanic monsters is recorded in *Les Mots,* Sartre's autobiography of his childhood (Sartre 1964a). There, he described that when he was eight years old, he discovered the power of creative writing. Whenever he started experiencing anguish, he took his heroes on wild adventures. Sartre's typical childhood heroes were geologists and deep-sea divers fighting various subterranean or undersea monsters—a giant octopus, a gigantic tarantula, or a twenty-ton crustacean—all of which are creatures that play an important role in psychedelic and Holotropic Breathwork sessions focusing on the perinatal level (BPM II). About this, Sartre said, "What flowed from my pen…was I myself, a child monster; it was my boredom with life, my fear of death, my dullness and my perversity…"

It seems that the mescaline session activated a COEX system associated with the second perinatal matrix and its effect continued long after the pharmacological action of mescaline had subsided. The layers of this COEX reached far back into Sartre's childhood; its most important common denominator was a sense of the pervasive presence of death. His father died at the age of thirty, less than two years after Sartre was born. His mother, concerned about her husband's disease, stopped lactating; Sartre had a strong reaction to weaning and developed severe enteritis.

His life from then on had a "funereal taste." At the age of five, he saw death as a tall, mad woman, dressed in black; when he looked at her, she muttered: "I will put that child in my pocket." As a child, Sartre responded strongly to the disease of his friend and to the death of his grandmother. When he was seven, he lived in a state of terror that the "shadowy mouth of death could open anywhere and snap me up."

When he looked in a mirror, he saw himself as "a jellyfish…hitting against the glass of the aquarium." Other children shunned him as a playmate and he felt abandoned and alone. In his daydreams, he would discover "a monstrous universe that was the underside of my impotence." He said about it: "I did not invent these horrors; I found them in my memory."

Many aspects of Sartre's problems and his work can be understood as a strong influence of BPM II: fear of death and insanity, the horror of engulfment, preoccupation with aquatic monsters, a sense of the absurdity of life and other elements of existentialist philosophy, loneliness, inferiority, and guilt. His famous play even carries the title *No Exit (Huit clos)* (Sartre 1994). In the critical years of his life, Sartre saw himself "strained to the breaking point between two extremes—being born and dying with each heartbeat." This strange experiential amalgam of dying and being born is again a characteristic feature of perinatal dynamics.

The tension reached unbearable proportions a few months before Sartre's thirtieth birthday. Using the strategy of denying death that Ernest Becker called the "immortality project" (Becker 1973), he attempted to rob death of its sting by writing and fantasizing that he would reach *post mortem* fame. However, his efforts at the time failed, and he did not succeed in getting published. He was also realizing that he was approaching the age at which his father died. His COEX system with death as the central theme was thus close to the surface when Sartre took mescaline.

It intensified and partially emerged into consciousness, but it was not resolved. Its elements appear throughout *La Nausée,* a book he started writing at the time of the mescaline session (Sartre 1964b). It seemed that working on it helped Sartre integrate the experience; it deals with issues such as nausea, suffocation, and scatological elements ("sticky rotten filth"). There are also references to sea monsters and the uncanny chestnut tree (the tree of death from Sartre's childhood described in *Les Mots).*

A more comprehensive discussion of the advantages of the expanded cartography for the analysis of artworks can be found in my book *Modern Consciousness Research and the Understanding of Art* (Grof 2015). An important part of this book is a selection of the paintings, drawings, and sculptures of the Swiss genius of fantastic realism Hans Ruedi Giger. There cannot be more obvious proof for the importance of the perinatal domain of the unconscious in understanding art than his creations.

Leonardo da Vinci (1452–1519) created his well known self-portrait
in the year 1512.

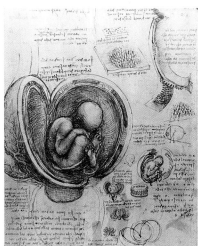

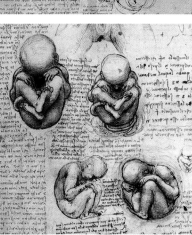

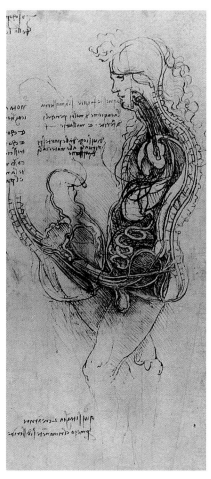

Sketches of fetuses in the uterus (top left, bottom left); *Copulation,* anatomy of sexual intercourse as imagined by Leonardo da Vinci.

Facing page: Leonardo da Vinci, *Last Supper (L'ultima cena),* a late fifteenth-century mural painting in the refectory of the Convent of Santa Maria delle Grazie in Milan (top).

Lenardo da Vinci's drawings of war machines for Duke Lodovico Sforza; cannon exploding into multiple balls (middle); rotating blades driving horses into the soldiers of the approaching army (bottom).

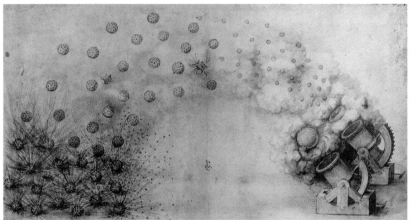

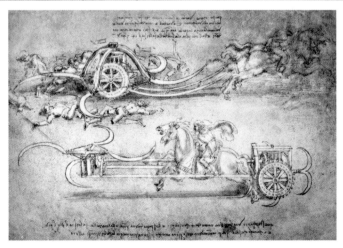

Leonardo da Vinci, *The Virgin and Child with St. Anne,* 1508. Musée du Louvre, Paris (top).

Line drawing of Leonardo's *The Virgin and Child with St. Anne* showing the hidden image of a vulture (according to Oskar Pfister).

84

Leonardo da Vinci, *Mona Lisa,* 1519. Musée du Louvre, Paris (top).

Leonardo da Vinci, *St. John the Baptist* with "Leonardesque smile." 1516. Musée du Louvre, Paris.

C. G. Jung's famous *Red Book,* in which he documented in writing and paintings his challenging experiences during his spiritual emergency (top).

Philemon, a spirit guide appearing in C. G. Jung's visions, as Jung portrayed him in his *Red Book*.

Yantra, a Tantric abstract archetypal symbol. There are nine hundred and sixty yantras, each representing the cosmic energy of a specific deity (top); Sri Yantra is the most sacred archetypal symbol of Tantra. It is called the mother of all yantras, because all other yantras are derived from it. In its three dimensional form, it is said to represent Mount Meru, the cosmic mountain at the center of the universe.

Kali and Shiva, at the end of one cycle and beginning of another; the river Ganges originating in Shiva's head, Rajasthan, nineteenth century (top left).

Shiva Ardhanareshvara, Shiva and Kali, an archetypal androgynous symbol, representing both the beginning of polarity during cosmogenesis or transcendence of duality at the end of the spiritual journey (top right).

Kali as Great Wisdom, nourishing all new life and herself with her own blood. The Nandi bull is the animal of Shiva, and the tiger an animal related to Kali (bottom).

Dante Alighieri (1265–1321), shown holding a copy of the *Divine Comedy*, next to the entrance to Hell, the seven terraces of Mount Purgatory, and the city of Florence, with the spheres of Heaven above (Domenico di Michelino's fresco in Dom Maria del Fiore).

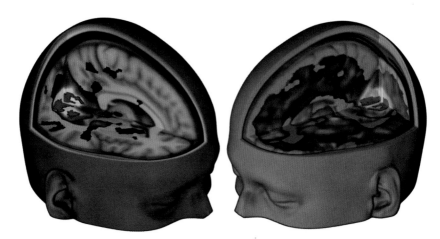

Neuroimaging with psychedelics. On the left side is a scan of the brain after ingestion of a placebo; on the right, a brain after ingestion of psilocybin (Robin Carhart-Harris 2016).

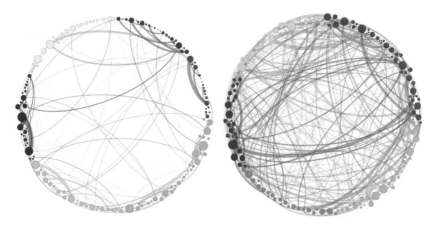

Communication between brain networks in people given a non-psychedelic compound (left) or psilocybin (right) (Petri et al 2014).

Mohammed and archangel Gabriel in Paradise meeting beautiful houris riding camels. From *Mirâj Nâmeh,* an Islamic manuscript written in a Turkish dialect, created in the fifteenth century.

Scene of divine judgment from the *Egyptian Book of the Dead*. The jackal-headed god Anubis is bringing the deceased Hunefer into the Hall of Judgment. There he weighs his heart (character) against the ostrich feather symbolizing the goddess of justice Maat. If he does not pass the judgment, he is devoured by Amemet, Devourer of Souls, a tri-form monster with the head of a crocodile, body of a lion, and bottom of a hippopotamus. The Ibis-headed god Thoth plays the role of an impartial judge (Papyrus in the British Museum, ca.1300 BC) (top).

Hunefer passed the judgment and Horus is taking him to Osiris and his two sisters, the goddesses Isis and Nephthys. On a lotus stand three sons of Horus, who personify the four canopic jars containing the entrails for mummification (Papyrus in the British Museum, ca.1300 BC).

The tomb of Sennedjem. In the upper register sits the sun god Ra in a solar boat holding an ankh; he is attended by two baboons celebrating the moment of sunrise. Below are the Fields of Laru where the deceased Sennedjem is enjoying his afterlife with his wife Iyneferti (top).

Triumphant moment of sunrise from the *Egyptian Book of the Dead*. Goddesses Isis and Nephthys sit at the djed, which symbolizes the vertebral column of their brother Osiris. The rising sun is supported by a personified Nile cross ankh, symbol of eternal life in the Beyond. Six Spirits of Dawn witness this event and at the moment of sunrise they turn into baboons.

Isis, the Great Mother Goddess, enchantress, sister and spouse of Osiris. Osiris conceived his son Horus while Isis took the form of a kite. Here she stands with long wings outspread as protectress on the shrine of the pharaoh Tutankhamen (Relief, tomb of Tutankhamen, Eighteenth Dynasty).

Authorship of this work is attributed to the legendary spiritual teacher Padmasambhava, who brought Buddhism to Tibet in the eighth century. He is depicted among various scenes of his life (top).

The profound wisdom that can lead to spiritual liberation is known as Prajñāpāramitā (transcendental wisdom); it is sometimes personified as a goddess.

The germinal mandala of the *Tibetan Book of the Dead* depicting the five transcendent Dhyani or Tathagata Buddhas; in the course of the journey through the bardos, it unfolds into a large number of peaceful and wrathful deities, dakinis, and animal-headed deities.

The principle deities, who are encountered between the time of death and seeking rebirth, are depicted in the center of the picture of the Buddha Heruka. Around four other terrifying Herukas dance fierce dakinis and guardian deities of the mandala. The small mandalas in the corners each contain one of the five transcendental Dhyani Buddhas with consort assistant Bodhisattvas (Tibetan thangka painting nineteenth century).

The Mandala of the Peaceful and Wrathful Deities, based on the *Bardo Thödol,* intended for preparation of the time of dying. Chemchok Heruka, in his consort. In the upper part of the mandala are the Peaceful Deities, while all around dance a ferocious host of humans and animals (Thangka from eighteenth century).

Fra Angelico: The Last Judgment in the church of Santa Maria degli Angeli in Florence (1430). Christ sits on a white throne surrounded by angels, Mary, John, and the saints. With his left hand he points down to Hell, his right hand up to Heaven. To Christ's right is paradise, with angels leading the saved through a beautiful garden. In the middle are the broken tombs of the risen dead, having come out of their graves to be judged. On Christ's left demons drive the damned into Hell, where the wicked are tormented (top).

A painting of the Last Judgment set the Christian pantheon of God the Father, Christ, and the Virgin Mary in a mandorla-shape opening in the heavens, among saints and angels, with Satan in Hell below (Bologna Pinacotheca).

Facing page: Hieronymus Bosch, *Ascent of the Blessed* (1505–1515). An array of angels help blessed humans souls toward salvation. All the figures in the painting are looking upwards toward the tunnel (Gallerie delle Accademia, Venice).

This page: In the Nauatl (Aztec) Borgia Codex, this painting shows the dynamic dance between Quetzalcoatl (Spirit) and Tezcatlipoca or Smoking Mirror (Matter). It beautifully portrays polarity and at the same time complementarity between Spirit and Matter.

A scene from the Bhagavad Gita: Arjuna insisting that Krishna reveal to him his entire Divine Being. Krishna agreed and manifested himself as a giant Cosmic Human, containing the entire universe. His belly was the earth plane (bhur-loka), above it seven ascending realms (lokas), and below it seven descending lokas.

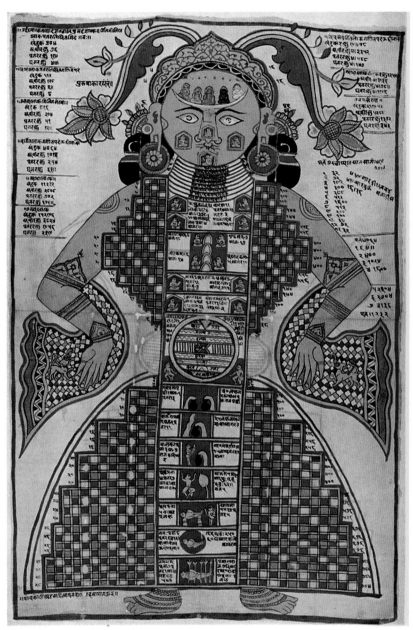

Jain Purushakara Yantra. The small circle around the waist of the figure depicts Jambudvipa, the terrestrial world, the realm where ordinary human beings live. Above and below are the celestial and infernal realms. This figure represents the human being as a microcosm that contains the entire macrocosm (Gouache on silk from Rajasthan, India, ca. 1780).

Adam Kadmon, the Primordial Man, "Makroanthropos" or "Makrokosmos." In Kabbalah, he came into being in the First Spiritual World after the contraction of God's Infinite Light. He is not the same physical Adam, the first man whom God created from the dust. The spiritual realm of Adam Kadmon corresponds to the Sefirah (divine attribute) of Keter ("Crown"). It is the divine will and program for subsequent creation.

Literature

Alpher R. A. and Herman, R. 2001. *Genesis of the Big Bang.* Oxford: Oxford University Press.

Becker, E. 1973. *The Denial of Death.* New York: The Free Press.

Bonaparte, M. 1949. *The Life and Works of Edgar Allan Poe.* London: Imago Publishing Co.

Cardinal, R. 1972. *Outsider Art.* New York: Praeger.

Freud, S. 1911. "Formulations Regarding the Two Principles in Mental Functioning." *Papers on Metapsychology; Papers on Applied Psycho-Analysis.* Vol. 4 of Collected Papers. London: Hogarth Press and the Institute of Psychoanalysis.

Freud, S. 1913. "The Case of the Three Caskets." *The Standard Edition of the Complete Psychological Works of Sigmund Freud, Volume XII* (1911-1913).

Freud, S. 1917. "A Childhood Recollection from Dichtung und Wahrheit." *The Standard Edition of the Complete Psychological Works of Sigmund Freud, Volume XVII* (1917-1919).

Freud, S. 1953. *The Interpretation of Dreams.* London: The Hogarth Press and the Institute of Psychoanalysis, Vol. IV.

Freud, S. 1957a. *Dostoevsky and Parricide.* London: The Hogarth Press and the Institute of Psychoanalysis, Vol. XI.

Freud, S. 1957b. *Leonardo da Vinci and A Memory of His Childhood.* London: The Hogarth Press and the Institute of Psychoanalysis, Vol. XI.

Freud, S. 2003. *Delusion and Dreams in Wilhelm Jensen's Gradiva.* Los Angeles, CA: Green Integer.

Friedman A. 1922. "On the Curvature of Space," *Gen. Rel. Grav.* 31:1991–2000.

Gamow, G. 1952. *Creation of the Universe.* New York: Viking Press.

Grof, S. 1998. *The Cosmic Game: Explorations of the Frontiers of Human Consciousness.* Albany, NY: State University New York (SUNY) Press.

Grof, S. 2009. Holotropic Research and Archetypal Astrology. Archai: *Journal of Archetypal Astrology* 1:50-66.

Grof, S. 2012. Two Case Studies: An Archetypal Astrological Analysis of Experiences in Psychedelic Sessions and Spiritual Emergencies. Archai: *Journal of Archetypal Astrology.* 4:11-126.

Grof, S. 2015. *Modern Consciousness Research and the Understanding of Art.*

Santa Cruz, CA: MAPS Publications.

Harman, W. 1984. *Higher Creativity: Liberating the Unconscious for Breakthrough Insights.* Los Angeles, CA: J. P. Tarcher.

Hillman, J. 1996. *The Soul's Code: In Search of Character and Calling.* New York: Random House.

Huxley, A. 1945. *Perennial Philosophy.* New York: Harper & Brothers.

Jung, C. G. 1956. *Symbols of Transformation.* Collected Works, vol. 5, Bollingen Series XX. Princeton, NJ: Princeton University Press.

Jung, C. G. 1975. *The Spirit in Man, Art, and Literature.* Collected Works, vol. 15, Bollingen Series XX. Princeton, NJ: Princeton University Press.

Jung, C. G. 1990. *Archetypes and the Collective Unconscious.* Collected Works, vol. 9 (Part 1). Bollingen Series XX. Princeton, NJ: Princeton University Press.

Miller, Miss Frank. 1906. "Quelques Faits d'Imagination Créatrice." *Archives de psychologie (Geneva)* V. 36-51.

Mookerjee, A. and Khanna, M. 1989. *The Tantric Way: Art, Science, Ritual.* London: Thames and Hudson.

Morgenthaler, W. 1992. *Madness and Art (Ein Geisteskranker als Künstler).* Lincoln, NE: University of Nebraska Press.

Neumann, E. 1974. *Art and the Creative Unconscious.: Leonardo da Vinci and the Mother Archetype.* Princeton, NJ: Princeton University Press.

Pfister, O. 1913. "Kryptolalie, Kryptographie und unbewusstes Vexierbild bei Normalen" (Cryptophasia, Cryptography, and the Unconscious Puzzle Picture in Normal People). *Jahrbuch fuer Psychoanalytische und Psychopathologische Forschungen.* 5, 115.

Prinzhorn, H. 1995. *Artistry of the Mentally Ill: A Contribution to the Psychology and Psychopathology of Configuration.* Vienna, New York: Springer Verlag.

Rank, O. 1989. *Art and Artist.* New York: W.W. Norton Company.

Riedlinger, T. 1982. "Sartre's Rite of Passage." *Journal of Transpersonal Psychology* 14: 105.

Sartre, J. P. 1964a. *The Words (Les Mots).* New York: George Braziller.

Sartre, J. P. 1964b. *Nausea (La Nausée).* New York: New Directions Publishing Corporation.

Sartre, J. P. 1994. *No Exit (Huit Clos).* New York: Samuel French.

Tarnas, R. 2006. *Cosmos and Psyche: Intimations of a New World View.* New York: Viking Press.

X

The Promethean Impulse:
Higher Creativity

Expanding the model of the psyche by adding the perinatal and transpersonal domains provides much deeper insights into works of art. Adding the transpersonal dimension—the collective unconscious and the archetypal dynamics—also makes it possible to understand the creative process itself as well as the phenomenon of genius, which Freud was not able to do.

We have already discussed Thomas Kuhn's book *The Structure of Scientific Revolutions,* in which he dispelled the myth that science has progressed linearly. Instead, he has replaced it with the theory that science has gone through a discontinuous series of periods governed by very different paradigms, which often contradicted each other (Kuhn 1962). What has not been sufficiently acknowledged by historians is how often the greatest scientific insights, discoveries, breakthroughs, and inventions appeared to their creators in the form of visions, dreams, fantasies, trance states, lightning flash epiphanies, and other types of holotropic states of consciousness.

In his remarkable book *Higher Creativity: Liberating the Unconscious for Breakthrough Insights,* Willis Harman illustrated that geniuses like Isaac Newton, René Descartes, Albert Einstein, Nikola Tesla, W. A. Mozart,

Giacomo Puccini, Richard Wagner, Rainer Maria Rilke, and Friedrich Nietzsche received their inspiration in holotropic states of consciousness and channeled cosmic creative energy (Harman 1984).

We usually learn about the final products of this process but hear very little about the special states of mind that were involved. Generations of historians have ignored what might have been some of the most important events in history. In his book, Willis Harman referred to what he called "the secret history of inspiration." These revelations have happened to scientists in different disciplines, mathematicians, painters, composers, writers, poets, founders of religions, prophets, and mystics.

Physicist, mathematician, and philosopher of the Vienna circle Philipp Frank showed in his book *Philosophy of Science* that the source of a scientific discovery or its basic axiom is often an archetypal motif. In the history of science, revolutionary ideas frequently emerged long before there was sufficient evidence to justify or support them (Frank 1957).

Just some examples of this includes pre-Socratic philosopher Anaximandros, who proposed a proto-evolutionary theory suggesting that all life

Friedrich Nietzsche (1844–1900), German classical scholar, philosopher, and cultural critic, one of the most influential of all modern thinkers.

originated in the ocean; Demokritos and Leucippus, who suggested in the fourth and fifth centuries B.C. that basic constituents of matter are atoms, or tiny indivisible particles; Nicolas Copernicus and Johannes Kepler, who drew their inspiration from the solar archetype; and in the seventh century, Huayan (Hwa Yen) Buddhist philosophers talked about holographic principles in the universe (Franck 1976). These and many other fascinating examples are explored in Willis Harman's book.

The idea of divine inspiration is beautifully represented in Michelangelo's paintings in the Vatican's Sistine Chapel, in which Michelangelo painted images of major and minor prophets. All of them have cherubim at their ears, but only the major ones are portrayed as listening. Divine inspiration, after all, requires an openness and readiness to receive it.

In his book *Ecce Homo,* Friedrich Nietzsche gave an eloquent description of the experience of divine inspiration involved in higher creativity:

> Has any one at the end of the nineteenth century any distinct notion of what poets of a stronger age understood by the word inspiration? If not, I will describe it. If one had the smallest vestige of superstition left in one, it would hardly be possible completely to set aside the idea that one is the mere incarnation, mouthpiece, or medium of an almighty power. The idea of revelation, in the sense that something which profoundly convulses and upsets one becomes suddenly visible and audible with indescribable certainty and accuracy—describes the simple fact. One hears—one does not seek; one takes—one does not ask who gives; a thought suddenly flashes up like lightning, it comes with necessity, without faltering—I never had any choice in the matter. (Nietzsche 1992)

Friedrich August Kekulé von Stradonitz

The most famous example of higher creativity is the story of Friedrich August Kekulé von Stradonitz, a nineteenth-century German chemist who was the founder of the structural theory of organic chemistry. After working for years trying to understand the structure of chemical compounds, he had a vision in which he saw the dance of smaller and larger atoms joining in various combinations, linking with each other and forming chains. It is certainly extraordinary that a vision which, according to him, spontaneously emerged while he was riding on the upper deck of a horse-drawn omnibus in London, could give him an insight into the intricate structure of chemical compounds.

A more specific insight came to Kekulé in a later vision when he was trying to understand the structure of benzene. It came in the form of a hypnagogic vision of Ouroboros, an archetypal snake swallowing his tail, which is an alchemical symbol representing cyclicity, eternal return, or endless creation and destruction. This was the discovery of the benzene ring (C_6H_6), which was called "the most brilliant piece of prediction in the entire history of science."

Friedrich August Kekulé von Stradonitz (1829–1896), German organic chemist who was the principal founder of the theory of chemical structure in organic chemistry (top).

The Archetype of Ouroboros, a 1478 drawing by Theodoroes Pelecanos. Gnostic, Hermetic, and alchemical symbol of eternal return, cyclicity, endless creation and destruction, life and death.

Dmitri Ivanovich Mendeleev

Very often, the solution to a problem comes as a lightning flash after days of fruitless struggle. This happened to the Russian chemist Dmitri Ivanovich Mendeleev. He worked hard trying to devise a way of organizing the chemical elements according to their atomic weight, but without success. Tired, he fell asleep and the solution appeared to him in a dream in which all the elements fell into place in the form that we now know as the Mendeleev Periodic Table of Elements. Only one place required correction. Mendeleev was nominated for the 1906 Nobel Prize in chemistry but died in 1907 without that honor.

Dimitri Ivanovitch Mendeleev (1834–1907), Russian chemist nominated for a Nobel prize for his periodic classification of the elements (top); Mendeleev's Periodic Table of Chemical Elements.

Otto Loewi

Another scientist whose Nobel Prize has to be credited to his dream life is German-born pharmacologist and psychobiologist Otto Loewi. At the beginning of his professional career, in a conversation with a colleague, Loewi had a fleeting hunch that the transmission of nerve impulses might involve not only electric current, but also a pharmacological agent. However, at the time, he was not able to come up with an experiment that would prove it.

Seventeen years later, he saw very clearly in a dream how it could be done. He jotted it down, but in the morning, he was not able to decipher his scribble. The next night, at three o'clock, the dream repeated itself. This time, Loewi got up and immediately went to the laboratory to carry out the experiment. The successful result, the discovery of the neuronal transmitter acetylcholine, became the foundation of the theory of chemical transmission of the neural impulse.

Niels Bohr

Niels Bohr, Danish physicist, made major contributions to the understanding of atomic structure and to quantum theory and had a dream about a planetary system as a model of the atom. This was the discovery for which he received the Nobel Prize for physics in 1922.

Niels Bohr (1885–1962), Nobel Prize-winning Danish physicist, inventor of the planetary model of the atom and of the complementarity principle; generally regarded as one of the foremost physicists of the twentieth century.

Paradox of the Newtonian-Cartesian Paradigm

In his book *The Tao of Physics,* Fritjof Capra described what he called the Newtonian-Cartesian paradigm as an ideology that had held Western science under the spell of mechanistic materialistic philosophy for three hundred years (Capra 1975). However, neither Newton nor Descartes were themselves materialists. In his principal work *Discourse on Method,* Descartes included a proof of the existence of God (Descartes 1960). Newton believed that the universe is a mechanical system, but that it has this form because God created it that way. Moreover, both Newton and Descartes can be used as prime representatives of what Harman called the "secret history of inspiration," an important aspect of the evolution of science that is seldom acknowledged by historians. Their extraordinary creativity originated in transcendental realms that were reached in holotropic states of consciousness.

Isaac Newton

The Royal Society of London planned to celebrate the tercentenary anniversary of Isaac Newton's birth in the year 1942. John Maynard Keynes, Newton's principal biographer, had been invited to present the keynote lecture. However, because of World War II, the celebrations did not take place until July 1946. Unfortunately, Keynes died in April 1946, three months before the celebrations took place, and his lecture "Newton, the Man" was delivered by his brother Geoffrey.

Keynes was the first person to see Newton's manuscript material, which had been hidden in a chest and kept secret until these papers were sold in the year 1936. He was fascinated by the esoteric and religious content of this material which revealed important aspects of Newton's personality that had been hidden from the public for more than two centuries. According to Keynes, Newton was very different from the conventional picture of him.

From the eighteenth century onward, Newton came to be thought of as the first and greatest of the modern age scientists, who taught us to think in a way that conforms to cold and uncompromising reason. According to Keynes, in view of the contents of the box which Newton packed up when he finally left Cambridge in 1696, Newton was not the first great scientist of the age of reason. He was the last of the magicians, the last of the Babylonians and Sumerians, the last great mind that looked out on the world with the same eyes as those who began to build our intellectual inheritance 10,000 years ago.

In Keynes' own words, "Isaac Newton, a posthumous child born with no father on Christmas Day, 1642, was the last wonder child to whom the Magi could do sincere and appropriate homage." A legend was built around Newton, which covered up the fact that Newton was profoundly neurotic. His deepest instincts were occult and esoteric; he was withdrawn from the world, haunted by a paralyzing fear of exposing his thoughts, his beliefs, and his discoveries to the inspection and criticism of society. He published nothing he had written except under the extreme pressure of friends.

Newton was an accomplished experimentalist known for his astronomical observations and his optical experiments, but this was not his most unique talent. His special gift was his ability to hold a problem in his mind for hours and days and weeks until it surrendered its secret. Then, being a supreme mathematical technician, he could dress it up for purposes of exposition, but it was his intuition which was preeminently extraordinary.

Augustus de Morgan, British nineteenth-century mathematician and logician, said about Newton that he was "so happy in his conjectures that he seemed to know much more than he could possibly have any means of proving." The mathematical proofs were dressed up later, but they were not the instrument of discovery. There is a story of how he informed the British astronomer and mathematician Edmond Halley of one of his most fundamental discoveries of planetary motion. "Yes," replied Halley, "but how do you know that? Have you proved it?" Newton was taken aback: "Why, I've known it for years," he replied. "If you'll give me a few days, I'll certainly find you a proof of it"—and in due course he did. Newton's experiments were not a means of discovery, but of verifying what he knew already.

Newton regarded the whole universe and all that is in it as a cryptogram set by God. God had put certain clues around the world to provide a sort of philosopher's treasure hunt for the esoteric brotherhood. He believed that these clues were to be found partly in the evidence of the heavens and in the constitution of elements. But Newton also found them in certain papers and traditions handed down by the brethren in an unbroken chain going back to the original cryptic revelations in Babylonia.

Nearly all of Newton's unpublished works on esoteric and theological matters were composed during the twenty-five years of his mathematical studies and his work on his magnum opus *Philosophiae Naturalis Principia Mathematica*. They include copious writings criticizing the Trinitarian doctrines and asserting that the revealed God was One God. This was a frightful secret, which Newton desperately tried to conceal all his life.

A large section of the material contained various apocalyptic writings from which Newton tried to learn the secret truths of the universe. A copious section was related to alchemy, including transmutation, the Philosopher's Stone, and the Elixir of Life. Newton was also trying to find meaning in cryptic verses and imitate the experiments of the initiates of past centuries. In these mixed and extraordinary studies, Newton had one foot in the Middle Ages and the other on the path of modern science.

Newton's friends, who were concerned about his involvement with esoteric matters, succeeded in getting him out of Cambridge and, for more

Sir Isaac Newton (1642–1727), English physicist and mathematician, who was the culminating figure of the scientific revolution of the seventeenth century.

than two decades, he reigned in London as the most famous man in Europe. He was knighted by Queen Anne and for nearly twenty-four years functioned as President of the Royal Society. Magic was quite forgotten; he became the Sage and Monarch of the Age of Reason. But he did not destroy the papers that he kept in a chest. They remained in the box to profoundly shock future generations.

John Maynard Keynes, who had the chance to study the content of Newton's chest, made this interesting comment about Newton: "As one broods over these queer collections, it seems easier to understand... this strange spirit, who was tempted by the Devil to believe at the time when...he was solving so much, that he could reach all the secrets of God and Nature by the pure power of mind—Copernicus and Faustus in one."

René Descartes

It is very rare for historians to be able to give a specific date for the beginning of great philosophical, scientific, and cultural movements, but here is an instance on which there is general agreement. Almost 400 years ago, on November 11, 1619, René Descartes, a twenty-three-year-old French aristocrat and soldier-philosopher, spent a night dreaming and a day thinking. In that time, he reformed the entire structure of European knowledge and laid the foundations of a new science, philosophy, and mathematics, as well as a new way of thinking about the world.

Ironically, Descartes' seminal work, *Discourse on Method* (Descartes 1960), which became the cornerstone of rationalism, was not a product of his reason; it was inspired by three dreams and a dream within a dream. As a soldier in the army of the Prince of Nassau, he was quartered in the town of Ulm, waiting for the war activities to resume in the spring. He was in an overheated room, in a feverish state, excited about the intellectual adventures on which he had embarked and writing down his ideas about "enthusiasm," which originated from the Greek *entheos,* meaning possession by the Divine Within.

That night, he had three dreams that turned out to be of astonishing importance. To an outside observer, they might seem relatively uninteresting and mundane. However, for Descartes, their enigmatic images held the key to a new revolutionary kind of knowledge. In the first dream, he experienced winds blowing from a church building toward a group of people who did not seem to be affected by the gale. After this dream, Descartes awoke and prayed for protection against the bad effects of this dream. In view of the benign nature of the dream, it is not clear why he needed this protection. After falling asleep again, he was filled with terror by a burst of noise like thunder. Believing that he was awake, he saw a shower of sparks filling his room. In the third and final dream, he saw himself holding a dictionary and some papers, one of which contained a poem beginning with the words: "What path should I follow in life?" An unknown man handed him a fragment of verse; the words *"Est et Non"* caught his mind's eye.

At the end of the third dream came an even more extraordinary state of consciousness: a dream within a dream. Descartes realized that the shower of sparks in his room was actually a dream and then he dreamed that he had interpreted the previous dream. In this dreamed interpretation, Descartes explained to himself that the dictionary represented the future unity of science—all the sciences grouped together. The sheaf of paper

René Descartes (1596–1650), French mathematician, scientist, and philosopher who has been called the father of modern philosophy.

represented the linkage of philosophy and wisdom. *"Est et Non"* signified Truth and Falsity in human attainment and in secular sciences.

Descartes understood the dreams to mean that he was the person destined to reform knowledge and unify the sciences, that the search for truth should be his career, and that his thoughts from the previous months, about knowledge and methods and a unifying system, would become the foundations for a new method of finding truth. Descartes himself attributed great significance to these dreams and made a pilgrimage from Venice to the Virgin Mary of Loretto as an act of giving thanks for the visions. Many scientists, though, including German philosopher Gottfried Wilhelm Leibniz and Dutch mathematician Christiaan Huygens, saw this part of his life as a manifestation of a disease that was compromising his thinking.

Albert Einstein

The activity from which Albert Einstein obtained the inspiration for his brilliant ideas has usually been referred to as "Einstein's thought experiments" *(Gedankenexperiment)*; however, this term is not really accurate. Psychologist Howard Gardner characterized Einstein's genius as stemming from his "logico-mathematical" mind (Gardner 1993). But Einstein himself wrote in his autobiographical notes, "I have no doubt that our thinking goes on for the most part without the use of symbols, and, furthermore, largely unconsciously" (Schilpp 1949).

He expanded on this theme in his remarks to Jacques Hadamard, stating, "The words or the language, as they are written or spoken, do not seem to play any role in my mechanism of thought. The psychical entities, which seem to serve as elements in thought are certain signs and more or less clear images which can be 'voluntarily' reproduced and combined... The above mentioned elements are, in my case, of visual and some of a muscular type" (Hadamard, 1945).

Einstein was mathematically challenged, and he worked with collaborators—all of whom were mathematicians—in a distinctly secondary step in his creative process, one that involved the translation of his private intuitions into public forms of communication. "I very rarely think in words at all," he wrote to Max Wertheimer. "A thought comes, and I may try to express it in words afterwards" (Wertheimer 1959). Einstein received his inspiration in images and physical feelings, which he then communicated through mathematical symbols with the help of his team of coworkers.

Below are a few examples of Einstein's "thought experiments," beginning with those that provided inspiration for his special theory of relativity.

1. Chasing the beam of light. Einstein started thinking about light when he was just sixteen years old. What would happen if you chased a beam of light as it moved through space? If you could somehow catch up to the light, Einstein reasoned, you would be able to observe the light frozen in space. But light cannot be frozen in space, otherwise it would cease to be light. Eventually Einstein realized that light cannot be slowed down and must always be moving away from him at the speed of light. Therefore, something else had to change; Einstein eventually realized that time itself had to change.

2. Train and lightning. Imagine you are standing on a train while your friend is standing outside the train, watching it pass by. If lightning struck on both ends of the train, your friend would see both bolts of lightning strike at the same time. On the train, however, you are closer to the bolt of lightning that the train is moving toward, so you see this lightning first because the light has a shorter distance to travel. This thought experiment showed that time moves differently for someone moving than for someone standing still, cementing Einstein's belief that time and space are relative, and *simultaneity does not exist*. This is a cornerstone in Einstein's special theory of relativity.

3. Elevator in empty space. In one of his famous visualization experiments, Einstein realized that gravity and acceleration appear to be the same phenomenon. This basic idea of the general theory of relativity emerged when he was imagining situations involving an elevator in empty space. Think about what would happen if that elevator suddenly went into a free-fall. The person inside would effectively weigh nothing and would float in space.

Next, imagine that same person in a motionless rocket ship so far from Earth that the force of gravity is practically zero. Just like in the free-falling elevator, he would also weigh nothing. Now, put the rocket in motion. As the rocket speeds up, the passenger's weight increases. To him, it feels just as if gravity had planted his feet firmly on the floor. Einstein realized that the force of gravity is just the acceleration that you feel as you move through space-time.

4. Orbiting the sun in space-time. If gravity is equivalent to acceleration, and if motion affects measurements of time and space (as shown in the special theory of relativity), then it follows that gravity does so as well. In particular, the gravity of any mass, such as our sun, has the effect of warping the space and time around it. For example, the angles of a triangle no longer add up to 180 degrees, and clocks tick more slowly the closer they are to a gravitational mass like the sun.

If there were nothing in our universe, the fabric of space-time would be flat. But if we add a mass, indentations form within it. Smaller objects that approach that large mass will follow the curve in space-time around it. Our nearest star, the sun, has formed such a shape in space-time, and our tiny planet Earth moves in this warped space-time, staying in orbit around the sun. Since energy and mass are equivalent, this applies to all forms of energy (including light). That would mean that even the trajectory of light would be bent in the presence of mass.

In November 1919, at the age of forty, Albert Einstein became an overnight celebrity thanks to a solar eclipse. Observations of the planet Venus in the *perihelium* (when its orbit was nearest to the sun) and measurements of its position had confirmed that light rays from distant stars were deflected by the gravity of the sun very close to the amount he had predicted in his theory of gravitation, the general relativity theory. Einstein became a hero. Humanity, exhausted and disgusted by the atrocities of World War I, was eager for some sign of dignity and nobility, and suddenly here was a humble scientific genius, seemingly interested only in pure intellectual pursuits and the search for truth.

General relativity may be the biggest leap of the scientific imagination in history. Unlike many previous scientific breakthroughs, such as the principle of natural selection, or the discovery of the physical existence of atoms, general relativity had little foundation in the theories or experiments of the time. No one except Einstein was thinking of gravity as equivalent to acceleration, as a geometrical phenomenon, as a bending of time and space. Although it is impossible to know, many physicists believe

Albert Einstein (1879–1955), German-born theoretical physicist, Nobelist, author of the special and general theories of relativity.

that, without Einstein and his unorthodox methods of higher creativity, it could have been another few decades or more before another physicist worked out the concepts and mathematics of general relativity.

Nikola Tesla

Nikola Tesla was a Serbian-American inventor, engineer, and physicist. He was born approximately at midnight, between July 9 and July 10, 1856, during a horrific lightning storm. During Tesla's birth, according to the story told by his family, the midwife wrung her hands and declared that the lightning was a bad omen. "This child will be a child of darkness," she reportedly said, to which Tesla's mother replied: "No, he will be a child of light." In retrospect, the mother's prediction for her son's future turned out to be prophetic.

In childhood, Tesla suffered from terrifying nightmares. He practiced vivid visualizations of pleasant scenes to ward off the terrifying ones. Later, this activity developed into a superb general capacity to visualize in three dimensions. He was allegedly capable of visualizing complex machines (such as the electric generator and electric motor) in their final form and function. His capacity to visualize was further enhanced by sitting in electric fields of millions of volts. He also had a favorite pet pigeon whose presence he felt greatly enhanced his imagination.

Tesla had what is known as a photographic memory, which he inherited from his mother. He was able to memorize books and images and stockpile visions for inventions in his head. His amazing photographic memory enabled him to devise and build complete inventions in his mind, which later in life caused some confusion with other inventors, engineers and financiers, who wanted to see Tesla's ideas on paper.

Tesla needed only two hours of sleep a night, although he occasionally took an afternoon nap. He claimed that he could hear a fly land in a room, and that he could hear thunderclaps hundreds of miles away. He also suffered from severe obsessive-compulsive disorder. He hated round objects and jewelry and could not stand the sight of pearls, to the extent that he refused to speak to women wearing them. When his secretary came to work wearing pearls, he sent her home for the day.

Tesla was known for having excessive hygiene habits, born out of a near-fatal bout of cholera when he was a teenager. He suffered from mysophobia (the pathological fear of dirt), wore white gloves, and ordered waiters to serve his meals with eighteen napkins so that he could polish all of his silverware before using it. He also calculated the cubic centimeters of space occupied by each bite of food, dish, or coffee cup and often counted his steps when walking.

He could not bear, "except at the point of a revolver," to touch another person's hair; he never married or had a long-lasting relationship, except a strictly platonic affair with a woman named Katherine Johnson. One of Tesla's biographers, a journalist who remained close to Tesla in his declining years, called Tesla "an absolute celibate," and confirmed that he rarely slept. In his autobiography, he referred to many of his "out of body experiences."

I am giving Tesla more space in this chapter because of the astonishing number and gigantic scope of the inventions engendered by his higher creativity. He registered more than three hundred patents, among them the alternating current (AC), the electric generator and electric motor, Tesla's coil, which generated millions of volts, and the wireless transmission of electricity. Tesla also had a patent for radio before Marconi, although he did not develop the finished product. His work became the basis of developments for radar, lasers, x-rays, lighting, and robotics, among many other areas.

In his autobiography, Tesla commented that as a child in remote Croatia, he saw a photograph of Niagara Falls and told his uncle that one day he would harness its energy. Some decades later, he did just that, calling it an "extraordinary coincidence." Westinghouse Electric Corporation entered a contract with Tesla to build the giant alternating current generator inside Niagara Falls. The generator made history, sending electrical power all the way to New York City and delivered an amazing amount of electricity—15,000 horsepower—to Buffalo twenty-six miles away in order to run the streetlights and street cars. A bust of Tesla now stands at Niagara Falls.

Tesla also gave one of his more unforgettable displays at the Chicago World's Fair of 1893, which he illuminated with alternating current for Westinghouse. The exposition covered more than 700 acres, cost more than $25 million to produce and featured 60,000 exhibitors. One famous legend surrounding Tesla was that he had caused an earthquake in Manhattan and nearly brought down the neighborhood when he attached an electro-mechanical oscillator to an iron pillar in his laboratory. Just as in an earthquake, people felt the vibrations and repercussions miles away. A policeman searching the building found Tesla destroying the small device that caused the havoc with a sledgehammer. Tesla told the reporters that by using the oscillator, he could destroy the Brooklyn Bridge in a few minutes.

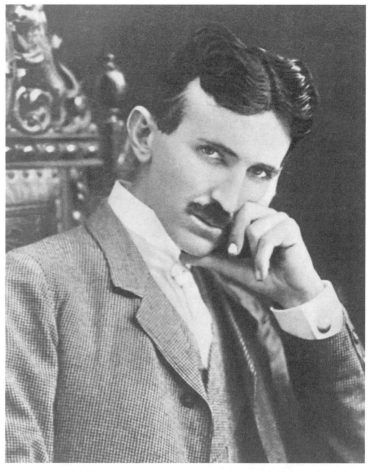

Nikola Tesla (1856–1943), Serbian-American inventor, electrical engineer, physicist, and futurist, creator of more than three hundred patents.

During his stay in Colorado Springs, Tesla conducted dangerous experiments with lightning and produced such a strong current that he knocked the Colorado Springs electric powerhouse out of commission by setting it on fire, thus plunging the entire city into darkness. Tesla sent a crew of engineers to repair the damage and returned electricity to Colorado Springs within a week. His experiments were allegedly also changing weather in the area.

A painful chapter of Tesla's life was his difficult relationship with his fellow inventor and bitter enemy, Thomas A. Edison. The two men differed so significantly that they disliked each other almost from the very first meeting. At the core of their conflict was the disagreement about which type of electricity should be used. Edison promoted direct current, which was more difficult to send over long distances because it required powerhouses every mile or so to get "pumped up." Tesla was able to increase the voltage of the alternating current simply and directly by using transformers.

Their argument took a bizarre form. Edison, a stubborn proponent of direct current, began electrocuting dogs and cats with alternating currents in front of audiences to show them how dangerous he thought alternating current truly was. Tesla countered with public performances during which

Nikola Tesla's experiments with high voltage electricity.

he used himself as a conductor, allowing hundreds of thousands of volts of alternating current to pass through his own body. His clothing would emit sparks and glimmers of halos hours after the demonstration. Tesla was finally able to convince Edison that alternating current was a far superior system of power generation than his own direct current.

Nikola Tesla, the genius who lit the world and whose discoveries in the field of alternating current advanced the United States and the rest of the world into the modern industrial era, was a very bad businessman and negotiator. After being repeatedly exploited and cheated out of his discoveries, he died a pauper. There are many scientists who believe that some of Tesla's fantastic utopian ideas will inspire projects in the future that will radically change the use of energy on our planet.

Srinivasi Ramanujan

These earlier examples mostly involved visual imagination, a function that is greatly enhanced in holotropic states. But higher creativity can even involve complex operations requiring logical thinking, such as higher mathematics. Srinivasi Ramanujan, an uneducated villager from a poor Indian family, was catapulted to the cutting edge of mathematics after a series of dreams in which the village goddess Namagiri taught him higher mathematical knowledge.

Ramanujan had already exhibited extraordinary mathematical skills during his rudimentary education. When he was fifteen years old, somebody gave him an outdated handbook of mathematics, which he read and from which he developed some basic mathematical knowledge. However, this was insignificant in comparison with the extraordinary amount of mathematical information that the goddess Namagiri imparted to him in his dreams.

After several unsuccessful attempts to get scholarship to government colleges due to his lack of general education and ignorance in non-mathematical subjects, Ramanujan attracted the attention of Ramachandra Rao, the Secretary of the Indian Mathematical Society. Rao, described as a "lover of mathematics," recognized that the young man's knowledge of mathematics was extraordinary and exceeded his own, thus opening the door into mathematical circles for him. Ramanujan sent his work to G. C. Hardy, a famous Cambridge mathematician and began corresponding with him.

Ramanujan was repeatedly invited to Cambridge by outstanding mathematicians who were deeply impressed and fascinated by his extraordinary and unorthodox mathematical talent, but his mother refused to let him go until she had a dream in which the goddess Namagiri ordered her not to stand in the way of his career. Ramanujan made stunning contributions to mathematics, in spite of his bad health and his untimely death at the age of thirty-three from what was diagnosed as tuberculosis or hepatic amoebiasis.

Ramanujan astonished Cambridge mathematicians by being able to instantly know the solution of complicated problems without working on them. Asked how he knew the answer, he answered: "It just came to my

Srinivasa Ramanujan (1887–1920), one of the greatest Indian mathematical geniuses.

mind." Sometimes it took him hours, even months to verify what came to him in an instant flash. Deeply religious, Ramanujan credited his substantial mathematical capacities to divinity. He once said: "An equation for me has no meaning unless it expresses a thought of God."

Mathematician and code-breaker Max Newman said about Ramanujan, "[He] arrived in England abreast and often ahead of contemporary mathematical knowledge. Thus, in a lone mighty sweep, he had succeeded in recreating in his field, through his own unaided powers, a rich half-century of European mathematics. One may doubt whether so prodigious a feat had ever been accomplished in the history of thought."

An extraordinary example of higher creativity tapping medieval archetypal sources is Wolfgang Pauli, a brilliant Austrian-Swiss theoretical physicist and Nobel prize winner whose friendship and cooperation with C. G. Jung was discussed earlier (pp. 35). Pauli drew inspiration for solving difficult problems in quantum physics and quantum electrodynamics from archetypal images and motifs that he encountered in his rich dream life. He also got important ideas for his work from alchemical texts and illustrations by sixteenth-century English physician, theosophist, and Rosicrucian Robert Fludd (Miller 2009).

Inspirations for the Great Religions

All great religions and spiritual systems of the world have been inspired and sustained by powerful holotropic experiences of their founders, as well as their prophets, saints, and mystics. These experiences, revealing the existence of numinous dimensions of reality, served as a vital source of all religious movements.

Gautama Buddha

Gautama Buddha, meditating in Bodh Gaya under the Bo tree, had an awe-inspiring visionary experience of Kama Mara, the master of the world illusion, who tried to divert him from his spiritual quest by exposing him to sexual seduction by his three voluptuous and salacious daughters and by instilling terror in him by bringing in his formidable army, hurricanes, and torrential rains. After having successfully resisted these temptations and braving these onslaughts, Buddha experienced illumination and spiritual awakening. On other occasions, he also envisioned and relived a long chain of his previous incarnations and experienced a profound liberation from karmic bonds. These experiences became an important inspiration for Buddha's teachings.

Mohammed

The Islamic text Miraj Nameh gives a description of the "miraculous journey of Mohammed," a powerful visionary state during which archangel Gabriel escorted Mohammed through the seven Muslim heavens, Paradise, and Hell (Gehenna). During this visionary journey, Mohammed experienced an "audience" with Allah in the seventh heaven. In a state described as "ecstasy approaching annihilation," he received a direct communication from Allah. This experience and additional mystical states that Mohammed had over a period of twenty-five years became the inspiration for the *suras* of the Qur'an and for the Muslim faith.

Biblical Visionaries

In the Judeo-Christian tradition, the Old Testament offers an impressive account of Moses' experience of Yahweh in the burning bush on Mount Sinai, the description of Abraham's interaction with the angel, the Israelites' collective vision of Yahweh in the clouds, Ezekiel's observation of the flaming chariot, and other visionary experiences. The New Testament describes Jesus' forty days' stay in the desert where he was tempted by the devil. The devil asked him to prove that he was the Son of God by turning stones into bread and by jumping down from the top of the temple. Jesus refused to do it and also rejected the devil's offer of all the kingdoms of the world.

Additional famous examples are Saul's blinding vision of Jesus on the way to Damascus and St. John's vision of the Apocalypse in his cave on the island Patmos. The Bible provides many other examples of direct communication with God and with the angels. The descriptions of the visions of St. Teresa of Avila, Hildegard von Bingen, temptations of St. Anthony, and visionary experiences of many other saints and Desert Fathers are well-documented parts of Christian history.

Helen Schucman and the Course in Miracles

Remarkable spiritual revelations or insights are not limited to remote history; they have continued through the present day. They are often received from a specified source, such as a discarnate being, spiritual guide, archetypal figure, or even God. An extraordinary example of higher creativity in this category is the story of Helen Schucman, a clinical and research psychologist and tenured Associate Professor of Medical Psychology at Columbia University in New York City.

At a time of great emotional stress and interpersonal tensions between herself and her friend and boss Bill Thetford, she started experiencing highly symbolic dreams and images and hearing what she referred to as "the VOICE." It seemed to be giving her a rapid inner dictation, not in words but by some form of telepathic transmission. To Helen's great surprise and consternation, the Voice introduced himself as Jesus.

Helen, who was Jewish, an atheistic scientist, psychologist, and educator working in a highly prestigious academic setting, was initially horrified that this was the onset of a psychotic break. But then she noticed that the Voice was accurately quoting long passages from the Bible, which she had not read, and was making very specific linguistic references to errors that had been made in various translations of these passages. She was also able to verify the accuracy of this information.

At Bill's suggestion and encouragement, Helen started recording all the communications in her notebook, jotting them down in shorthand; the next day she read her notes to Bill, and he typed them. She could interrupt the writing at any time and pick it back up again later. As she decided to embark on this giant project, Helen surprised herself by beginning her writing with the sentence: "THIS IS A COURSE IN MIRACLES." She felt that this was a special assignment that she had "somewhere, sometime, somehow, agreed to complete."

The result of this cooperation between Helen and Bill was a thick manuscript entitled *A Course in Miracles,* which was a book containing a self-study curriculum that promised to assist its readers in achieving spiritual transformation (Anonymous 1975). The underlying assertion of the work is that the greatest "miracle" that one may achieve is the act of gaining full "awareness of love's presence" in one's own life. Helen felt a strong urge to publish her manuscript and share it with the world, but she was afraid that she would be considered crazy and that she would destroy her academic reputation.

When *A Course in Miracles* was finally published, it quickly became a bestseller and a sensation not only among transpersonal psychologists, but also for the general public. It was soon followed by the *Workbook for Students,* a volume consisting of 365 lessons, each offering an exercise for one day of the year, and the *Manual for Teachers.* This three-volume set has now been translated into more than thirty languages and sold more than two million copies.

Helen Schucman, Ph.D. (1909–1981), clinical and research psychologist at Columbia University in New York City, who channeled the book *A Course in Miracles.*

Roberto Assagioli

Sources identified as spiritual can sometimes communicate in psychological language. Roberto Assagioli was an Italian psychiatrist and pioneer in the fields of humanistic and transpersonal psychology. He created the psychological school known as psychosynthesis, which integrates psychology and spirituality. I had the great pleasure to spend a day with Roberto in his house in Florence several months before his death. As I mentioned in Volume I, he shared something that he did not officially speak or write about: that he had received some of the basic ideas for his psychotherapeutic system by channeling the messages from a spiritual guide who called himself the Tibetan. According to Roberto, the Tibetan was the same entity to whom Alice Bailey credited the voluminous series of her books. For Roberto, these messages came in psychological language; for Alice Bailey they took the form of metaphysical terminology.

Roberto Assagioli (1887–1974), Italian psychotherapist and pioneer in humanistic and transpersonal psychology, founder of the psychological school called psychosynthesis.

Carl Gustav Jung

C. G. Jung described a similar situation in his own life. At the time of his stormy "spiritual emergency," he connected with several fantasy figures with whom he was able to have meaningful discussions. The most important of them was a spiritual guide who called himself Philemon. Jung saw him first in a dream as an old man with kingfisher wings and with the horns of a bull flying across the sky, carrying a bundle of keys. Jung was struck by a strange synchronicity associated with this dream because he found a dead kingfisher in the garden, a bird that is rarely seen around Zürich.

Jung developed a connection with Philemon and was able to carry on long conversations with him during his strolls around the lake. He discovered that this spirit guide seemed to have independent existence and autonomy and had an intelligence superior to his own. Like Assagioli, Jung credited Philemon as the source of some important ideas in his teachings. His experiences with fantasy figures were described in the legendary *Red Book* (Jung 2009).

C. G. Jung (1875–1961), Swiss psychiatrist and pioneer in depth psychology, in his office in Küssnacht.

Jung experienced another extraordinary episode of higher creativity as well. After finishing the discussions with Philemon, he started having the feeling that his house was invaded by a crowd of spirits who were so tightly packed that it made it difficult for him to breathe. It was interesting that other family members shared Jung's feeling that strange things were happening in the house. His eldest daughter saw a white figure in her room and his second daughter reported that twice during the night her blankets had been snatched away. His nine-year-old son had a nightmare the same night and in the morning asked for crayons (which he never did) and sketched an eerie picture of a fisherman and an angel and a devil fighting over him.

At one point, the doorbell started to ring insistently, but when the maid answered the door, there was nobody there. Jung slipped into one of his trances and asked what it all meant. The answer of the spirits was: "We have come back from Jerusalem, where we found not what we sought." Jung sat down and started writing at a hectic pace; as soon as he began, the haunting stopped.

Within three days, he had completed an essay that was later published as "Septem Sermones ad Mortuos" (Seven Sermons to the Dead), arguably the most fascinating work he ever wrote. It was a text outlining the basic tenets of the Gnostic tradition and it was signed by the Alexandrian Gnostic philosopher Basilides. The forceful automatic writing released Jung from his severe writer's block; for three years before this episode, he had not been able to write anything.

Rainer Maria Rilke

The Austrian-Bohemian poet Rainer Maria Rilke wrote his *Sonnets to Orpheus,* a cycle of fifty-five sonnets inspired by Ovid's *Metamorphoses,* over a period of three weeks, experiencing what he described as a "savage creative storm." Within a few days, he completed the first section of twenty-six sonnets. For the next few days, he focused on the *Duino Elegies,* a work with which he had struggled for years, during which he suffered from paralyzing depression.

Rilke finished the work and, immediately after, returned to work on the

Sonnets and completed the following section of twenty-nine sonnets in less than two weeks. He wrote them down in their final form without having to change a single word. Writing to his former lover, Lou Andreas Salomé, he described this three-week period as "a boundless storm, a hurricane of the spirit" and of its impact on him, he said, "whatever inside me is like thread and webbing, framework, it all cracked and bent. No thought of food."

Elias Howe

Higher creativity does not always result in discoveries worth a Nobel Prize or in musical compositions that will enchant countless future generations. It can also occur in relatively mundane situations, as we see in the following example, which actually has a certain element of humor. Elias Howe, the inventor of the lockstitch sewing machine, worked on this project for several years without success, experimenting with needles that had the hole in the middle of the shank.

The solution came in a nightmare in which he was captured by natives and taken to their king. The monarch roared at him: "I command you on pain of death to finish this machine at once!" As he was taken in utmost horror to his execution, he noticed that the warriors had spears with an eye-shaped hole in their heads. He realized that he had found the solution; he needed needles with an eye near the point. After waking up, he instantly made a whittled model of the eye-pointed needle that was needed for the successful completion of the project.

Higher Creativity in Music

The history of music abounds with remarkable examples of higher creativity. One night in 1713, Giuseppe Tartini, a Venetian composer and violinist, dreamed that he had made a pact with the devil for his soul. Everything went as he wished, and his new servant anticipated his every desire. Among other things, he gave him his violin to see if he could play. Tartini said about this experience: "How great was my astonishment on hearing a sonata so wonderful and so beautiful, played with such great art and intel-ligence, as I had never even conceived in my boldest flights of fantasy." He felt so enraptured and enchanted that he lost his breath and awoke.

He immediately grasped his violin in order to retain, in part at least, the beautiful music of his dream, but without success. He could not even come close to what he had heard in the dream. He still considered the music, which he had composed at that time, to be the best he ever wrote, and called it the "Devil's Trill." The difference between it and what he had heard in his dream, though, was so great that he felt like destroying his violin and giving up playing forever. Then he realized that it was not pos-sible for him to live without the enjoyment that playing music gave him and he continued to play.

Giacomo Puccini credited his masterpiece Madama Butterfly to God; he said about it: "I did not write Madama Butterfly; it was God. I was just holding the pen." Wolfgang Amadeus Mozart related that entire sympho-nies appeared in his head in their final form; he just had to write them down. Richard Wagner allegedly hallucinated the music that he was writ-ing. In a discussion with the original composer Engelbert Humperdinck in 1880, Wagner said: "Atheistic upbringing is fatal. No atheist has ever created anything of great and lasting value."

Johannes Brahms expressed the same opinion in a conversation with vi-olinist Joseph Joachim: "I know several young composers who are atheists. I have read their scores, and I assure you, Joseph, that they are doomed to speedy oblivion, because they are utterly lacking in inspiration. Their works are purely cerebral…No atheist has ever been or ever will be a great composer." Charles Francois Gounod answered a female admirer, who asked him how he could invent such lovely melodies, "God, Madame, sends me down some of his angels and they whisper sweet melodies in my ear."

The Effect of Chemical Substances on Creativity

The English Romantic poet, Samuel Taylor Coleridge, was a regular user of opium *(laudanum),* which was prescribed to him for the treatment of rheumatism and other ailments as a relaxant, analgesic, and antidepressant. His poem "Xanadu" was inspired by opium-induced visions of the legendary imperial palace of Genghis Khan's grandson Kublai Khan. After he awakened from the opium dream, he had a vivid form of the entire poem in its mind, but his effortless spontaneous writing was interrupted by a visitor and the poem remained an unfinished fragment.

Hector Berlioz composed his *Symphonie fantastique* under the influence of opium. Leonard Bernstein described the symphony as the first musical expedition into psychedelia because of its hallucinatory and dream-like nature. According to Bernstein: "Berlioz tells it like it is. You take a trip, you wind up screaming at your own funeral." This was a reference to the movement of the symphony called *March to the Scaffold,* describing the composer's walk to his own execution.

Psychedelics and Creativity

The extraordinary effect of psychedelic substances on creativity deserves special attention. In the 1960s, Willis Harman, Robert McKim, Robert Mogar, James Fadiman, and Myron Stolaroff conducted a pilot study of the effects of psychedelics on the creative process, using the administration of mescaline to enhance inspiration and problem-solving in a group of twenty-six highly talented individuals. These included physicists, math-ematicians, architects, psychologists, one furniture designer, one commercial artist, and one sales manager. Nineteen of the subjects had had no previous experience with psychedelics (Harman et al. 1966).

Each participant was required to bring a professional problem they had been working on for at least three months, and a desire to solve it. The participants reported experiences of enhanced functioning: lower inhibition and anxiety, capacity to restructure problems in a larger context, enhanced fluency and flexibility of ideation, heightened capacity for visual imagery and fantasy, increased ability to concentrate, heightened empathy with people, more access to unconscious data, increased motivation to obtain closure, and ability to visualize the completed solution.

As mentioned earlier, James Fadiman is currently conducting a study on microdosing with LSD for the improvement of normal functioning (Fadiman 2017). Microdosing (or sub-perceptual dosing) means taking a sub-threshold dose, which for LSD is 10–20 micrograms. The purpose of microdosing is to enhance normal cognitive and executive functionality (nootropic effect), rather than to achieve a non-ordinary state of consciousness. Volunteers participating in the study include a wide variety of professionals in the field of science and artists. Early results suggest that the subjects continue to experience normal functioning but with increased creative focus and emotional clarity.

In 1993, molecular biologist and DNA chemist Kary Mullis received a Nobel Prize for his development of the Polymerase Chain Reaction (PCR) that allows the amplification of specific DNA sequences; it is a central technique in biochemistry and molecular biology. During a symposium in Basel celebrating Albert Hofmann's 100th anniversary, Albert Hofmann revealed that Kary Mullis told him that LSD had helped him discover the Polymerase Chain Reaction. In a 1994 interview for "California Monthly," Mullis mentioned that in the 1960s and early 1970s, he took "plenty of LSD" and said about it: "It was certainly much more important than any courses I ever took."

Francis Crick, the Nobel-Prize-winning father of modern genetics, often used small doses of LSD to boost his power of thought. At one point, he allegedly told his friend Kemp that he had had a vision of the double helix DNA molecule during an LSD experience, which helped him to unravel its structure. This discovery won him the Nobel Prize.

In his non-fiction book *What the Dormouse Said: How the Sixties Counterculture Shaped the Personal Computer Industry,* John Markoff described the history of the personal computer. He showed that there was a direct connection between psychedelic use in the American counterculture of the 1950s and 1960s and the development of the computer industry (Markoff 2005). Steve Jobs said that taking LSD was among the two or three most important things he had done in his life. He stated that people around him who did not share his countercultural roots and had not taken LSD could not fully follow and relate to his thinking.

Douglas Engelbart, early computer and Internet pioneer, who invented the computer mouse and the technique of "copy and paste" was one of many engineers who participated in guided LSD sessions in studies on the connection between LSD and enhanced creativity at the International Foundation for Advanced Study (IFAS), which was founded by Myron

Kary Mullis (1944–), Nobel Prize-winning American biochemist, who invented the poly-merase chain reaction (PCR), which has become the central technique in biochemistry and molecular biology. Mullis attributed this discovery to his experimentations with LSD (top left); Francis Crick (1916–2004), British molecular biologist, biophysicist, and neuroscientist, who codiscovered with James Watson the double helix structure of the DNA molecule (top right); Douglas Engelbart (1925–2013), American engineer and inventor, early computer and internet pioneer, and creator of the computer mouse (bottom left); Steven Jobs (1955–2011), American inventor, designer and entrepreneur, and cofounder, chief executive, and chairman of Apple Computer (bottom right).

Stolaroff. He described how LSD enhanced his creative process and believed that LSD inspired major advancements in collective intelligence.

Mark Pesce, the co-inventor of virtual reality's coding language, VRML, agreed that there is a definite relationship between chemical mind expansion and advances in computer technology. He said: "To a man and a woman, the people behind virtual reality were acid heads." Kevin Herbert, who worked for CISCO Systems in the early days, said that he solved his toughest technical problems while tripping to drum solos by the Grateful Dead.

He stated: "When I'm on LSD and hearing something that's pure rhythm, it takes me to another world and into another brain state where I've stopped thinking and started knowing." He also said, "It must be changing something about the internal communication in my brain. Whatever my inner process is that lets me solve problems, it works differently, or maybe different parts of my brain are used." When Herbert has a particularly intractable programming problem, or finds himself pondering a big career decision, he deploys LSD-25. He also intervened to stop drug testing of employees at CISCO.

Neuroimaging of Brains Under the Influence of Psychedelics

The influence of psychedelic substances, such as LSD, psilocybin, and mescaline, can lead to profound breakthroughs in innovation and creativity. Sophisticated techniques of neuroimaging reveal functional changes corresponding to an opening and increase in communication between brain pathways. Brain scans using functional magnetic resonance imaging (fMRI), which measures brain activity by detecting associated changes in blood flow, as well as magnetoencephalography (MEG), which measures brain oscillations, can be used to discover what happens in the brain as a result of taking psychedelics.

When we compare the communication pathways between different regions in the brain after ingestion of a placebo versus ingestion of psilocybin, we observe remarkable differences. In the brain after a placebo, neuronal communication is confined to particular communities or regions of the brain, forming groups of closely connected neurons known as cliques.

After ingestion of psilocybin, communication across the brain becomes incomparably more open and liberated, and there are fewer observed neuronal cliques (Carhart-Harris 2016). This free and unimpeded communication in the brain has the potential to resolve emotional and conceptual blockages and engender unexpected new ideas and connections. This is very likely the mechanism which underlies the observed enhancements in creativity after ingestion of psychedelics, as well as the deepening and acceleration of the process of psychotherapy. The changes in the brain under psychedelics seem to be functionally similar in some ways to the brains of infants, with an increased sense of freshness, newness, and curiosity, while also maintaining the intelligence of the adult brain.

Literature

Anonymous 1975. *A Course in Miracles.* New York: Foundation for Inner Peace.

Capra, F. 1975. *The Tao of Physics.* Chicago, IL: University of Chicago Press.

Carhart-Harris, R. 2016. "Psychedelics: Lifting the Veil." San Raphael, CA: TEDxWarwic.

Carhart-Harris, R., et al. 2016. "Neural correlates of the LSD experience revealed by multimodal neuroimaging." *Proceedings of the National Academy of Sciences* 113.17: 4853-4858.

Descartes, R. 1960. *Discourse on Method and Meditations.* New York: The Liberal Arts Press.

Fadiman, F. 2017. A Researcher Wants to Test the Effects of Microdosing on Cognitive Ability and Productivity. *Futurism* August 10.

Franck, F. 1976. *Book of Angelus Silesius.* New York: Random House.

Frank, P. 1957. *Philosophy of Science.* Englewood-Cliffs, NJ: Prentice Hall.

Gardner, H. E. 1993. *Creating Minds: An Anatomy of Creativity Seen Through the Lives of Freud, Einstein, Picasso, Stravinsky, Eliot, Graham and Gandhi.* New York: Basic Books.

Hadamard, J. 1945. *An Essay on the Psychology of Invention in the Mathematical Field.* Princeton NJ: Princeton University Press.

Harman, W. et al. 1966. "Psychedelic Agents in Creative Problem-Solving:

A Pilot Study". *Psychological Reports* 1966 Aug:19(1): 211-2.

Harman, W. 1984. *Higher Creativity: Liberating the Unconscious for Breakthrough Insights.* Los Angeles, CA: J. P. Tarcher.

Jung, C. G. 2009. *The Red Book: Liber Novus.* New York/London: W. W. Norton & Co.

Keynes, J. M. 1946. *Newton, the Man.* http://www-history.mcs.st-and. ac.uk/Extras/Keynes_Newton.html

Kuhn, T. 1962. *The Structure of Scientific Revolutions.* Chicago, IL: University of Chicago Press.

Markoff, J. 2005. *What the Dormouse Said: How the Sixties Counterculture Shaped the Personal Computer Industry.* New York: Viking Press, Penguin Group (USA) Inc.

Miller, A. 2009. *Deciphering the Cosmic Number: The Strange Friendship of Wolfgang Pauli and Carl Jung.* New York: W. W. Norton & Co.

Nietzsche, F. 1992. *Ecce Homo.* New York: Penguin Classics.

Petri, Giovanni, et al. 2014. "Homological scaffolds of brain functional networks." *Journal of The Royal Society Interface* 11.101: 20140873.

Schilpp, P. (ed). 1949. *Albert Einstein: Philosopher-Scientist.* Evanston IL: Library of Living Philosophers.

Wertheimer M. 1945. *Productive Thinking.* New York: Harper.

XI

Archetypes:
Guiding Principles of the Psyche and the Cosmos

Archetypes are cosmic primordial patterns and governing principles; they are universals that function as templates for the particulars of the material world. As Jungian psychologist James Hillman pointed out in his ground-breaking book *Re-Visioning Psychology*, the term archetype can be applied to a broad range of objects, processes, and situations (Hillman 1977). It could be, for example, the immaterial potential of structures, like invisible forms of crystals that can materialize in a solution; snowflakes or patterns of ice that can form on the windowpane; instinctual behavior in animals; the genres and topoi in literature; the basic syndromes in psychiatry; the paradigmatic thought models in science; and the world-wide figures, rituals, and relationships in anthropology.

There are many metaphors for describing the archetypes. According to Hillman, "There is no place without Gods and no activity that does not enact them. Every fantasy, every experience has its archetypal reason. There is nothing that does not belong to one God or another." In this chapter, we will explore the aspects of the archetypes that are most relevant for psychonauts undergoing inner journeys and practitioners working with holotropic states of consciousness.

The Greek term ἀρχέτυπος means "first-molded" (from ἀρχή, meaning "beginning" or "origin" and τύπος, meaning "pattern," "model," or "type"). Archetypes are abstract universal matrices that are themselves transphenomenal, but they can manifest in many different ways and on many different levels. Richard Tarnas described three important perspectives from which archetypes can be seen in his book *Cosmos and Psyche: Intimations of a New World View* (Tarnas 2006):

1. as **mythological principles** (Homer, Greek tragedy, world mythology)

2. as **philosophical principles** (philosophy of Socrates, Plato, and Aristotle)

3. as **psychological principles** (psychology of C. G. Jung)

The mythological manifestations of archetypes can be traced back to the dawn of human history. They have played an important role in the shamanic lore and in the ritual and spiritual life of native and ancient cultures. The figure of the shaman, in and of itself, is an archetype that has manifested throughout the ages in many human groups and in many countries. The universal image of the shaman has existed in many variations and inflections, reaching back probably 30–40,000 years into the Paleolithic era.

In the chapter on the history of psychonautics, we discussed the images of Paleolithic shamans from the walls of the caves in southern France: the Sorcerer and Beast Master in Les Trois Frères, the shaman in the hunting scene from the Lascaux cave, and the Dancer from Le Gabillou. Additional archetypal images from the Paleolithic era are the Venus figures and figurines symbolizing female fertility: Venus of Willendorf, Venus of Dolní Věstonice, Venus of Laussel, Venus of Hohle Fels, Vénus impudique, and many others.

The initiatory crisis of novice shamans in various cultures has characteristic archetypal sequences: the journey into the underworld, attack by evil spirits, severe emotional and physical ordeals, and experiences of annihilation, dismemberment and psychospiritual death and rebirth, followed by a magical journey into the solar realm. Many cultures have rich eschatological imagery, including the posthumous journey of the soul, the abodes of the Beyond (paradises, heavens, and hells), and scenes of judgment. The archetypal iconography in the ancient Books of the Dead is especially rich (the Tibetan *Bardo Thödol,* Egyptian *Pert em Hru,* Mayan *Ceramic Book of the Dead,* Aztec *Codex Borgia,* and the European *Ars Moriendi)* (Grof 1994, 2006b). India abounds with stunning archetypal sculptures, reliefs, carvings, and paintings of this nature.

The artistry and sophistication of archetypal symbolism reached the culmination point in the Tantric traditions of the three major Indian religions—Hinduism, Buddhism, and Jainism. Intricate figurative paintings and sculptures represent the dynamics of the Serpent Power *(Kundalini),* maps of the subtle body and its energetic centers *(chakras),* different aspects of the two main deities of Tantra (Shiva and Mahakali), and various stages of cosmogony and of the spiritual journey (Mookerjee and Khanna 1977).

Intricate Tantric abstract symbolism makes it possible to portray various deities and spiritual themes as *yantras,* abstract images composed of points, lines, triangles, squares, spirals, and stylized lotus blossoms. Within Vajrayana (Tibetan Mahayana Buddhism), there are scroll paintings called *thangkas* which are used as meditational aids and teaching devices. These feature *mandalas,* complex images combining rich figurative archetypal iconography with geometric symbolism. Many of them depict scenes from the *bardos,* the intermediate state between incarnations. Similar rich iconography can be found in Chinese and Japanese Buddhism. These depict peaceful and wrathful deities, heavens and hells, episodes from Buddha's life and his previous incarnations *(jatakas),* and many other motifs.

James Hillman (1926–2011), American Jungian psychologist, founder of archetypal psychology.

Rich pantheons of archetypal figures, realms, and stories existed in other ancient cultures as well: Egypt, Babylonia, Assyria, North and pre-Hispanic America, African kingdoms and tribes, Australian Aborigines and other indigenous cultures. In the Homeric epics and Greek drama, archetypes take the form of gods *(archai)*, demigods, and legendary heroes, such as Zeus, Hera, Poseidon, Hades, Apollo, Artemis, Aphrodite, Hermes, Heracles, Jason, Theseus or the Centaurs. Greek mythology also offers complex archetypal scenes—the gods' feasts on Olympus, scenes in Tartaros the underworld and in the paradisean Elysian Fields, the battle of the Titans with the Olympian Gods, and the labors of Heracles. This rich archetypal world provided inspiration for Greek sculptors and painters and the artists of the Italian renaissance.

The Greek culture also articulated, in great detail, another major perspective on archetypes—seeing them as philosophical principles. The tendency to interpret the world in terms of archetypal principles was one of the most striking characteristics of Greek philosophy and culture. The classical archetypal perspective was formulated by Plato. He was building on the early philosophical discussions about the first universal principles *(archai)* by the Presocratics (Heraclitus, Thales, Anaximenes, and Anaximander). They discussed whether these principles were fire, water, air, or a limitless boundless substance *(apeiron)*. Plato also drew on Pythagoras' teachings on transcendent mathematical forms and, particularly, on the wisdom of his teacher Socrates.

For Plato, archetypes were transcendent universal principles superordinated to the world of particulars; they formed and informed the material world. In Plato's terminology, archetypes were called *Ideas* or *Forms*, coming from the Greek word *eidos*, meaning pattern, essential quality, or nature of something. It did not mean *idea* as it is understood in the Western world—the product of an individual human psyche. The archetypes possessed an independent existence in a "realm beyond heaven" *(huperouranios topos)*, which was not accessible to ordinary human senses. They could be experienced in holotropic states of consciousness by initiates in ancient mysteries and in temple incubation in the temples of Apollo, or apprehended by the *enlightened intellect* (German *Vernunft*, not *Verstand*).

According to Plato, the only real knowledge is the knowledge of the Forms. In his dialogue *Timaeus*, he gives the reason for this. The Form "keeps its own shape unchangingly, it has not been brought into being and is not destroyed" (Plato 1988). For example, something is beautiful to the extent to which the archetype of Beauty is present in it or the extent to which it partakes in the archetype of Beauty. However, the archetype of Beauty itself is eternal and cannot be either added to or diminished.

The concept of archetype (Form, Idea) does not apply just to abstract qualities, but also to material objects, animals, and people. What makes the key a key is that it contains the Keyness archetype and the dog is a dog to the extent to which it partakes in the archetype of Dogness. We can also talk about the archetype of Humanness, which is Anthropos, the Cosmic Man. Each archetype has its nondescript general form as well as many specific inflections and variations. Alex Grey's remarkable collection of images called *Sacred Mirrors* shows humans of different races, gender, and age and their skeletal, muscular, nervous, and circulatory system, as well as their subtle bodies (*nadis, chakras, meridians,* and *auras).* In biology, we can talk about the archetype of the skeleton of vertebrates and the specific analogs that its parts can take in different species. For example, analogs of human or simian forearms and hands would be the wings of birds or bats, the front legs of felines and the flippers of whales, dolphins, sea lions, and penguins.

Excellent examples of archetypal domains are mathematics and geometry. Like Pythagoras, Plato did not see numbers as something that the human mind invented for ordering and counting material objects, but as transcendent numinous principles woven into the very fabric of existence. Above the door to the Platonic Academy in Athens was an inscription: "Let no one ignorant of geometry enter here."

Hungarian-American physicist, mathematician, and Nobel Prize winner Eugene Wigner published the essay "Unreasonable Effectiveness of Mathematics in Natural Sciences," in which he expressed his astonishment that mathematics, allegedly a product of the human mind, can model and even predict phenomena in the material world. He wrote, "The enormous usefulness of mathematics in the natural sciences is something bordering on the mysterious and there is no rational explanation for it" (Wigner 1960).

Jungian psychologist Marie-Louise von Franz wrote a book called *Number and Time* about the archetypal meaning of the first four numbers (integers). She presented many specific examples, drawing both on psychology and hard sciences, and concluded that "Natural number is the common ordering factor of both physical and psychic manifestations of energy, and is consequently the element that draws psyche and matter together" (von Franz 1974).

Von Franz, Pauli, and Jung saw this as an indication of the existence of *Unus mundus,* a psychophysical reality beyond the split into matter and psyche, a potential world out of which causeless new creations can emerge. Observer and the observed phenomenon come from the same source. Synchronistic events show the moment when this potential world incarnates into the concrete.

Geometrical figures, such as the triangle, square, circle, rectangle, pentacle, six-pointed star, spiral and double spiral and Platonic solids (tetrahedron, cube, octahedron, dodecahedron, icosahedron), sphere, pyramid, and cone would be seen in Platonic philosophy as transcendental Ideas. Additional examples of sacred geometry are π (pi), the golden section, the chambered nautilus shape, or the Fibonacci series. More recent examples are fractals, computer-generated graphic representations of nonlinear equations emulating the shapes of trees, ferns, vegetables, sea shells, and ocean shores, etc. Swiss researcher Hans Jenny was able to create archetypal shapes by vibrating plates covered with lycopodium powder at various frequencies. He described his experiments in the book *Cymatic*

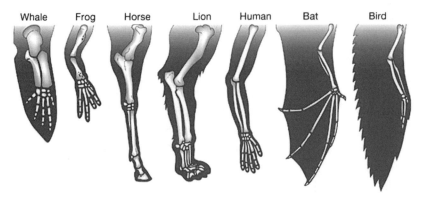

The skeleton of vertebrates is an archetype which in different species manifest as variations of this universal pattern. For example, whales, dolphins, and seals have flippers; the analog in frogs is webbed arms, horses and lions front limbs, simians and humans arms, and bats and birds wings.

Soundscapes (Jenny 1992).

The concept of Ideas is closely related to being and becoming. The world of particulars is mercurial, subjected to constant change, and nothing ever remains the same. This is the reason why Buddha warned that attachment to material things is a source of human suffering. The world of Ideas is superior in comparison with the material world; it is real, eternal, reliable and always remains the same. The Ideas are enduring, which makes them similar to gods. This is why Plato believed that the only real knowledge is the knowledge of Forms.

Plato's student and successor Aristotle brought a more empiricist approach to the concept of universal forms, one supported by rationalism that is based on logical analysis that was secular rather than spiritual and epiphanic. In the Aristotelian perspective, the forms lost their numinosity but gained a new recognition for their dynamic and teleological character as being concretely embodied in the empirical world and in the processes of life.

For Aristotle, the universal forms primarily exist in things, not above or beyond them. Moreover, they not only give form and essential qualities to concrete particulars, but also dynamically transmute them from within, from potentiality to actuality and maturity. Aristotle's archetypes would guide the development of an acorn into an oak tree, a caterpillar into a butterfly, an embryo into a mature organism, and a child into an adult. After the essential character of the forms has been fully actualized, decay occurs as the forms gradually "lose their hold."

In biology, the problem is not only what gives the final form to different organisms—a mosquito, parrot, whale, or human being—but also what is the nature of the force that is capable of guiding their development through the millions of cellular divisions in all the stages of embryogenesis, from the fertilized egg to a mature form. It was the study of embryogenesis of various forms of life and their ability to compensate for noxious experimental intervention that inspired Hans Driesch to postulate the existence of an intelligent force in nature *(entelechy)* and to found vitalism (Driesch 1914).

The problem of universals, more specifically Plato and Aristotle's concepts of archetypes, was one of the central themes in the debates of medieval Scholastic philosophers. They were divided into three groups: the

Realists defended Plato's original idea that archetypes had independent existence in a realm that lay outside of our universe. The Nominalists asserted that universals are mere names, abstractions from what we see in the material world. The third group, the Conceptualists, claimed that universals exist, but only in the mind; they have no external or substantial reality.

The idea of the archetypal or universal underwent important developments in the later classical, medieval, and Renaissance periods. Realism reached its culmination in the philosophy and art of the High Renaissance. In the following centuries, with the development of empiricist science, the concept of archetypes radically shifted toward nominalist philosophy. The archetypal perspective remained vital in the arts, in classical and mythological studies, and in Romanticism. It seemed that the archetypal vision was all but extinguished by the increasing emphasis on reason.

Immanuel Kant's discovery of *a priori* categories and forms of the human mind, which order and condition all human knowledge and experience, and the ensuing revolution in philosophy, brought a re-emergence of the archetypal perspective (Kant 1999). It caused a radical shift from the object of knowledge to the knowing subject that influenced virtually every field of modern thought. In the twentieth century, the concept of archetypes underwent an unexpected renaissance. It was foreshadowed by Friedrich Nietzsche's book *The Birth of Tragedy* and his discussion of the Dionysian and Apollonian principles shaping human culture (Nietzsche 1967) and increased exponentially with the development of depth psychology.

Sigmund Freud had a keen interest in mythology and was a passionate collector of antiquities. His former apartment and office at Berggasse 19 in Vienna is now a museum replete with Greek, Roman, and Egyptian artifacts from his own personal collection. Freud's term Oedipus complex was inspired by the tragedy *Oedipus Rex* by the Greek playwright Sophocles, and in his latest formulation of psychoanalysis, he chose the mythological names Eros and Thanatos for the two drives competing in the human psyche. However, Freud saw mythological stories as reflections of the problems and conflicts that children have in the nuclear family; he did not achieve a real understanding of the transpersonal domain and of the archetypes.

C. G. Jung added an important new chapter to the history of archetypes by defining them as psychological principles and bringing supportive evidence for the realistic perspective. Jung's thinking was influenced by Kant's critical epistemology and Freud's instinct theory, but he eventually transcended both of them. His understanding of the human psyche represented a major extension beyond Freud's biographical model. Like Freud, Jung put great emphasis on the unconscious and its dynamics, but his concept of it was radically different than Freud's.

Jung's epoch-making departure from Freud's psychoanalysis started when he was analyzing a collection of poetry and prose of the American writer Miss Frank Miller *(Miller Fantasies)* (Miller 1906). During this work, he discovered that many motifs in her writings had parallels in the literature of various countries around the world and different historical periods. He was able to find the same phenomenon when he was analyzing the dreams of his patients, fantasies and delusions of schizophrenics, and his own dreams.

He concluded that we do not only have the Freudian individual unconscious, a psychobiological junkyard of rejected instinctual tendencies, repressed memories, and subconsciously assimilated prohibitions, but also a collective unconscious. He saw this vast domain in the psyche as a manifestation of an intelligent and creative cosmic force, which binds us to all humanity, nature, and to the entire cosmos.

The collective unconscious has a historical domain that contains the entire history of humanity, while the archetypal domain harbors the cultural heritage of humanity—mythologies of all the cultures that have ever existed. In holotropic states, we can experience mythological motifs from these cultures even if we do not have any intellectual knowledge of them. Exploring the collective unconscious, Jung discovered the archetypes, or universal principles governing its dynamics.

He first referred to them as "primordial images," using a term that he had borrowed from Jacob Burkhardt. Later he called them "dominants of the collective unconscious" and finally settled on "archetypes." According to the understanding that has emerged from Jungian psychology, scholarly mythological research, and modern consciousness research, archetypes are timeless primordial cosmic principles underlying and informing the fabric of the material world (Jung 1959).

Jung initially thought that archetypes were not transindividual, but intrapsychic patterns hardwired into the brain, which he compared to animal instincts. A major step in his understanding of archetypes was his discovery of synchronicity. As a result, Jung came to regard archetypes as expressions not only of a collective unconscious shared by all human beings, but also of a larger matrix of being and meaning that informs and encompasses both the physical world and the human psyche.

In the postmodern period, archetypes became increasingly influential not only in post-Jungian psychology, but also in other fields such as anthropology, mythology, religious studies, philosophy of science, process philosophy, astrology, and others. The concept of archetypes was elaborated, refined and enriched through an increased awareness of archetypes' fluid, evolving, multivalent, and participatory nature (Tarnas 2006).

Archetypes in Psychiatry and Psychology

Modern consciousness research has shown that in holotropic states, archetypes can be directly experienced and bring new information about mythologies of the world that are otherwise unknown to the subject. In my books, I have given many examples of situations in which my clients experienced or even embodied archetypal figures and witnessed mythological sequences (Grof 2006a, 2006b). Jung described an interesting observation of his that occurred during Grand Rounds in a locked psychiatric ward. At one point, he noticed a chronic psychotic patient who was staring very intently out of the window. He asked him what he was watching. The patient responded: "Don't you see it? The sun has a penis and is making wind by moving it back and forth." Jung later discovered, to his great surprise, what this patient experienced was a motif from Mithraic mythology.

Archetypes have profound theoretical and practical implications for psychiatry, psychology, and psychotherapy. They play an important role in the genesis of emotional and psychosomatic symptoms as part of COEX systems. Understanding archetypal dynamics is thus essential for healing and transformation. This is closely related to the inner self-healing intelligence of the psyche (Jung's individuation process) and the healing potential of archetypal figures or cosmic energies that ancient and native cultures saw as divine.

Some examples of this include the archetype of Apollo in the Greek temple incubation, the deities of the Caribbean and South American syncretistic religions (the *loa* in Voodoo or the *orishas* in Umbanda and Santeria) and the Serpent Power (Kundalini) described in the Indian scriptures. Many psychonauts experimenting with sacred plants experience guidance from what appear to be the spirits of these plants in their sessions, such as Mescalito from peyote or the Great Mother Goddess Pachamama from ayahuasca.

Of particular interest in this regard is a complex archetypal sequence known as the "Hero's Journey." It is very important not only for psychiatry and psychotherapy, but also for comparative religion because it plays a key role in the ritual and spiritual history of humanity. It is an archetypal pattern that is essential for understanding shamanism, rites of passage, the ancient mysteries of death and rebirth, and the great religions of the world. The concept of the Hero's Journey emerged from the research of Joseph Campbell, the greatest mythologist of the twentieth century. He first described this motif in his 1947 classic *The Hero with a Thousand Faces* (Campbell 1947). He referred to it as a "monomyth" because of its universal and ubiquitous nature, which transcends historical and geographical boundaries.

Campbell later demonstrated, in joint seminars with leaders of programs at the Esalen Institute in Big Sur, California (John Perry, Sam Keen, Chungliang Al Huang, and Stanislav and Christina Grof), how this archetypal sequence is essential for understanding a broad range of phenomena, including shamanic initiatory crises, rites of passage, ancient mysteries of death and rebirth, Dante Alighieri's *Divine Comedy,* the lives of saints and mystics, sociopolitical events, and spiritual emergencies.

The work with holotropic states has shown beyond any reasonable doubt that archetypal experiences are not erratic products of brain pathology of unknown origin ("endogenous psychoses"), but creations of Anima mundi emerging into individual consciousness (Grof and Grof 1991, Grof 2000). The discovery of systematic correlations of planetary transits with the timing and content of holotropic states of consciousness is the most powerful evidence for this fact that I have seen.

Another critical proof is the phenomenology of John Perry's Renewal Process, a type of spiritual emergency that mimics the themes of royal

New Year's dramas that were performed in ancient cultures during the "archaic era of incarnated myth" (Perry 1998). The work with holotropic states has also revealed the existence of the perinatal domain of the unconscious that contains a unique mixture of fetal and archetypal elements.

The Archetypes and Science

Modern materialistic science joined the centuries-old philosophical argument between the Nominalists and Realists and emphatically decided in favor of the Nominalists. The existence of hidden invisible dimensions of reality is an idea that is alien to materialistic science, unless these are material in nature and can be made accessible through the use of devices that extend the range of our senses, such as microscopes, telescopes, or sensors detecting various bands of electromagnetic radiation.

Joseph Campbell (1904–1987), American professor of comparative mythology and religion; his best known work is *The Hero with a Thousand Faces*.

Academic and clinical psychiatrists use a very narrow conceptual framework that limits the human psyche to postnatal biography and the Freudian individual unconscious. According to them, the archetypal beings and realms are not ontologically real; they are figments of human imagination or pathological products of the brain that require treatment with tranquilizing medication.

In holotropic states of consciousness, the archetypal figures and domains can be experienced in a way that is as convincing as—or more convincing than—our experience of the material world; they can also be subjected to consensual validation. Deep personal experiences of this realm help us realize that the worldviews found in ancient and native cultures are not based on ignorance, superstition, primitive "magical thinking," or psy-

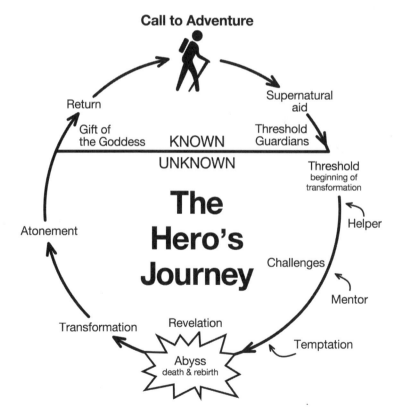

Joseph Campbell's diagram of the Hero's Journey, an archetypal "monomyth" story that exists in various inflections in all historical periods and all the parts of the world.

chotic visions, but on authentic experiences of alternate realities.

Archetypal figures fall into three distinct categories. The first one includes personages embodying various universal roles and principles. The most famous of them are the Great Mother Goddess, the Terrible Mother Goddess, the Wise Old Man, the Eternal Youths (Puer Aeternus and Puella Aeterna), the Lovers, Death, and the Trickster. Jung also discovered that men harbor in their unconscious a generalized representation of the feminine principle, which he called Anima. For her counterpart, the generalized representation of the masculine principle in the unconscious of women, he used the term Animus. The unconscious representation of the dark, destructive aspect of human personality carries the name Shadow in Jungian psychology.

The archetypal figures of the second category represent deities and demons related to specific cultures, geographical areas, and historical periods. For example, instead of a generalized universal image of the Great Mother Goddess, we can experience one of her specific culture-bound forms, such as the Christian Virgin Mary, Sumerian Inanna, Egyptian Isis, Greek Hera, Hindu Lakshmi or Parvati, and many others.

Similarly, specific examples of the Terrible Mother Goddess would be the Indian Kali, pre-Columbian serpent-headed Coatlicue, Greek Medusa or Hekate, Balinese Rangda, or the Hawaiian Pele. It is important to emphasize that the images, which emerge into consciousness in holotropic states, can be drawn from the mythology of any culture in human history. They do not have to be limited to our own racial and cultural heritage.

The third group of archetypal figures are holographic agglomerates which represent an age, gender, race, culture, role, profession, etc.—the Soldier, the Child, the Mother, the Jew, the Conquistador, the Tyrant, the Martyr, etc. These images are from the different collective experiences of these categories—the Jews from all historical periods, all the soldiers who have fought on the battlefields of the world, all the mothers or children of the world, and so on. Similarly, it is possible to experientially differentiate the archetype of the Wolf from the experience of the consciousness of a wolf pack.

Many times over the years, I have observed that my clients, participants in workshops, and trainees in psychedelic and Holotropic Breathwork sessions experienced obscure archetypal figures and motifs from little known cultures, which I was later able to identify. Frequently, I did this with the help of my close friend Joseph Campbell, who was a "walking encyclopedia of world mythology." The most remarkable examples of this kind that I remember was an experience from the mythology of the Malekulan culture of New Guinea and another one from the Inuit Eskimo mythology (the cases of Otto and Alex in *The Ultimate Journey,* Grof 2006b).

Archetypes play an important role in the genesis of scientific theories and in scientific discoveries. As Philipp Frank has shown in his remarkable book *Philosophy of Science: The Link between Science and Philosophy,* the source of the basic axiom of a scientific theory or the idea that leads to a scientific discovery is often an archetypal motif. In the history of science, revolutionary ideas often emerge long before there is sufficient evidence to justify or support them (Frank 1957).

The Ionian philosopher Anaximander proposed, in the sixth century BC, a proto-evolutionary theory suggesting that all life originated in the ocean. Greek philosophers Demokritos (fourth century BC) and Leucippus (fifth century BC) formulated an atomic theory of matter, suggesting that the material world consists of tiny indivisible particles (a-tomos, meaning one that cannot be cut any further). Nicolaus Copernicus and Johannes Kepler drew the inspiration for their astronomical theories from the solar archetype, and German chemist Friedrich August Kekulé von Stradonitz was inspired in his discovery of the benzene ring by a vision of the archetype Uroboros, a snake devouring its tail, as we have seen.

There is also increasing awareness of the importance of archetypal patterns in various scientific disciplines. Johann Wolfgang von Goethe was fascinated by the building plan of plants, especially by the archetypal leaf concept, which considers floral organs to be modified leaves. Goethe formulated a theory of plant metamorphosis in which the archetypal form of the plant is to be found in the leaf. He wrote: "From top to bottom, a plant is all leaf, united so inseparably with the future bud that one cannot be imagined without the other." Goethe's research has created the foundations for many domains of modern plant biology.

British-American anthropologist, biologist, and philosopher Gregory Bateson was fascinated by the "pattern that connects" in nature and in evolutionary theory; he considered it the main feature that differentiates living organisms from inorganic objects (Bateson 1980). British plant physiologist and parapsychologist Rupert Sheldrake formulated the theory of morphogenetic fields and morphic resonance to account for the existence of forms and order in nature (Sheldrake 1981).

In his discussion of the nature of morphogenetic fields, Sheldrake made references to archetypes. He pointed out that the morphogenetic fields have the properties that the immutable Platonic forms found in the "mathematical world of perfection;" as we saw earlier, these forms exist outside of time. However, Sheldrake has another hypothesis involving formative causation that has Aristotelian features. Here nature itself can produce forms utilizing evolutionary creativity.

Archetypes, Religion, and Spirituality

The discovery that the archetypal world is ontologically real gives legitimacy to the spiritual worldview, the spiritual quest, and to religious activity that involves direct experience. It makes it possible to distinguish organized religions based on belief, with their dogmatism, ritualism, moralism, and secular ambitions, from the authentic spirituality that is found in the

Johann Wolfgang von Goethe (1728–1749), important German writer, statesman, and natural scientist.

monastic and mystical branches of religions and in groups emphasizing spiritual practice and direct experience.

Spirituality is based on personal experiences of non-ordinary aspects and dimensions of reality. It does not require a special place or an officially appointed person mediating contact with the divine. The mystics do not need churches or temples. The context in which they experience the sacred dimensions of reality, including their own divinity, are their bodies, psyches, and nature. Instead of officiating priests, they need a supportive group of fellow seekers or the guidance of a teacher who is more advanced on the inner journey than they are themselves.

By comparison, organized religion is an institutionalized group activity that takes place in a designated location, such as a sanctuary, church, or temple, and at a specified time and involves a system of appointed officials who might or might not have had personal experiences of spiritual realities. Once a religion becomes organized, it often completely loses the connection with its spiritual source and becomes a secular institution that exploits human spiritual needs without satisfying them.

Gregory Bateson (1904–1980), British-American anthropologist, biologist, cyberneticist, and philosopher, who was fascinated by the archetype that defines the phenomenon of life, or "pattern that connects".

Organized religions tend to create hierarchical systems focusing on the pursuit of power, control, politics, money, possessions, and other secular concerns. Under these circumstances, religious hierarchy as a rule dislikes and discourages direct spiritual experiences in its members, because they foster independence and cannot be effectively controlled. When this is the case, genuine spiritual life continues mostly in the monastic orders, mystical branches, and ecstatic sects of the religions involved. Historically, mystics did not have easy relationships with organized religions of the same creed, as exemplified by the fate of Joan of Arc and many victims of the Inquisition, and in the story of the martyrdom of Sufi Hallaj and the persecution of the Sufis in Muslim countries.

During his 1937 Dwight Harrington Terry lecture at Yale University, C. G. Jung suggested to those in the audience for whom the rituals of conventional religion had lost their efficacy that they might consider moving beyond the confines of established religion and practice direct experiential encounters with the unconscious. Properly followed, this intrapsychic ritual could bring an "immediate religious experience" and lead to the emergence of a highly personalized spiritual wholeness (Jung 1937).

What Jung had in mind in 1937 was a ritual to be enacted within the sacred circle of one's psyche. His discovery of synchronicity dramatically transformed his earlier notion of this ritual. The idea of an "immediate religious experience" may now be understood as referring to a ritual which is to be enacted within the sacred circle of nature as a whole. Jung's definition of true religion was "the network of genuine spiritual seekers transcending the boundaries of space and time."

Search for a New Planetary Myth

Scholars such as Arnold Toynbee and Joseph Campbell noticed that all past cultures were governed by an underlying myth or a combination of myths. Joseph Campbell often asked the question: "What are the myths that are driving the Western civilization?" He himself emphasized the importance of the myth of the search for the Holy Grail in its relation to the individualism characterizing Western society. King Arthur's knights decided not to search for the Holy Grail as a group, but each chose his own individual path in the woods. We can also think about two major myths of the modern era that Richard Tarnas explores in his *The Passion of the Western Mind:* Paradise Lost vs. The Ascent of Man (Tarnas 1991). The motifs of the Psychospiritual Death/Rebirth, Abduction and Rape of the Feminine, and a variety of others, including Faust, Sorcerer's Apprentice, Frankenstein, and Prodigal Son seem to be equally appropriate.

Joseph Campbell also often asked: "What will be the myth of the future?" and he expressed his hope that it would involve overcoming fragmentation and creating a planetary civilization, where people would live in harmony with others and with nature, benefiting from the astonishing discoveries of science and technology, but using them with a wisdom that comes from a deep, spiritual understanding (Hoffman's "New Atlantis"). Achieving this goal would also involve Psychospiritual Rebirth and Liberation and The Return of the Feminine. Since we are talking about planetary

Richard Tarnas (1950–), depth psychologist, cultural historian, philosopher, and archetypal astrologer.

civilization, I would like to mention a very interesting observation that seems especially relevant.

One of the most surprising discoveries in my work with psychedelics and with Holotropic Breathwork was the ease with which my clients, trainees, and workshop participants in holotropic states of consciousness transcended historical and geographical boundaries and experienced archetypal figures, motifs, and domains from so many cultures in human history. Michael and Sandra Harner observed a similarly wide cross-cultural range of experiences in 1,500 Westerners who were exposed to shamanic drumming (Harner 2012).

Over the years, during my own psychedelic sessions, I have experienced episodes from different mythologies and religions of the world, including Hindu, Buddhist, Tibetan Buddhist, Muslim, Christian, ancient Egyptian, Shinto, Australian Aborigine, Native American, and South American. This must be a new phenomenon, because many cultures used powerful mind-expanding technologies, including psychedelic plants, and if the entire collective unconscious had been as easily accessible for them as it seems to be for modern subjects, we would not have distinct culture-specific mythologies.

We have to assume that, for example, the Tibetans experienced primarily Tibetan deities and for the Huichol Indians, primarily Mexico Huichol deities. There are no descriptions of the Deer Spirit or Grandfather Fire in the *Bardo Thödol* or those of the Dhyani Buddhas in the Huichol lore. We can discover different inflections of the same archetypes, but not culture-specific forms related to other cultural groups.

It seems that this increased accessibility of various domains in the collective unconscious parallels what is happening in the material world on planet Earth. Until the end of the fifteenth century, Europeans did not know anything about the New World and its inhabitants and vice versa. Many human groups in remote parts of the world remained unknown to the rest of the world until the modern era. Tibet was relatively isolated until the Chinese invasion in 1949. Today telephone, short-wave radio, television, jet travel, and, more recently, the Internet have dissolved many of the old boundaries. Let us hope that what is happening in the inner and the outer world are indications that we are moving toward a truly global civilization.

Dangers of Archetypes for Psychonauts

The most common danger associated with the experiences of the archetypal world is what C. G. Jung called "inflation." It means assuming the numinosity and luster of the archetypal world for oneself and attaching it to one's body/ego. According to Joseph Campbell, echoing Karlfried Graf Durckheim, "a useful deity (archetypal figure) has to be transparent to the transcendent." It has to point to the Absolute, but not be mistaken for it. Making the archetypes opaque and worshipping them is another important danger and pitfall on the spiritual journey.

This results in religions that unite people within its radius who are willing to believe and worship in their particular way, but separate them from everyone else, dividing the world into rival groups: Christians/pagans, Muslims/infidels, Jews/goyim, etc. Even differences in interpreting the basic tenets of the same religion can result in internecine encounters and centuries of bloodshed, as we see in the centuries of atrocities between Catholics and Protestants, and Sunnis and Shiites. The ability to see through or beyond the archetypes to the Absolute, which is the source of all religions, determines whether the result will be a mystical worldview or idolatry.

The realization of the ontological reality of the archetypal world validates the ritual and spiritual life of pre-industrial cultures—shamanism, rites of passage, mysteries of death and rebirth, and the great religions and spiritual philosophies of the East and West. Of these, the rites of passage are of particular importance for modern society. According to scholars such as Margaret Mead and Mircea Eliade, the fact that the industrial civilization has lost meaningful, socially sanctioned rites of passage contributes significantly to the ills of modern society, particularly of the young generation—sexual acting out, drug abuse, and violence.

In 1973, Joan Halifax and I, who were at that time newlyweds, were invited by anthropologist Margaret Mead and her daughter Catherine Bateson to a small working conference entitled "Ritual: Reconciliation in Change." The conference was sponsored by the Wenner-Gren Foundation, a small anthropological association located in Lower Manhattan in New York City, and took place at Burg Wartenstein in Austria. There were eighteen participants in this conference and all of us had to write pre-prints, since Margaret hated formal lectures. The meeting lasted six days and we met twice a day around the castle's giant round table for brainstorming sessions. The topic was Margaret's idea, mentioned above, that the problems we have with teenagers are caused by the fact that the industrial civilization has lost rites of passage.

The task of the discussion was to determine if it was possible to artificially recreate rites of passage or if they have to emerge organically from the history of the tribe or culture. All of us recognized the importance of rites of passage and were interested in the possibility of recreating them using some combination of already available techniques, such as ropes courses, outward bound/survivor kind of approaches, stays in wilderness, and fire-walking.

Due to the political climate, it was clear that it was not realistic to consider using psychedelic plants and substances for this purpose, which would be a logical choice in view of the many centuries of experiences from native cultures. The group came to the conclusion that non-pharmacological experiential therapies would be a reasonable temporary substitute. Unfortunately, Margaret was not able to overcome the administrative challenges and implement her interesting idea. The efforts to reinstitute rites of passage have continued to this day.

Additional validation of the ontological reality of archetypes came from informal experimentation with psychedelics, entheogens, and with powerful non-drug experiential techniques (Grof 2000, 2006a, Metzner 20). Of the many experiences involving the archetypal world I myself have had in psychedelic sessions, the most interesting one happened in a session with a high dose of MDMA (in a pilot study conducted by Sasha Shulgin and Leo Zeff).

About fifty minutes into the session, I started experiencing strong activation in the lower part of my body. My pelvis was vibrating and releasing powerful streams of energy in ecstatic jolts. At one point, this exploding energy swept me along in an intoxicating frenzy into a whirling cosmic vortex of creation and destruction. In the center of this monstrous hurricane of primordial forces were four herculean archetypal figures performing what seemed to be the ultimate cosmic saber dance. They had strong Mongolian features with protruding cheekbones, oblique eyes, and clean-shaven heads decorated each with a large braided ponytail.

Whirling around in a frantic dance craze, they were brandishing large weapons that looked like scythes or L-shaped scimitars; all four of these combined formed a rapidly rotating swastika. I intuitively understood that this monumental archetypal scene was related to the beginning of the process of creation and simultaneously to the final stage of the spiritual journey. In the cosmogenetic process (with its movement from the primordial unity to the worlds of plurality), the blades of the scimitars represented the force that is splitting and fragmenting the unified field of cosmic consciousness and creative energy into countless individual units.

In relation to the spiritual journey, they also seemed to represent the

Margaret Mead (1901–1978), American cultural anthropologist who was famous for her research focusing on sexuality and child-bearing in traditional cultures in the South Pacific and Southeast Asia. She was married to Gregory Bateson and they together conducted research in New Guinea and Bali.

stage at which the seeker's consciousness transcends separation and polarity and reaches the state of original undifferentiated unity. Here the scimitars functioned like a blender, transforming the individual separate units into an amorphous mush. The direction of this process seemed to be related to the clockwise and counterclockwise rotation of the blades (represented by the peaceful and ominous versions of the swastika). Projected into the material world, this archetypal motif seemed to be related to growth and development (the fertilized egg or seed dividing and becoming an organism) or destruction of forms (wars, natural catastrophes, decay). Then the experience opened up into an unimaginable panorama of scenes of destruction.

In these visions, natural disasters, such as volcanic eruptions, earthquakes, crashing meteors, forest fires, floods and tidal waves were combined with images of human made desolation: burning cities attacked by air-raids and rocket fire, entire blocks of collapsing high-rise buildings, mass death, and the horrors of war. Heading this wave of total annihilation were four archetypal images of macabre riders symbolizing the end of the world. I realized that these were the Four Horsemen of the Apocalypse (pestilence, war, famine, and death) on colorful horses. The continuing vibrations and jolts of my pelvis now became synchronized with the movements of this ominous horseback riding and I joined the dance, becoming one of them, or possibly all four of them at the same time, leaving my own identity behind.

Suddenly, there was a rapid change of scenery and I had a vision of the cave from Plato's Republic. In this work, Plato describes a group of people who spend their whole lives chained in a cave, facing a blank wall. They watch shadows projected on the wall by things passing in front of the cave entrance. According to Plato, the shadows are as close as the prisoners get to seeing reality. The enlightened philosopher is like a prisoner who is freed from this illusion and comes to understand that the shadows on the wall are illusory, as he can perceive the true form of reality rather than the mere shadows that are seen by the prisoners. This was followed by a profound and convincing realization that the material world of our everyday life is not made of *stuff*, but that it is a virtual reality created by cosmic consciousness through an infinitely complex and sophisticated orchestration of experiences. It is a divine play that the Hindus call *lila,* created by a cosmic illusion or *maya*.

The final major scene of the session was a magnificent ornate theater stage featuring a parade of personified universal principles, or archetypes, which were cosmic actors, who create the illusion of the phenomenal world through a complex interplay. They were protean personages with many facets, levels, and dimensions of meaning that kept changing their

Four Horsemen of the Apocalypse from the *Book of Revelation* by John of Patmos. Albrecht Dürer (1498).

forms in extremely intricate holographic interpenetration as I was observing them. Each of them seemed to simultaneously represent the essence of his or her function as well as all the concrete manifestations of this element in the world of matter.

There was Maya, the mysterious ethereal principle symbolizing the world illusion; Anima, embodying the eternal Female; a Mars-like personification of war and aggression; the Lovers, representing all the sexual dramas and romances throughout the ages; the royal figure of the Ruler; the withdrawn Hermit; the elusive Trickster; and many others. As they were passing across the stage, they bowed in my direction, as if they were expecting appreciation for their stellar performance in the divine play of the universe.

This experience brought me a deep understanding of the meaning of the archetypal motif of the Apocalypse. It suddenly seemed profoundly wrong to see it as being exclusively related to the physical destruction of the material world. It is certainly possible that the Apocalypse will actually manifest on a planetary scale as a historical event, which is the potential of all archetypes. There are many examples of situations in which archetypal motifs and energies broke through the boundary that usually separates the archetypal realm from the material world and shaped history. The giant

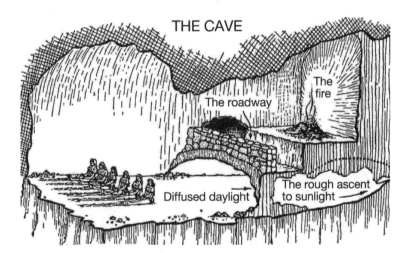

The *Allegory of the Cave* that Plato wrote in his Socratic dialogue *Republic* around 380 BC.

asteroid that killed the dinosaurs sixty-five million years ago, the wars of all ages, the crucifixion of Jesus, the medieval Witches' Sabbath and Dance of Death, the hell of the Nazi concentration camps, and the Buddhist hot hell of Hiroshima are just a few salient examples.

The primary importance of the archetype of the Apocalypse, though, is that it functions as an important landmark on the spiritual journey. It emerges into the consciousness of the seeker at a time when he or she recognizes the illusory nature of the material world. As the universe reveals its true essence as a virtual reality, as a cosmic play of consciousness, the world of matter is destroyed in the psyche of the individual.

It crossed my mind that this might also be the meaning of the "end of the world" referred to in the Mayan prophecy. In this case, it would relate to a radical inner transformation that humanity would go through during the period of the sun's transit over the axis of the galaxy (lasting at least seventy-two years, during which the body of the sun would be in contact with the galactic axis). We would thus be now in the middle of this period. The magnitude of this transformation would be comparable to the transition of humanity from the age of Neanderthals to the age of Cro-Magnons (during the previous transit of this kind about 26,000 years, one "Platonic Year" ago) or from the age of hunters and gatherers to the age of agriculture and the building of cities (the precessional transit of the sun on the other side of the galaxy, approximately 13,000 years, or half a "Platonic Year" ago).

Literature

Bateson, G. 1980. *Mind in Nature: A Necessary Unity.* New York: E. P. Dutton.

Campbell, J. 1947. *The Hero with A Thousand Faces.* Princeton, NJ: Princeton University Press.

Driesch, H. 1914. *The History and Theory of Vitalism* (C. K. Ogden transl.). London: Macmillan.

Frank, P. 1957. *Philosophy of Science: The Link between Science and Philosophy.* Englewood Cliffs, NJ: Prentice-Hall.

Franz, M.-L. von. 1974. *Number and Time: Reflections Leading Toward a*

Unification of Depth Psychology and Physics. Stuttgart: Ernst Klett Verlag.

Grof, C. and Grof, S. 1991. *The Stormy Search for the Self: A Guide to Personal Growth through Transformational Crises*. Los Angeles, CA: J. P. Tarcher.

Grof, S., 1994. *Books of the Dead: Manuals for Living and Dying*. London: Thames and Hudson.

Grof, S. 2000. *Psychology of the Future: Lessons from Modern Consciousness Research*. Albany, NY: State University of New York (SUNY) Press.

Grof, S. 2006a. *When the Impossible Happens*. Louisville, CO: Sounds True.

Grof, S., 2006b. *The Ultimate Journey: Consciousness and the Mystery of Death*. Santa Cruz, CA: MAPS Publications.

Grof, S. and Grof, C. 2011. *Holotropic Breathwork: A New Approach to Self-Exploration and Therapy*. Albany, NY: State University of New York (SUNY) Press.

Harner, M. 2012. *Cave and Cosmos: Shamanic Encounters with Another Reality*. Berkeley: North Atlantic Books.

Hillman, J. 1977. *Re-Visioning Psychology*. New York: Harper Collins.

Jenny, H. 1992. *Cymatic Soundscapes*. Epping, NH: MACROmedia.

Jung, C. G. 1937. *Religion and Psychology*. Dwight Harrington Terry lecture at Yale University during Jung's visit to United States.

Jung, C. G. 1959. *Archetypes and the Collective Unconscious*. Collected Works, vol. 9,1. Bollingen Series XX, Princeton, NJ: Princeton University Press.

Kant, I. 1999. *Critique of Pure Reason*. Cambridge, MA: Cambridge University Press.

Metzner, R. 2013. *The Toad and the Jaguar. A Field Report of Underground Research on a Visionary Medicine*. Berkeley, CA: Regent Press.

Miller, Miss Frank. 1906. "Quelques Faits d'Imagination Créatrice." *Archives de psychologie (Geneva)* V. 36-51.

Mookerjee, A. and Khanna, M. 1977. London: Thames and Hudson.

Nietzsche, F. 1967. *The Birth of Tragedy and the Case of Wagner* (translated by Walter Kaufmann). Visalia, CA: Vintage Press.

Perry, J. W. 1998. *Trials of the Visionary Mind: Spiritual Emergency and the Renewal Process*. Albany, NY: State University of New York (SUNY) Press.

Plato. 1986. *Symposium*. Chicago, IL: University of Chicago Press.

Plato. 1988. *Timaeus*. Salem, NH: Ayers Co. Publishers.

Sheldrake, R. 1981. *A New Science of Life*. Los Angeles, CA: J. P. Tarcher.

Tarnas, R. 1991. *The Passion of the Western Mind*. New York: Harmony Books.

Tarnas, R. 2006. *Cosmos and Psyche: Intimations of a New Worldview*. New York: Viking Press.

Wigner, E. 1960. "Unreasonable Effectiveness of Mathematics in Natural Sciences." In: *Communications in Pure and Applied Mathematics,* vol. 13, No. I. New York: John Wiley & Sons.

XII

Roots of Human Violence and Greed:
Consciousness Research and Human Survival

Since time immemorial, the propensity toward unbridled violence and insatiable greed have been two elemental forces driving human history. The number and nature of the atrocities that have been committed throughout the ages in various countries of the world—many of them in the name of God—are truly astonishing and shocking. Countless millions of soldiers and civilians have been killed in wars and revolutions and other forms of bloodshed. In the past, these violent events had tragic consequences for the individuals, who were directly involved in them, and for their immediate families. However, they did not threaten the future of the human species as a whole and certainly did not represent a danger for the ecosystem and for the biosphere of the planet. Also during this time, hunting, gathering, and farming were sustainable human activities.

Even after the most violent wars, nature was able to recycle all the aftermath and completely recover within several decades. This situation changed very radically over the course of the twentieth century due to rapid technological progress, the exponential growth of industrial production and pollution, the massive population explosion, and particularly the development of atomic and hydrogen bombs, chemical and biological warfare, and other weapons of mass destruction.

We are facing a global crisis of unprecedented proportions and have the dubious privilege of being the first species in history that has achieved the capacity to eradicate itself and, in the process, threaten the evolution of life on this planet. Diplomatic negotiations, administrative and legal measures, economic and social sanctions, military interventions, and other similar efforts have had very little success; as a matter of fact, they have often produced more problems than they solved. It is obvious why they had to fail: the strategies used to alleviate this crisis are rooted in the same ideology that created it in the first place. And, as Albert Einstein pointed out, it is impossible to solve problems with the same level of thinking that created them.

It has become increasingly clear that the crisis we are facing reflects the level of consciousness evolution of the human species and that its successful resolution, or at least alleviation, would have to include a radical inner transformation of humanity on a large scale. The observations that have come from the research of holotropic states of consciousness provide new insights into the nature and roots of human aggression and greed, and may lead to effective strategies for alleviating the destructive and self-destructive tendencies of the human species.

Anatomy of Human Destructiveness

The scientific understanding of human aggression began with Darwin's epoch-making book on the evolution of species in the middle of the nineteenth century (Darwin 1952). The attempts to explain human aggression from our animal origins generated such theoretical concepts as Desmond Morris's image of the "naked ape" (Morris 1967), Robert Ardrey's idea of the "territorial imperative" (Ardrey 1961), Paul MacLean's "triune brain" (McLean 1973) and Richard Dawkins's sociobiological explanations interpreting aggression in terms of genetic strategies of the "selfish gene" (Dawkins 1976).

More refined models of behavior developed by pioneers in ethology, such as Nobel laureates Konrad Lorenz and Nikolaas Tinbergen, complemented the mechanical emphasis on instincts through the study of ritualistic and motivational elements (Lorenz 1963, Tinbergen 1965). However, as Erich Fromm demonstrated in his groundbreaking book *Anatomy of Human Destructiveness* (Fromm 1973), any theories asserting that the human disposition to violence simply reflects our animal origins are inadequate and unconvincing. Animals exhibit aggression when they are hungry, competing for sex or defending their territory. With rare exceptions, such as the occasional violent group raids of the chimpanzees against neighboring groups (Wrangham and Peterson 1996), animals do not prey on their own kind. The nature and scope of human violence—Erich Fromm's "malignant aggression"—has no parallels in the animal kingdom.

The realization that human aggression cannot be adequately explained as a result of phylogenetic evolution led to the formulation of psychodynamic and psychosocial theories that consider a significant part of human aggression to be learned behavior. This trend began in the late 1930s and was initiated by the work of Dollard and Miller (Dollard et al. 1939). The authors of psychodynamic theories made attempts to explain the specifically human aggression as a reaction to various psychotraumatic situations that the human infant and child experience during the extended period of dependency—physical, emotional, and sexual abuse, lack of love, sense of insecurity, inadequate satisfaction of basic biological needs, emotional deprivation, abandonment, and rejection.

However, explanations of this kind fall painfully short of accounting for extreme forms of individual violence, such as the serial murders by the Boston Strangler, Geoffrey Dahmer, the Son of Sam, or Ted Bundy. They also do not have a plausible explanation for "running amok," the indiscriminate killing of multiple people in public places followed by suicide (or killing) of the perpetrator. "Running amok" was long considered to be an exotic culture-bound syndrome limited to Malaysia. In the last several decades, it has been repeatedly observed in the western industrial countries, including mass killing among teenagers on school campuses.

There also is no plausible psychodynamic explanation for the religiously motivated combination of violence and suicide. In WWII, Japanese kamikaze warriors conducted suicidal missions to destroy American battleships and sacrifice their lives for their Emperor, whom they considered to be God. In recent decades, Muslim fundamentalists have been committing mass murders, expecting to obtain blissful existence in the Muslim paradise as the reward for their actions (see pp. 284, Volume I).

Current psychodynamic and psychosocial theories are even less convincing when it comes to bestial acts committed by entire groups, like the Sharon Tate murders of Charles Manson's gang, the My Lai massacre of more than five hundred unarmed Vietnamese villagers by American soldiers, the torture and abuse of prisoners in the Abu Ghraib prison, and atrocities that occur during prison uprisings.

They fail completely when it comes to mass societal phenomena that involve entire nations, such as Nazism, Communism, bloody wars and revolutions, genocide, and concentration camps. Psychoanalytic theories do not explain Hitler's Holocaust, Stalin's Gulag Archipelago and the mass murders of many millions of farmers, Ukrainians and Armenians, Mao's Cultural Revolution in China and genocide in Tibet.

Perinatal Roots of Violence

There is no doubt that traumatic experiences and the frustration of basic needs in childhood and infancy represent important sources of aggression. However, psychedelic research and deep experiential psychotherapies have revealed additional, much more significant roots of violence in the deep recesses of the human psyche that lie beyond (or beneath) postnatal biography. The feelings of vital threat, pain, and suffocation experienced for many hours during the passage through the birth canal generate enormous amounts of murderous aggression that remains repressed and stored in the organism.

As Sigmund Freud pointed out in his book *Mourning and Melancholia,* repressed aggression turns into depression and self-destructive impulses (Freud 1917). Perinatal energies and emotions, by their very nature, represent a mixture of murderous and suicidal drives. The reliving of birth in various forms of experiential psychotherapy is not limited to the replay of the emotional feelings and physical sensations experienced during the passage through the birth canal; it is typically accompanied by a variety of experiences from the collective unconscious portraying scenes of unimaginable violence.

Among these are often powerful sequences depicting wars, revolutions, racial riots, concentration camps, totalitarianism, and genocide. Spon-

A painting representing reliving of the onset of delivery (BPM II) in a high-dose LSD session experienced as engulfment by a giant Maelstrom. The little boat with a skeleton suggests the impending encounter with death (top). Drawing of an engulfing whirlpool experienced in a high-dose LSD session of Harriette Francis, a professional painter. A mandala made of skulls and ribcages, like the boat with a skeleton in the above picture, heralds an imminent profound encounter with death.

Economic and political crises are often depicted in cartoons as engulfment or drowning. In this picture, the crisis is portrayed as engulfment by a giant Maelstrom.

Crisis in the White House portrayed as collapsing and being swallowed by the earth.

International crisis in the Middle East, representing Syria as a perinatal Maelstrom engulfing all the countries involved in this conflict.

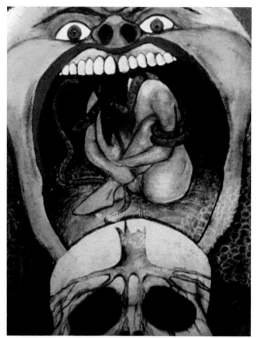

A painting depicting an experience of engulfment from a Holotropic Breathwork session related to the beginning of BPM II. Snakes are common perinatal symbols, the skull suggests an impending encounter with death, and the tree is an allusion to the placenta and the archetypal World Tree.

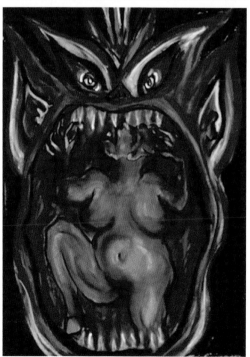

A painting from an LSD session depicting the experience of being engulfed at the onset of the birth process. The aggressive energy of the oral attack represents the onslaught of the uterine contractions; the suffering caused by pain and choking is turning the victim into an evil being.

Crisis of the American army in Lebanon depicted as a stream of marching soldiers being engulfed by a giant skull and disappearing into the underworld.

An Arab monster swallowing an American luxury car symbolizing the loss of American lifestyle after OPEC quixotically increased the price of petroleum.

A political cartoon representing Great Britain's loss of Hong Kong to China by showing the city being swallowed by a giant Chinese dragon.

The Hong Kong Blues

A political cartoon satirizing Barack Obama's military difficulties in Iraq by depicting him swallowed by a giant dragon or crocodile.

Cartoons representing situations that seem unsuccessful and hopeless often use the perinatal symbolism of the journey into an underworld labyrinth, as in this cartoon symbolizing American financial crisis by showing Uncle Sam finding that he is in the belly of a whale.

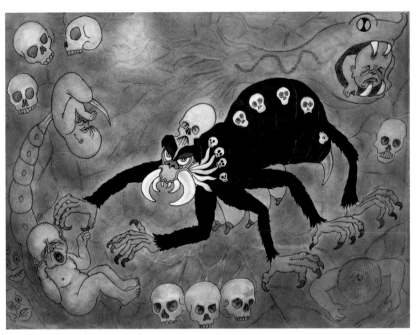

A monstrous Devouring Mother-Spider exposing helpless fetuses to diabolical tortures. A vision encountered in a high-dose LSD session governed by BPM II (top).

A cartoon from a Soviet newspaper criticizing the United States for bringing dangerous nuclear weapons to Western Europe by portraying Uncle Sam as a colossal spider with rockets for legs.

A drawing representing a giant spider, a vision from a Holotropic Breathwork training session governed by BPM II (top).

The threat that Saddam Hussein posed for Iraqi people symbolized by an image portraying him as a gigantic arachnoid monster.

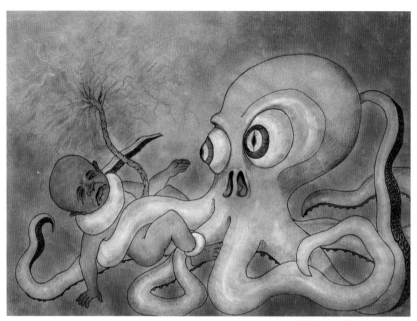

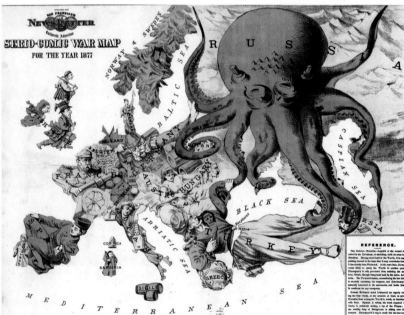

A painting portraying an episode from a high-dose LSD session dominated by the onset of BPM II. The uterine contractions are experienced as an attack by a giant octopus-like creature (top); a political cartoon portraying Czarist Russia as a colossal octopus threatening Europe.

Japan attacking Dutch Indonesia portrayed as a giant octopus with tentacles grabbing individual islands (top).

Serbian President Slobodan Milošević portrayed as a vicious giant octopus taking over Yugoslavia.

A painting from a high-dose LSD session related to BPM II. The female reproductive system was experienced as a combination of a giant press, a prison, and a torture chamber.

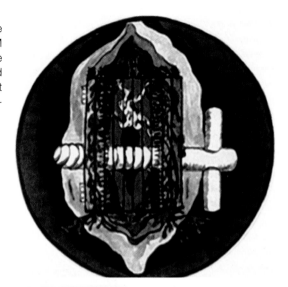

An episode from artist Harriette Francis' birth experience in a high-dose LSD session, in which she felt crushed under a giant boulder with the face of her mother.

A self-portrait of the Swiss genius of fantastic realism Hansruedi Giger on a poster advertizing one of his exhibitions. Giger was aware that he was drawing his inspirations from the memory of his birth.

Economic crisis described by using perinatal language and images of crushing pressure (top left).

A cartoon depicting Jimmy Carter's financial trouble by showing him in a perinatal crisis (top right).

Economic crisis portrayed and described in a way applicable to the trauma of birth (bottom left).

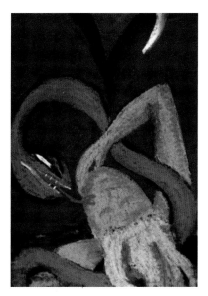

A painting from a high-dose LSD session portraying the inside of the uterus in BPM II as a snake pit (top left); the struggle in the birth canal experienced in an LSD session as a vicious fight with a constrictor snake (top right).

A drawing from a Holotropic Breathwork session in which the constriction by uterine contractions in BPM II was experienced as being entwined and crushed by a giant boa constrictor.

A cartoon portraying the fight of former American President Theodore Roosevelt with his political enemies by showing him as baby Hercules killing the giant snakes which the goddess Hera sent to kill him (top left); a Communist political cartoon from pre-WW II Germany showing the Nazi party as a vicious dangerous viper (top right).

A political cartoon depicts the problems of the U.S. military in the Middle East by showing Uncle Sam trapped in a snake pit.

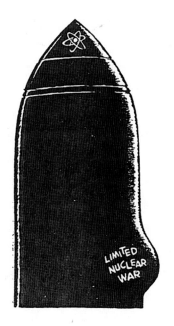

A political cartoon mocking the concept of "limited nuclear war" by comparing it with pregnancy (top).

A political cartoon demonstrating unconscious association between atomic weapons and pregnancy: Saddam Hussein pregnant with atomic weapons.

A political cartoon calling for a leader who would be able to show America the way out of the tunnel (top).

A political cartoon depicting Bill Clinton's victory as rebirth (middle).

A drawing depicting rebirth and triumphant emergence from the birth canal experienced in a Holotropic Breathwork session (bottom).

taneous emergence of this imagery associated with the reliving of birth suggests that the perinatal level might actually be an important source of extreme forms of human violence. Naturally, wars and revolutions are extremely complex phenomena that have historical, economic, political, religious, and other dimensions. My intention here is not to offer a reductionistic explanation replacing all the other causes, but to add some new insights concerning the psychological and spiritual dimensions of these forms of social psychopathology that have been neglected or received only cursory attention in earlier theories.

The images of violent sociopolitical events accompanying the reliving of biological birth tend to appear in very specific connection with the four Basic Perinatal Matrices (BPMs) associated with the reliving of the consecutive stages of the birth process (see pp. 150, Volume I).

While reliving episodes of undisturbed intrauterine existence (BPM I), we typically experience images from human societies with an ideal social structure, from cultures that live in complete harmony with nature, or from future utopian societies where all major conflicts have been resolved. Memories of intrauterine disturbances, such as those of a toxic womb, Rh incompatibility between the maternal organism and the fetus, imminent miscarriage, or attempted abortion are accompanied by images of human groups living in industrial areas where nature is polluted and spoiled, or in societies with insidious social order and all-pervading paranoia.

Experiences associated with the first clinical stage of birth (BPM II), during which the uterus periodically contracts but the cervix is not yet open, present a diametrically different picture. They portray oppressive and abusive totalitarian societies with closed borders, victimizing their populations, and "choking" personal freedom, such as Czarist Russia, Stalin's Gulag Archipelago, Hitler's Third Reich, Eastern European Soviet satellites, Mao Tse-tung's China, South American military dictatorships, or South African apartheid. While experiencing these scenes, we experience emotional and physical torture. We identify exclusively with the victims and feel deep sympathy for the downtrodden and the underdog; it is impossible to imagine that this nightmarish situation will ever end.

The experiences accompanying reliving of the second clinical stage of delivery (BPM III), when the cervix is dilated and continued contractions propel the fetus through the narrow passage of the birth canal, feature a rich panoply of violent scenes: bloody wars and revolutions, human or animal slaughter, mutilation, sexual abuse, and murder. These scenes often contain demonic elements and repulsive scatological motifs. Additional frequent concomitants of BPM III are visions of burning cities, rocket launches, and explosions of nuclear bombs. Here we are not limited to the role of victims but can participate in three roles—of the victim, the perpetrator, and an emotionally involved observer.

The reliving of the third clinical stage of delivery (BPM IV), the actual moment of birth and the separation from the mother, is typically associated with images of victory in wars and revolutions, liberation of prisoners, and the success of collective efforts, such as patriotic or nationalistic movements. At this point, we can also experience visions of triumphant celebrations and parades or exciting post-war reconstruction.

In 1975, I described these observations, linking sociopolitical phenomena to stages of biological birth, in my book *Realms of the Human Unconscious* (Grof 1975). Shortly after its publication, I received an enthusiastic letter from Lloyd de Mause, New York psychoanalyst and journalist, and one of the founders of psychohistory, which is a discipline that applies the findings of depth psychology to the study of history and political science. Psychohistorians explore such issues as the relationship between the childhood of political leaders and their system of values and the process of decision-making, or the influence of child-rearing practices on the nature

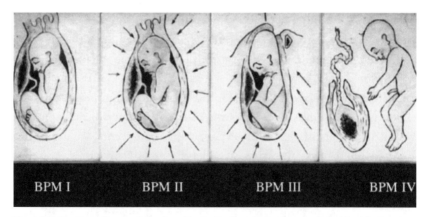

Stanislav Grof's *schema of the four Basic Perinatal Matrices,* painted for his first lecture about the importance of the trauma of birth. Conference on LSD Psychotherapy, Amsterdam 1966.

of revolutions of that particular historical period.

Lloyd de Mause was very interested in my findings concerning the trauma of birth and its possible sociopolitical implications, because they provided independent support for his own research. For some time, de Mause had been studying the psychodynamics of the periods immediately preceding wars and revolutions. He was interested in discovering how military leaders succeed in mobilizing masses of peaceful civilians and transforming them into killing machines practically overnight. His approach to this problem was very original and creative. In addition to the analysis of traditional historical sources, he drew data of great psychological importance from caricatures, jokes, dreams, personal imagery, slips of the tongue, side comments of speakers, and even doodles and scribbles on the edge of the rough drafts of political documents.

By the time he contacted me, he had analyzed seventeen situations preceding the outbreak of wars and revolutionary upheavals, spanning many centuries, from antiquity to recent times. He was struck by the extraordinary abundance of figures of speech, metaphors, and images related to biological birth that he found in this material. Military leaders and politicians of all ages describing a critical situation or declaring war typically

Lloyd de Mause (1931–), American psychoanalyst, journalist, political scientist, and founder of *The Journal of Psychohistory.*

used terms that applied equally to perinatal distress (de Mause 1975).

They accused the enemy of choking and strangling their people, squeezing the last breath out of their lungs, constricting them, and not giving them enough space to live (Hitler's: "Wir haben nicht genug Lebensraum," meaning "We don't have enough space to live"). Equally frequent were allusions to dark caves, tunnels, and confusing labyrinths, dangerous abysses into which one might be pushed, and the threat of engulfment by treacherous quicksand or a terrifying whirlpool.

Similarly, the offer for the crisis' resolution had the form of perinatal images. The leader promised to rescue his nation from an ominous labyrinth, to lead it to the light on the other side of the tunnel, and to create a situation where the dangerous aggressor and oppressor will be overcome, and everybody will again breathe freely. Lloyd de Mause's historical examples at the time included such famous personages as Alexander the Great, Napoleon Bonaparte, Samuel Adams, Kaiser Wilhelm II, Adolf Hitler, Nikita Khrushchev, and John F. Kennedy.

Samuel Adams, talking about the American Revolution, referred to "the child of Independence now struggling for birth." In 1914, Kaiser Wilhelm stated that "the Monarchy has been seized by the throat and forced to choose between letting itself be strangled and making a last ditch effort to defend itself against attack." During the Cuban missile crisis, Krushchev wrote to Kennedy, pleading that the two nations not "come to a clash, like blind moles battling to death in a tunnel."

Even more explicit was the coded message used by Japanese ambassador Kurusu when he phoned Tokyo to signal that negotiations with Roosevelt had broken down and that it was all right to go ahead with the bombing of Pearl Harbor. He announced that the "birth of the child is imminent" and asked how things were in Japan: "Does it seem as if the child might be born?" The reply was: "Yes, the birth of the child seems imminent." Interestingly, the American intelligence listening in recognized the meaning of the "war-as-birth" code.

More recent examples can be found in Osama bin Laden's videotape, where he threatens to turn the United States into a "choking hell" and in the speech of U.S. Secretary of State Condoleezza Rice, who described the acute crisis in Lebanon as "birth pangs of the New Middle East." Particularly chilling was the use of perinatal language in connection with the explosion of the atomic bomb in Hiroshima. The airplane was given the name of the pilot's mother, Enola Gay, the atomic bomb itself carried a painted nickname, "The Little Boy," and the agreed-upon message sent to Washington as a signal of successful detonation was "The baby is born." It would not be too far-fetched to also see the image of a newborn behind the nickname of the Nagasaki bomb, "Fat Man."

Since the time of our correspondence, Lloyd de Mause collected many additional historical examples and refined his thesis that the memory of the birth trauma plays an important role as a source of motivation for violent social activity. The relationship between nuclear warfare and birth is of such relevance that I would like to explore it further using the material from a fascinating paper by Carol Cohn, "Sex and Death in the Rational World of the Defense Intellectuals" (Cohn 1987).

The defense intellectuals (DIs) are civilians who move in and out of government, working sometimes as administrative officials or consultants, sometimes at universities and think tanks. They create the theory that informs and legitimates U.S. nuclear strategic practice—where to place nuclear missiles, how to manage the arms race, how to deter the use of nuclear weapons, how to fight a nuclear war if the deterrence fails, what is the strategy of the first strike, and how to explain why it is not safe to live without nuclear weapons.

Activist Daniel Ellsberg, author of the 1971 explosive book *The Pentagon Papers* (Ellsberg 1971), revealed the diabolical nature and apocalyptic scale of the doomsday schemes and scenarios of these individuals in his recent sequel *The Doomsday Machine.* According to the experts' estimates, the first nuclear strike on the Soviet Union was expected to kill 370 million people in Europe, dying immediately or in the aftermath of this attack; whether countries like Denmark and Sweden would survive would depend on the direction of the wind at that time. There is no doubt that American defense intellectuals have like-minded opponents on the other side. It is hard to believe that this is a story about our species.

Carol Cohn attended a two-week summer seminar on nuclear weapons, nuclear strategic doctrine, and arms control. She was so fascinated by what had transpired there that she spent the following year immersed in the almost entirely male world of defense intellectuals (except for the secretaries). She collected some extremely interesting facts that confirmed the perinatal dimension in nuclear warfare. In her own terminology, this material confirms the "male birth" and "male creation" as important motifs underlying the psychology of nuclear warfare.

She uses the following historical examples to illustrate her point of view: in 1942, Ernest Lawrence sent a telegram to a Chicago group of physicists who were developing the nuclear bomb, which read, "Congratulations to the new parents. Can hardly wait to see the new arrival." At Los Alamos, the atom bomb was referred to as "Oppenheimer's baby." Richard Feynman wrote in his article "Los Alamos from Below" that when he was temporarily on leave after his wife's death, he received a telegram that read, "The baby is expected on such and such a day."

At Lawrence Livermore laboratories, the hydrogen bomb was referred to as "Teller's baby," although those who wanted to disparage Edward Teller's contribution claimed he was not the bomb's father, but its mother. They claimed that Stanislaw Ulam was the real father, as he had all the important ideas and "conceived it"; Teller only "carried it" after that. Terms related to motherhood were also used regarding the provision of "nurturance"—the maintenance of the missiles.

General Grove sent a triumphant coded cable to Secretary of War Henry Stimson at the Potsdam conference, reporting the success of the first atomic test: "Doctor has just returned most enthusiastic and confident that the little boy is as husky as his big brother. The light in his eyes was discernible from here to Highhold [Stimson's country home] and I could have heard his screams from here to my farm." Stimson, in turn, informed Churchill by writing him a note that read: "Babies satisfactorily born."

William L. Laurence, who witnessed the test of the first atomic bomb, wrote: "The big boom came about a hundred seconds after the great flash—the first cry of a new-born world." Edward Teller's exultant telegram to Los Alamos, announcing the successful test of the hydrogen bomb "Mike" at the Eniwetok atoll in the Marshall Islands read: "It's a boy."

According to Carol Cohn, "male scientists gave birth to a progeny with the ultimate power of domination over female Nature." Further support for the pivotal role of the perinatal domain of the unconscious in war psychology can be found in Sam Keen's excellent book *The Faces of the Enemy*. Keen brought together an outstanding collection of war posters, propaganda cartoons, and caricatures from many historical periods and countries (Keen 1998).

He demonstrated that the way the enemy is described and portrayed during a war or revolution is a stereotype that shows only minimal variations and has very little to do with the actual characteristics of the country and its inhabitants. This material also typically disregards the diversity and heterogeneity characterizing the population of each country and makes blatant generalizations: "This is what the Germans, Americans, Japanese, Russians, etc. are like!"

Keen was able to divide these images into several archetypal categories. He did not specifically refer to the perinatal domain of the unconscious, but the analysis of his picture material reveals a preponderance of symbolic images that are characteristic of BPM II and BPM III. The enemy is typically depicted as a dangerous octopus, a vicious dragon, a multi-headed hydra, a giant venomous tarantula, an engulfing Leviathan, or ominous snakes, particularly vipers and boa constrictors. Scenes depicting strangulation or crushing, ominous whirlpools, and treacherous quicksand also abound in pictures from the time of wars, revolutions, and political crises.

The juxtaposition of pictures from holotropic states of consciousness that focus on the reliving of birth with the historical pictorial documentation collected by Lloyd de Mause and Sam Keen represents strong evidence for the perinatal roots of human violence. According to the new insights, provided jointly by observations from consciousness research and through the findings of psychohistory, we all carry in our deep unconscious powerful energies, emotions, and painful physical sensations associated with the trauma of birth that have not been adequately processed and assimilated.

This aspect of our psyche can be completely unconscious for many people, until and unless they embark on in-depth self-exploration with the use of psychedelics or other powerful experiential techniques of psychotherapy, such as Holotropic Breathwork, primal therapy, or rebirthing. Others can have varying degrees of awareness of the perinatal level of the unconscious. The activation of this material can lead to serious individual psychopathology, including unmotivated violence.

Lloyd de Mause suggested that, for unknown reasons, the influence of inner perinatal elements can increase simultaneously in a large number of people. This creates an atmosphere of general tension, anxiety, and anticipation. The leader is an individual who is under a stronger influence of the perinatal dynamics than an average person. He also has the ability to disown his unacceptable feelings (the Shadow in Jung's terminology) and to project them onto the external situation. The collective discomfort is blamed on the enemy and a military intervention is offered as a solution.

In his groundbreaking book *Cosmos and Psyche,* Richard Tarnas presented fascinating material that might throw interesting light on the problem of increased collective tension preceding the onset of wars and revolutions as described by de Mause (Tarnas 2006). In his meticulous historical research, which extended for more than thirty years, Tarnas was able to show that throughout history, wars and revolutions showed correlations with specific astrological transits. His findings strongly suggest that archetypal forces play a critical role in shaping human history.

Wars and revolutions provide an opportunity to disregard the psychological defenses that ordinarily keep the dangerous unconscious forces in check. Superego, the psychological force that demands restraint and civilized behavior, is replaced by what Freud called "war superego." We receive praise and medals for violence, murder, indiscriminate destruction, and pillaging, the same behaviors that in peacetime are unacceptable and would land us in prison or worse. Similarly, sexual violence has been a common practice during wartime and has been generally tolerated. As a matter of fact, military leaders have often promised their soldiers unlimited sexual access to women in the besieged cities and conquered territories to motivate them for battle.

Once the war erupts, the destructive and self-destructive perinatal impulses are freely acted out. The themes that we normally encounter in certain stages of the process of inner exploration and transformation (BPM II and III) now become parts of our everyday life, either directly or in the form of television news. Various no-exit situations, sadomasochistic orgies and sexual violence, bestial and demonic behavior, the unleashing of enormous explosive energies, and scatological scenes, which belong to standard perinatal imagery, are all enacted in wars and revolutions with extraordinary vividness and power.

Witnessing scenes of destruction and acting out of violent unconscious impulses, whether it occurs on the individual scale or collectively in wars and revolutions, does not result in healing and transformation as it would in an inner confrontation with these elements in a therapeutic context.

The experience is not generated by our own unconscious, lacks the element of deep introspection, and does not lead to insights.

The situation is fully externalized and the connection with the deep dynamics of the psyche is missing. Naturally, there is also no therapeutic intention and motivation for change and transformation. Thus, the goal of the underlying birth fantasy, which represents the deepest driving force of such violent events, is not achieved, even if the war or revolution has been brought to a successful closure. The most triumphant external victory does not deliver what was expected and hoped for—an inner sense of emotional liberation and psychospiritual rebirth.

Since many of the clients with whom I worked in Prague had experienced both the Nazi occupation and the Stalinist regime, the work with them generated some fascinating insights into the relationship between perinatal dynamics and the institution of both the Nazi concentration camps and Communism. As we have all seen throughout history, after the intoxicating, initial feelings of triumph when the revolution is won, there comes at first a sober awakening and later, bitter disappointment.

It usually does not take long until a facsimile of the old oppressive system starts emerging from the ruins of the dead dream, since the destructive and self-destructive forces have not been resolved and continue to operate in the unconscious of everyone involved. This happens again and again in human history, whether the event involved is the French Revolution, the Bolshevik Revolution in Russia, the Communist revolution in China, or any of the other violent upheavals associated with great hopes and expectations.

Insights and issues related to Communist ideology typically emerged in the treatment of my clients at the time when they were struggling with perinatal energies and emotions. It soon became obvious that the passionate fervor that revolutionaries feel toward the oppressors and their regimes also receives a powerful psychological reinforcement from their revolt against the inner prison of their perinatal memories.

Conversely, the need to coerce and dominate others is an external displacement of the need to overcome the fear of being overwhelmed by one's own unconscious. The murderous entanglement of the oppressor and the revolutionary is thus an externalized replica of the situation experienced in the birth canal. A similar emotional entanglement also seems to exist between criminals and police.

The Communist vision contains an element of psychological truth that has made it appealing to large numbers of people. The basic notion that a violent experience of a revolutionary nature is necessary to terminate suffering and oppression, and institute a situation of greater harmony is correct when understood as related to the process of reliving birth and the ensuing inner transformation. However, it is dangerously false when it is projected on the external world as a political ideology of violent revolutions. The fallacy lies in the fact that what on a deeper level is essentially an archetypal pattern of psychospiritual death and rebirth takes the form of an atheistic and anti-spiritual program.

Paradoxically, Communism has many features in common with organized religions in that it exploits people's spiritual needs, while not only failing to satisfy them, but actively suppressing any genuine spiritual search. The parallel of Communism with organized religion goes so far that Stalin, at the height of his power, was declared infallible, even though he was expressing authoritative opinions in disciplines in which he had no actual knowledge.

Communist revolutions have been extremely successful in their destructive phase but, instead of creating the promised ideal utopian society, their victories bred regimes in which oppression, cruelty, and injustice ruled supreme. After the economically ruined and politically corrupt Soviet Union collapsed, and the Communist world fell apart, it became obvious to all people with sane judgment that this giant historical experiment, conducted at the cost of tens of millions of human lives and unimaginable human suffering, was a colossal failure. If the above observations are correct, no external interventions have a chance to create a better world unless they are associated with a profound transformation of human beings.

The observations from the study of holotropic states also threw some important light on the psychology of Nazism and concentration camps. Over a number of years, professor Jan Bastiaans in Leyden, Holland conducted LSD therapy with people suffering from "concentration camp syndrome," a condition that developed in former inmates many years after their incarceration. Bastiaans also worked with former *kapos* (concentration camp prisoners given authority over other prisoners by the SS) on their issues of profound guilt.

An artistic description of this work can be found in the book *Shivitti* written by a former inmate, Ka-Tzetnik 135633, who underwent a series of therapeutic sessions with Bastiaans (Ka-Tzetnik 1989). Bastiaans himself wrote a paper describing his work, called "Man in the Concentration Camp and the Concentration Camp in Man" (Bastiaans 1955). There he pointed out, without specifying it, that the concentration camps are a projection of a certain domain which exists in the human unconscious, "Before there was a man in the concentration camp, there was a concentration camp in man."

The study of holotropic states of consciousness makes it possible to identify the realm of the psyche Bastiaans was talking about. The perinatal domain of the unconscious certainly fits his description. Closer examination of the general and specific conditions in the Nazi concentration camps reveals that they were a diabolical and realistic enactment of the nightmarish atmosphere that characterizes the reliving of biological birth.

The barbed-wire barriers, high-voltage fences, watch towers with submachine guns, minefields, and packs of trained dogs certainly created a hellish and almost archetypal image of an utterly hopeless and oppressive no-exit situation that is characteristic of BPM II. At the same time, the elements of violence, bestiality, scatology, and sexual abuse of women and men, including rape and sadistic practices, all belong to the phenomenology of BPM III.

In concentration camps, the sexual abuse happened at random on the individual level, as well as in the context of the "houses of dolls," institutions providing "entertainment" for the officers. The only escape out of this hell was death, whether by a bullet, hunger, disease, or suffocation in the gas chambers. The books by Ka-Tzetnik 135633, *House of Dolls* and *Sunrise Over Hell* (Ka-Tzetnik 1955 and 1977), offer a shattering description of the life in concentration camps.

The bestiality of the SS seemed to have been focused particularly on pregnant women and little children, which brings further support for the perinatal hypothesis. The most powerful passage from Terrence des Près's book *The Survivor* is, without any doubt, the description of a truck full of babies dumped into a fire, followed by a scene in which pregnant women are beaten with clubs and whips, torn by dogs, dragged around by the hair, kicked in the bellies, and then thrown into the crematorium while still alive (des Près 1976).

The perinatal nature of the irrational impulses manifesting in the camps is also evident in the scatological behavior of the SS. Throwing eating bowls into the latrines and asking the inmates to retrieve them and forcing the inmates to urinate into each other's mouths were practices that, besides their bestiality, brought the danger of epidemics. Had the concentration camps been simply institutions for the isolation of political enemies and for providing cheap slave labor, maintenance of hygienic rules would have been a primary concern of the organizers, as is the case in any facility accommodating large numbers of people. In Buchenwald alone, as a result of these perverted practices, twenty-seven inmates drowned in feces in the course of a single month.

The convincing depth and intensity of many experiences of collective violence that contain such perinatal features suggest that they originate in the deep unconscious. When our experiential self-exploration reaches the memory of the birth trauma, we connect with an immense pool of painful memories of the human species and gain access to other peoples' experiences who were once in a similar predicament. It is not hard to imagine that the perinatal level of our unconscious, which "knows" so intimately the history of human violence, is actually partially responsible for wars, revolutions, genocide, and similar atrocities.

The nature and scope of the brutalities of human history associated with perinatal experiences is truly astonishing. Christopher Bache, after having carefully analyzed various aspects of this phenomenon, came to an interesting conclusion. He suggests that the memories of the violence perpetrated throughout the ages in human history have contaminated the field of collective unconscious in the same way in which the traumas from our infancy and childhood pollute our individual unconscious. According to Bache, it might be possible that when we start experiencing these collective memories, our inner process transcends the framework of personal therapy and we participate in the cleansing and healing of the field of consciousness of the human species (Bache 2000).

The role of the birth trauma as a source of violence and self-destructive tendencies has been confirmed by clinical studies. For example, there seems to be an important correlation between difficult birth and criminality (Litt 1974, Kandel and Mednick 1991, Raine, Brennan, and Mednick

1995). In a similar way, aggression directed inward, particularly suicide, seems to be psychogenetically linked to difficult birth (Appleby 1998).

The Scandinavian researcher Bertil Jacobson found a close correlation between specific forms of self-destructive behavior and the type of birth. Suicides involving asphyxiation were associated with suffocation at birth, violent suicides with mechanical birth trauma, and drug addiction that led to suicide with opiate and/or barbiturate administration during labor (Jacobson et al. 1987).

Transpersonal Roots of Violence

The research of holotropic states has revealed that the roots of human violence reach even deeper than the perinatal level of the psyche. Significant additional sources of aggression can be found in the transpersonal domain, including scenes of torture and killing in past life experiences, mythological figures of wrathful deities and demonic entities, and grand archetypal destructive scenes, such as the Nordic Ragnarok (the Doom or Twilight of the Gods), Archangel Michael fighting the demonic hordes, Zoroastrian Battle of Ahura Mazda's forces of Light against Ahriman's Forces of Darkness, or the Apocalypse from the New Testament.

C. G. Jung showed that the archetypes of the collective unconscious have a powerful influence not only on the behavior of individuals, but also on the events of human history (Jung 1954). From his point of view, entire nations and cultural groups might be enacting important archetypal themes in their behavior. Jung believed that many aspects of the German Nazi movement could be understood as possession of the German nation by the archetype of Wotan, an "ancient god of storm and frenzy" (Jung 1947). In his brilliant book *A Terrible Love of War,* James Hillman amassed convincing evidence that war is a formidable archetypal force that has irresistible power over individuals and nations (Hillman 2004).

In many instances, military, political, and religious leaders use not only perinatal, but also archetypal images and spiritual symbolism to achieve their goals (Grof 1985). Medieval crusaders were asked to sacrifice their lives for Jesus in a war that would recover the Holy Land from the Mohammedans. Adolf Hitler exploited the mythological motifs of the supremacy of the Nordic race and of the Millennial Empire, as well as the ancient Vedic symbols of the swastika and the solar eagle. Ayatollah Khomeini and Osama bin Laden ignited the imagination of their Muslim followers by references to *jihad,* the Holy War against the infidels. American president Ronald Reagan referred to the Soviet Union as the Evil Empire and George W. Bush used references to the Axis of Evil and Armageddon in his political speeches.

Carol Cohn discussed not only the perinatal in her paper, but also the transpersonal symbolism associated with the language used in relation to nuclear weaponry and doctrine (Cohn 1987). The authors of the strategic doctrine refer to members of their community as the "nuclear priesthood." The first atomic test was called Trinity, as in the unity of Father, Son, and the Holy Ghost, the male forces of creation. From her feminist perspective, Cohn saw this as an effort by male scientists to appropriate and claim ultimate creative power. The scientists who worked on the atomic bomb and witnessed the test described it in the following way: "It was as though we stood at the first day of creation." Robert Oppenheimer thought of Krishna's words to Arjuna in the *Bhagavad Gītā:* "I am become Death, the destroyer of worlds."

Biographical Determinants of Greed

Sigmund Freud saw greed as a phenomenon related to problems during the nursing period. According to him, frustration or overindulgence during the oral phase of libidinal development can reinforce the primitive infantile need to incorporate objects to such an extent that, in adulthood, it is transferred in a sublimated form to a variety of other objects and situations.

When the acquisitive drive focuses on money, psychoanalysts attribute it to fixation on the anal stage of libidinal development; this is based on Freud's discovery of a symbolic association between feces and gold. Insatiable sexual appetite is then considered to be the result of phallic fixation. Many other unrelenting human pursuits are then interpreted in terms of sublimation of such phallic instinctual urges. Modern consciousness research has found these interpretations to be superficial and inadequate. It has discovered significant additional sources of acquisitiveness and greed on the perinatal and transpersonal levels of the unconscious.

Perinatal Sources of Greed

In the course of biographically oriented psychotherapy, many people discover that their life has been inauthentic in certain specific sectors of interpersonal relations. For example, problems with parental authority can lead to specific patterns of difficulty with authority figures, repeated dysfunctional patterns in sexual relationships can be traced to parents as models for sexual behavior, strong sibling rivalry can color and distort future peer relationships, and so on.

When the process of experiential self-exploration reaches the perinatal level, we typically discover that our life up to that point has been largely inauthentic in its totality, not just in certain partial segments. We find, to our surprise and astonishment, that our entire life strategy has been misdirected and therefore incapable of providing genuine satisfaction. The reason for this is that we were primarily motivated in our choices and behavior by our fear of death and by unconscious forces associated with biological birth, which we had not adequately processed and integrated.

In other words, during biological birth, we completed the process physically but not emotionally. When our field of consciousness is strongly influenced by the underlying memory of the struggle in the birth canal, it leads to a feeling of discomfort and dissatisfaction with the present situation. This discontent can focus on a large spectrum of issues: unsatisfactory physical appearance, inadequate resources and material possessions, low social position and influence, insufficient amount of power and fame, and many others. Like the fetus stuck in the birth canal, we feel a strong drive and urge to get to a better situation that lies somewhere in the future.

Whatever the reality of our present circumstances, we do not find them satisfactory. Our fantasies keep creating images of a future situation that appears more fulfilling than the present one. It seems that—until we reach it—our life will only be preparation for a better future, not "the kind of life we want or feel we should have." This results in a life pattern that people involved in experiential self-exploration have described as a "treadmill" or "rat-race" type of existence.

Existentialist philosophers talk about "auto-projecting" into the future. This strategy is a basic fallacy of human life. It is essentially a losing strategy, whether or not we achieve the goals that we have set for ourselves, since these external goals cannot deliver the satisfaction that we expect from them. We can never get enough of the substitutes that we don't really want or need.

When the goal is not reached, the continuing dissatisfaction is attributed to the fact that we have failed to reach the aspired corrective state. When we do succeed in reaching the goal of our aspirations, it also typically does not have much influence on our basic life feelings. The continuing dissatisfaction is then blamed either on the fact that the choice of the goal was not correct or that it was not ambitious enough. The result is either substitution of the old goal with a different one or an augmentated version of the same type of goal.

In any case, the failure is not correctly diagnosed as being an inevitable result of a fundamentally wrong strategy of life that is incapable of providing satisfaction. This fallacious pattern applied on a large scale is responsible for the reckless irrational pursuit of various grandiose goals that results in great suffering and problems in the world. This unfulfilling pursuit of various goals can be played out on any level of affluence, importance, and fame, since it never brings true satisfaction. Joseph Campbell described this situation as "reaching the top of the ladder then finding that it is leaning against the wrong wall." The only strategy that can significantly reduce this irrational drive is full conscious reliving and integration of the trauma of birth in systematic inner self-exploration, and reaching the nourishing memories of the completed birth (BPM IV), the good womb (BPM I), and positive transpersonal states.

Transpersonal Roots of Insatiable Greed

Modern consciousness research and experiential psychotherapy have discovered that the deepest source of our dissatisfaction and striving for perfection is ultimately transpersonal in nature. In Dante Alighieri's words: "The [desire for perfection] is that desire which always makes every pleasure appear incomplete, for there is no joy or pleasure so great in this life that it can quench the thirst in our Soul" (Alighieri 1990).

In the most general sense, the deepest transpersonal roots of insatiable greed can best be understood in terms of Ken Wilber's concept of the Atman Project (Wilber 1980). Our true nature is divine (Brahman, Buddha, the Tao, God, Cosmic Christ, Allah) and, although the process of incarnation separates and alienates us from our source, the awareness of this fact is never completely lost.

The deepest motivating force of the psyche on all levels of consciousness evolution is to return to the experience of our divinity. However, the constraining conditions which surround the consecutive stages of ego development stand in the way of attaining this experience. Real transcendence requires the death of the separate self, dying to the exclusive autonomous subject. Due to the fear of annihilation and grasping onto the ego, the individual has to settle for Atman substitutes or surrogates, which are specific for each particular stage.

For the fetus and the newborn, this means the satisfaction experienced in the good womb or on the good breast. For an infant, this is the experience of age-specific physiological satisfaction and security. For the adult, the range of possible Atman Projects is large: besides food and sex, it also includes money, fame, power, appearance, knowledge, and many others. Since our deep sense that our true identity is the totality of cosmic creation and the creative principle itself, substitutes of any degree and scope (the Atman Projects) will always remain unsatisfactory.

Only the experience of our divinity in a holotropic state of consciousness can ever fulfill our deepest need. The ultimate solution for insatiable greed is in the inner world, not in secular pursuits of any kind. The great thirteenth-century Persian mystic and poet Rumi made it very clear:

> All the hopes, desires, loves, and affections that people have for different things—fathers, mothers, friends, heavens, the earth, gardens, palaces, sciences, works, food, drink—the saint knows that these are desires for God and all those things are veils. When men leave this world and see the King without these veils, then they will know that all were veils and coverings, that the object of their desire was in reality that One Thing. (Rumi 1983)

Psychology of Survival

The insights from consciousness research and from transpersonal psychology can be put to practical use in alleviating the crisis we are facing in the modern world. This work has shown that the roots of human violence are much deeper and more formidable than traditional psychology ever imagined. However, it has also discovered extremely effective therapeutic strategies that have the potential to assuage and transform the human propensity toward violence.

Efforts to change humanity would have to start with psychological prevention at a very early age. The data from prenatal and perinatal psychology indicate that much could be achieved by changing the conditions of pregnancy, delivery, and early postnatal care. This would include improving the emotional preparation of the mother during pregnancy, practicing natural childbirth, creating a psychospiritually informed birth environment, and cultivating emotionally nourishing contact between the mother and the child in the postpartum period. The circumstances of birth play an important role in creating a disposition to violence and self-destructive tendencies or, conversely, to loving behavior and healthy interpersonal relationships.

French obstetrician Michel Odent has shown how the hormones involved in the birth process and in nursing and maternal behavior participate in this imprinting. The catecholamines (adrenaline and noradrenaline) play an important role in the stress of the labor and, in evolution, they functioned as mediators of the mother's fight/flight response when birth was occurring in unprotected natural environments with dangerous predators.

Oxytocin, prolactin, and endorphins are known to induce parental behavior in animals and foster dependency and attachment. Today, the environment of the delivering mothers is physically safe, but the busy, noisy, and chaotic milieu of many hospitals induces anxiety and unnecessarily engages the catecholamine system. It imprints the picture of a world that is potentially dangerous and requires aggressive responses in the mind of the newborn. This interferes with the hormones that mediate positive interindividual imprinting and bonding. It is, therefore, essential to provide a quiet, safe, and private environment for birthing (Odent 1995).

Much has been written about the importance of child rearing and about disastrous emotional consequences of traumatic conditions in infancy and childhood. Certainly, this is an area where continued education and guidance are necessary. However, to apply the theoretically known principles, the parents must themselves reach sufficient emotional stability and maturity. It is well known that emotional problems are passed from generation to generation like a curse.

Humanistic and transpersonal psychologies have developed effective experiential methods of self-exploration, healing, and personality transformation. Some of these come from Western therapeutic traditions, while others represent modern adaptations of ancient and native spiritual practices. Besides offering emotional healing, these approaches have the potential to return genuine experiential spirituality into Western culture and overcome the alienation of modern humanity. Some of these approaches have a very favorable ratio between professional helpers and clients, and others use the healing potential of the group dynamics.

Systematic responsible work with psychedelics and other forms of holotropic states of consciousness can bring more than healing of emotional and psychosomatic disorders. It can facilitate deep psychospiritual transformation and changes in the hierarchy of values. This includes a significant decrease of aggression, as well as the development of compassion, a sense of inner peace, improved self-image, self-acceptance, and the acceptance of others. Some of these changes are identical with those that Abraham Maslow described in people who had experienced spontaneous mystical states ("peak experiences"), such as self-actualization and self-realization, a genuine sense for truth, beauty, and goodness ("metavalues") and a tendency to incorporate these virtues into one's life ("metamotivations").

People involved in responsible psychonautics also describe increased zest, *joie de vivre,* and an enhanced ability to enjoy the simple things in life, such as walks in nature, listening to music, interacting with other people, love-making, and savoring food. As the content of the perinatal level of the unconscious emerges into consciousness and is integrated, it results in radical personality changes. The experience of psychospiritual death and rebirth and a conscious connection with positive postnatal and prenatal memories reduce irrational drives and ambitions. This causes a shift of emphasis from the past and future to the present moment.

Some of these changes have important implications for human society at large. One frequent result of responsible psychonautics is the increase of racial, sexual, political, and religious tolerance. Differences among people appear to be interesting and enriching rather than threatening, whether they are related to gender, race, color, language, political conviction, or religious belief. Another frequent change is the replacement of competitiveness with synergy and cooperation.

Many psychonauts discover the power and efficacy of the Taoist *wu wei* (creative quietude, doing by being), when life is not governed by ambitious drives and begins to resemble instead the soft martial arts or surfing. With this life strategy, more is accomplished with less effort and the results are not only personally satisfying, but also serve the larger community. Very frequently, this can be associated with remarkable, helpful synchronicities, such as the unexpected appearance of the right people, information, and resources.

The process of spiritual opening and transformation typically deepens further as a result of transpersonal experiences. The changes in people who have them resemble those that astronauts and cosmonauts experienced as a result of their space travels. The remarkable effect that cosmic space has on astronauts was evident in the stories of eight American astronauts in Mickey Lemle's remarkable documentary *The Other Side of the Moon* (Lemle 1990), including Louis Armstrong, Edgar Mitchell, Buzz Aldrin, and Rusty Schweickart. Like the astronauts, psychonauts start seeing the Earth as a beautiful blue jewel shining in the dark night of the giant Cosmos, and as Buckminster Fuller's "Spaceship Earth," which all of humanity shares. This leads to a feeling that all of us are global citizens before we are Russians, Czechs, Germans, or Americans.

Identification with other people, entire human groups, animals, and plant life tends to bring a sense of wonder and love of nature and of all creation. This is based on an almost cellular awareness that the boundaries in the universe are arbitrary and that each of us is ultimately identical with the entire web of existence. It becomes evident how deeply we are embedded in nature and that we cannot damage the natural environment—polluting the air, the water, and the soil where we grow our food—without damaging ourselves. This awareness leads to great ecological sensitivity and determination to protect nature.

Last, but not least, responsible psychonautics tends to awaken spirituality of a non-denominational, non-chauvinistic, universal, all-encompassing, and mystical nature that is very authentic and convincing, because it is based on deep personal experience. It has the power to undermine and replace both the atheistic, monistic-materialistic worldview and rigid, fundamentalist belief systems which are founded on the literal understanding of religious scriptures.

It is obvious that the inner transformation described above would increase our chances for survival if it could occur on a sufficiently large scale. Many of the people with whom we have worked saw humanity at a critical crossroad, facing either collective annihilation or an evolutionary jump in consciousness of unprecedented proportions. Psychedelic pioneer Terence McKenna put it very succinctly: "The history of the silly monkey is over, one way or another." Our species either undergoes a profound inner transformation or may face extinction.

We seem to be involved in a dramatic race for time that has no precedent in the entire history of humanity. What is at stake is nothing less than the future of our species and of life on this planet. If we continue the old strategies, which are clearly extremely destructive and self-destructive, it is unlikely that the human species will survive. However, if a sufficient number of people could undergo the process of deep inner psychospiritual transformation, we might reach a level of consciousness evolution that we would lead us to deserve the name we have so proudly given to our species: *Homo sapiens sapiens*.

Literature

Alighieri, D. 1990. *Il Convivio*. (R. H. Lansing, transl.). New York: Garland.

Appleby, L. 1998. 8. "Violent Suicide and Obstetric Complications." *British Medical Journal* 14: 1333–1334.

Ardrey, R. 1961. *African Genesis*. New York: Atheneum.

Bache, C. 2000. *Dark Night, Early Dawn: Steps to a Deep Ecology of Mind*. Albany, NY: State University of New York (SUNY) Press.

Bastiaans, J. 1955. *Man in the Concentration Camp and the Concentration*

Camp in Man. Unpublished manuscript. Leyden, Holland.

Cohn, C. 1987. Sex and Death in the Rational World of the Defense Intellectuals. *Journal of Women in Culture and Society.* 12, pp. 687-718.

Darwin, C. 1952. *The Origin of Species and the Descent of Man.* Chicago, IL: Encyclopaedia Britannica, (originally published in 1859).

Dawkins, R. 1976. *The Selfish Gene.* New York: Oxford University Press.

Dollard, J. et al. 1939. *Frustration and Aggression.* New Haven, CN: Yale University Press.

Ellsberg, D. 1971. *The Pentagon Papers.*

Ellsberg, D. 2018. *The Doomsday Machine: Confessions of a Nuclear War Planner.* New York/London: Bloomsberry Publishing.

Freud, S. 1917. "Mourning and Melancholia." *The Standard Edition of the Complete Psychological Works of Sigmund Freud, Volume XIV* (1914-1916).

Fromm, E. 1973. *The Anatomy of Human Destructiveness.* New York: Holt, Rinehart & Winson.

Grof, S. 1975. *Realms of the Human Unconscious: Observations from LSD Research.* New York: Viking Press.

Grof, S. 1985. *Beyond the Brain: Birth, Death, and Transcendence in Psychotherapy.* Albany, NY: State University of New York (SUNY) Press.

Grof, S. 2000. *Psychology of the Future: Lessons from Modern Consciousness Research.* Albany, NY: State University of New York (SUNY) Press.

Hillman, J. 2004. *A Terrible Love of War.* New York: The Penguin Press.

Jacobson, B. et al. 1987. Perinatal Origin of Adult Self-Destructive Behavior. Acta psychiat. Scand. 6:364-371.

Jung, C. G. 1947. *Wotan: Essays on Contemporary Events* (London: Kegan Paul.

Jung, C. G. 1954. *Archetypes of the Collective Unconscious.* Collected Works IX.1. Princeton, NJ: Princeton University Press.

Kandel, E. and Mednik, S.A. 1991. Perinatal Complications Predict Violent Offending. *Criminology* 29 (3): 509-519.

Ka-Tzetnik 135633. 1955. *The House of Dolls.* New York: Pyramid Books.

Ka-Tzetnik 135633. 1977. *Sunrise Over Hell.* London: W. A. Allen.

Ka-Tzetnik 135633. 1989. *Shivitti: A Vision.* San Francisco, CA: Harper & Row.

Keen, S. 1998. *Faces of the Enemy: Reflections of the Hostile Imagination.*

San Francisco: Harper.

Lemle, M. 1990. *The Other Side of the Moon.* Lemle Pictures, Inc.

Litt, S. 1974. "A Study Of Perinatal Complications As A Factor In Criminal Behavior." *Criminology* 12 (1), 125–126.

Lorenz, K. 1963. *On Aggression.* New York, Harcourt: Brace, & World, Inc.

MacLean, P. 1973. "A Triune Concept of the Brain and Behavior. Lecture 1. Man's Reptilian and Limbic Inheritance" in: T.J Boag &D. Campbell (Eds.), *The Hincks Memorial Lectures.* University of Toronto Press, Toronto, Ontario, pp. 6-66.

Mause, L. de. (ed.). 1975. *The Independence of Psychohistory.* New York: The New Psychohistory.

McKenna, T. 1992. *Food of the Gods: The Search for the Original Tree of Knowledge.* New York: Bantam,

Morris, D., 1967. *The Naked Ape: A Zoologist's Study of the Human Animal.* New York: McGraw-Hill.

Odent, M. 1995. Odent, M. 1995. "Prevention of Violence or Genesis of Love? Which Perspective?" Lecture at the Fourteenth International Transpersonal Conference in Santa Clara, CA.

Près, T. Des. 1976. *The Survivor: An Anatomy of Life in the Death Camps.* Oxford: Oxford University Press.

Raine, A., Brennan, P., Mednick, S. A. 1995. Birth Complications Combined with Early Maternal Rejection at Age 1 Predispose to Violent Crime at Age 18 Years. *Obstetrical and Gynecological Survey* 50 (11):775-776.

Rumi, 1983. Translated by W. Chittick in *Sufi Path of Love.* Albany, NY: State University of New York (SUNY) Press.

Tarnas, R. 2006. *Cosmos and Psyche: Intimations of A New World View.* New York: Viking Press.

Tinbergen, N. 1965. *Animal Behavior.* New York: Time-Life.

Wilber, K. 1980. *The Atman Project: A Transpersonal View of Human Development.* Wheaton, IL Theosophical Publishing House.

Wrangham R., Peterson, D. 1996. *Demonic Males: Apes and the Origins of Human Violence.* New York: Houghton Mifflin Company.

XIII

Psyche and Thanatos:
Psychospiritual Dimensions of Death and Dying

It would be hard to imagine a subject that is more universal and more personally relevant for every single human being than death and dying. Over the course of our lives, all of us will lose relatives, friends, teachers, acquaintances, and important public figures, and eventually face our own biological demise. In view of this, it is quite remarkable that until the late 1960s, the Western industrial civilization showed an almost complete lack of interest in the subject of death and dying.

This was true not only for the general population, but also for scientists and professionals involved in disciplines that should have been keenly interested in this subject, such as medicine, psychiatry, psychology, philosophy, and theology. The only plausible explanation for this situation is fear and a massive denial of death that exists in modern industrial civilization.

American cultural anthropologist Ernest Becker showed in his book *The Denial of Death* that modern society is ultimately an elaborate, symbolic defense mechanism against facing our mortality. He suggested that people are trying to overcome their fear of death by creating "immortality projects," which make it possible for them to imagine that they become part of something larger than themselves, something that survives death. According to Becker, the clashes of the immortality projects of different people are responsible for most of the evil in the world—human conflicts, wars, bigotry, genocide, and racism (Becker 1973).

The disinterest of modern society in regard to death is even more striking when we compare it with the situation in ancient and pre-industrial cultures. Their attitude toward death and dying was diametrically different. Death played a central role in their cosmologies, philosophies, spiritual and ritual life, and mythologies, as well as in everyday life. The practical importance of this difference becomes obvious when we compare the situation of a person facing death in these two different historical and cultural environments.

An average person dying in one of the Western industrial societies has a pragmatic and materialistic worldview or is at least profoundly influenced by their exposure to it. According to mainstream academic Western science, the history of the universe is the history of developing matter. Life, consciousness, and intelligence are more or less accidental and insignificant side products of this development. They appeared on the scene after many billions of years of evolution of passive and inert matter in an infinitesimally small part of an immense universe. In a world where only what is material, tangible, and measurable is real, there is no place for spirituality of any kind.

Although religious activities are generally practiced, socially sanctioned, or even formally encouraged, from a strictly scientific point of view, any involvement with spirituality appears to be irrational and indicates emotional and intellectual immaturity, stemming from either a lack of education, superstition, or regression to primitive magical thinking. Direct experiences of spiritual realities are seen and diagnosed as manifestations of psychosis, a serious mental disease. Religion, bereft of its experiential component, has largely lost the connection to its deep spiritual sources and as a result has become empty, meaningless, and increasingly irrelevant in the life of an average Westerner.

In this form, religion cannot compete with the persuasiveness of materialistic science backed up by technological triumphs. Under these circumstances, religion has ceased to be a vital force during our life, as well as at the time of dying and death. Its references to life after death, posthumous adventures of the soul, and abodes of the Beyond, such as heaven and hell, have been relegated to the realm of fairy tales and handbooks of psychiatry.

The entire ritual and spiritual history of humanity has been pathologized.

At the cradle of all the great religions of the world were perinatal and transpersonal experiences of their founders, prophets, and saints. We can think here, for example, about Buddha's encounter with Kama Mara and his army or his reliving of various episodes from his past incarnations accompanied by "tearing of the karmic bonds". The Old Testament describes Moses' vision of Jehovah in the burning bush and the New Testament relates Jesus' temptation by the devil during his stay in the desert, Saul's blinding vision of Jesus on the Way to Damascus, and St. John's experience of the Apocalypse. Islamic scriptures portray the journey of Mohammed through the seven heavens, paradise, and hell in the company of the archangel Gabriel. According to traditional psychiatry, all these experiences are indicative of severe psychopathology, a mental disease of the individuals involved.

There is an abundance of psychiatric literature in articles and books discussing what would be the best clinical diagnosis for various famous spiritual figures, some of them of the stature of the Buddha, Jesus, Mohammed, Ramakrishna, or Saint Anthony. Visionary experiences of the transpersonal realms are usually attributed to severe psychosis of the schizophrenic type or to epilepsy, as it is in the case of Mohammed. St. John of the Cross has been labeled a "hereditary degenerate" and St. Teresa of Avila a "hysterical psychotic."

Mainstream anthropologists have argued whether shamans are schizophrenics, borderline psychotics, or epileptics. There is even a paper applying psychopathological criteria to meditation. It is entitled "Buddhist Training as Artificial Catatonia" and its author is the famous psychoanalyst and founder of psychosomatic medicine Franz Alexander (Alexander 1931).

According to Western neuroscience, consciousness is an epiphenomenon of matter, a product of the physiological processes in the brain, and thus critically dependent on the body. The death of the body, more specifically of the brain, is then seen as the absolute end of any form of conscious activity. Belief in the posthumous journey of the soul, afterlife, or reincarnation is usually dismissed as a product of wishful thinking of people who are unable to accept the obvious biological imperative of death, the absolute nature of which has been scientifically proven beyond any reasonable doubt. Very few people, including most scientists, realize that we have absolutely no proof that consciousness is actually produced by the brain and not even a remote notion of how something like that could possibly happen. In spite of it, this basic metaphysical assumption remains one of the leading myths of Western materialistic science and has a profound influence on our entire society.

This attitude effectively inhibited scientific interest in the experiences of dying patients and of individuals in near-death situations until the late 1960s. The rare reports on this subject received very little attention, whether they came in the form of books for the general public, such as Jess E. Weisse's *The Vestibule* (Weisse 1972) and Jean-Baptiste Delacour's *Glimpses of the Beyond* (Delacour 1974), or scientific research, such as the study of deathbed observations of physicians and nurses conducted by Karlis Osis (Osis 1961).

Since the publication of Raymond Moody's international bestseller *Life After Life* in 1975, Elizabeth Kübler-Ross, Ken Ring, Michael Sabom, and other pioneers of thanatology have amassed impressive evidence about the extraordinary characteristics of near-death experiences, from accurate extrasensory perceptions during out-of-body experiences to profound personality changes that followed them (Kübler-Ross 1969, Moody 1975, Ring 1982, Sabom 1982).

The material from these studies has been widely publicized and used by the media in everything from TV talk shows to Hollywood movies. Yet, these potentially paradigm-shattering observations that could revolutionize our understanding of the nature of consciousness and its relationship to the brain are still dismissed by most professionals as irrelevant hallucinations produced by a biological crisis. They are also not routinely recorded and examined as an important part of the patients' medical history, and no specific psychological support is being offered in most of the medical facilities that would help to integrate these challenging events.

People dying in Western societies also often lack effective human support that would ease their transition. We try to protect ourselves from the emotional discomfort that death induces. The industrial world tends to remove sick and dying people to hospitals and nursing homes. The emphasis is on life-support systems and the mechanical prolongation of life, often beyond any reasonable limits, rather than the quality of the human environment.

The family system has disintegrated, and children often live far from their parents and grandparents. At the time of a medical crisis, the contact is often minimal and formal. In addition, mental health professionals, who have developed specific forms of psychological support and counseling for a large variety of emotional crises, have given almost no attention to the dying. Those facing the most profound of all imaginable crises, one that simultaneously affects the biological, emotional, interpersonal, social, philosophical, and spiritual aspects of the individual, remain the only ones for whom meaningful help is not available.

All this occurs in the much larger context of the collective denial of impermanence and mortality that characterizes Western industrial civilization. Much of our encounter with death comes in a sanitized form, where a team of professionals mitigates its immediate impact. In its extreme expression, as exemplified by Los Angeles' Forest Lawn Memorial Park and Mortuaries, it includes postmortem barbers and hairdressers, tailors, make-up experts, and plastic surgeons who make a wide variety of cosmetic adjustments to the corpse before it is shown to relatives and friends.

The media helps to create more distance from death by diluting it into empty statistics when it is reporting, in a matter of fact way, about the thousands of victims who died in wars, revolutions, genocidal raids, and natural catastrophes. Movies and TV shows further trivialize death by capitalizing on violence. They immunize modern audiences against its emotional relevance by exposing them to countless scenes of dying, killing, and murder in the context of entertainment. Killing and destruction is also the most popular ploy in the digital games played by millions of children, adolescents, and adults.

In general, the conditions of life in modern technological countries do not offer much ideological or psychological support for people who are facing death. This contrasts very sharply with the situation encountered by those dying in one of the ancient and pre-industrial societies. Their cosmologies, philosophies, mythologies, as well as spiritual and ritual life, contain a clear message that death is not the absolute and irrevocable end of everything, that life or existence continues in some form after the time of biological demise.

Another characteristic aspect of ancient and pre-industrial cultures that colors the experience of dying is their acceptance of death as an integral part of existence. Throughout their life, people living in these cultures get used to spending time around dying people, handling corpses, observing cremation, and living with their remnants. For a Westerner, a visit to a place like Benares, India where this attitude is expressed in its extreme form, can be a profound culture shock.

In addition, people dying in pre-industrial cultures typically die in the context of an extended family, clan, or tribe. They thus can receive meaningful emotional support from people whom they intimately know. It is also important to mention powerful rituals conducted at the time of death that are designed to assist individuals facing the ultimate transition, or even specific guidance for the dying, such as the approach described in the *Tibetan Book of the Dead (Bardo Thödol).*

In Tibetan Buddhism, death is seen as a unique opportunity for spiritual liberation from the cycles of death and rebirth or, if we do not achieve liberation, a period that determines our next incarnation. In this context, it is possible to see the intermediate state between lives *(bardo)* as being, in a way, more important than incarnate existence. It is then essential to prepare for this time by systematic practice during our lifetime.

An extremely important factor influencing the attitude toward death and the experience of dying in pre-industrial cultures has been experiential training for dying involving holotropic states of consciousness. We have already discussed the use of these states in shamanism, in the rites of passage, in the ancient mysteries of death and rebirth, and in the work with "technologies of the sacred," which are developed in the context of the great religions of the world (pp. 4, Volume I). All these situations offer the practice of "dying before dying." Initiates in these events have an opportunity to experience psychospiritual death and rebirth, which frees them from the fear of death and transforms their experience of dying.

This includes various systems of yoga, the theory and practice of Buddhism, Taoism, Tibetan Vajrayana, Sufism, Christian mysticism, Kabbalah, and many others. These systems developed effective forms of prayers, meditations, movement meditations, breathing exercises, and other powerful techniques for inducing holotropic states with profoundly spiritual components. Like the experiences of shamans, initiates in the rites of passage, and neophytes in ancient mysteries, these procedures offered adepts the possibility of confronting impermanence and mortality, transcending their fear of death, and radically transforming their quality of being in the world.

The description of the resources available to dying people in pre-industrial cultures would not be complete without mentioning the books of the dead, such as the Tibetan *Bardo Thödol*, as we have seen, the Egyptian *Pert em hru*, the Aztec *Codex Borgia*, or the European *Ars moriendi*. When the ancient books of the dead first came to the attention of Western scholars, they were considered to be fictitious descriptions of the posthumous journey of the soul, and as such, wishful fabrications of people who were unable to accept the grim reality of death. They were put in the same category as fairy tales—imaginary creations of human fantasy that had definite artistic beauty, but no relevance for everyday reality.

However, a deeper study of these texts revealed that they had been used as guides in the context of sacred mysteries and spiritual practices and very likely described the experiences of the initiates and practitioners. From this new perspective, presenting the books of the dead as manuals for the dying appeared to be a clever disguise invented by the priests to obscure their real function and protect their deeper esoteric meaning and message from the uninitiated. However, the remaining problem was to discover the exact nature of the procedures used by the ancient spiritual systems in order to induce these states.

Modern research focusing on holotropic states brought unexpected new insights into this area. The systematic study of the experiences in psychedelic sessions, powerful non-drug forms of psychotherapy, and spontaneously occurring psychospiritual crises ("spiritual emergencies") showed that in all these situations, people can encounter an entire spectrum of unusual experiences, including sequences of agony and dying, passing through hell, facing divine judgment, being reborn, reaching the celestial realms, and confronting memories from previous incarnations. These states were strikingly similar to those described in the eschatological texts of ancient and pre-industrial cultures.

Another missing piece of the puzzle was provided by thanatology, the new scientific discipline that specifically studies death and dying. Thanatological studies of near-death states such as Raymond Moody's *Life After Life* (Moody 1975), Kenneth Ring's *Life at Death* and *Heading Toward*

Omega (Ring 1982, 1985), Pim van Lommel's *Consciousness Beyond Life* (van Lommel 1919), Michael Sabom's *Recollections of Death* (Sabom 1982), Bruce Greyson and Charles Flynn's *The Near Death Experience* (Greyson and Flynn 1984) showed that the experiences associated with life-threatening situations bear a deep resemblance to the descriptions from the ancient books of the dead, as well as those reported by subjects in psychedelic sessions and modern experiential psychotherapy.

It has thus become clear that the ancient eschatological texts are actually maps of the inner territories of the psyche as encountered in profound holotropic states, including those associated with biological dying. The experiences involved seem to transcend race and culture and originate in the collective unconscious, as described by C. G. Jung. It is possible to spend one's entire lifetime without ever experiencing these realms or even without being aware of their existence, until one is catapulted into them at the time of biological death.

However, for some people, this experiential area becomes available during their lifetime in a variety of situations, including psychedelic sessions or some other powerful forms of self-exploration, whether through serious spiritual practice, participation in shamanic rituals, or during spontaneous psychospiritual crises. This opens up the possibility of an experiential exploration of these territories of the psyche on their own terms, so that the encounter with death does not come as a complete surprise at the time of biological demise. The German Augustinian monk Abraham a Sancta Clara, who lived in the seventeenth century, expressed the importance of the experiential practice of dying in a succinct way: "The man who dies before he dies does not die when he dies."

This "dying before dying" has two important consequences: it liberates the individual from the fear of death and changes his or her attitude toward it, as well as influencing the actual experience of dying at the time of the biological demise. However, this elimination of the fear of death also transforms the individual's way of being in the world. For this reason, there is no fundamental difference between the preparation for death and the practice of dying, on the one hand, and spiritual practice leading to enlightenment on the other. This is the reason why the ancient books of the dead could be used in both situations.

As we have seen, many aspects of life in pre-industrial cultures make the psychological situation of dying people significantly easier in comparison with the Western technological civilization. Naturally, the question that immediately arises is whether this advantage was to a great extent due to a lack of reliable information about the nature of reality and to wishful self-deception. If that were the case, a significant part of our difficulties in facing death would simply be the toll we have to pay for our deeper knowledge of the universal scheme of things and we might prefer to bear the consequences of knowing the truth. However, closer examination of the existing evidence clearly shows that this is not the case.

The single most important factor responsible for the most fundamental differences between the worldview of Western industrial countries and all other human groups throughout history is not the superiority of materialistic science over primitive superstition, but the profound ignorance of modern humanity concerning holotropic states of consciousness. The only way the Newtonian-Cartesian worldview of Western science can be maintained is by systematic suppression or misinterpretation of all the evidence

The Great Staircase of the World: Symbolic representation of the fatal trajectory of human life. The steps begin at birth, culminate in the prime of life, and end in old age and death. The infant cradle on the left forms a sharp contrast to the coffin on the right as its mirror image. Isaac Jasparde, 1654.

generated by consciousness studies, whether its source is history, anthropology, comparative religion, or various areas of modern research, such as parapsychology, thanatology, psychedelic therapy, sensory deprivation, experiential psychotherapies, or therapy with individuals in psychospiritual crises ("spiritual emergencies").

The systematic practice of various forms of holotropic states of consciousness, which characterizes the ritual and spiritual life of ancient and aboriginal cultures, inevitably leads to an understanding of the nature of reality and of the relationship between consciousness and matter that is fundamentally different from the belief system of technological societies. I have yet to meet a single Western academician who has done extensive inner work involving holotropic states and continues to subscribe to the current scientific understanding of consciousness, psyche, human nature, and the nature of reality as taught in Western universities.

This is entirely independent on the educational background, IQ, and specific area of expertise of the individual involved. The difference regarding the possibility of consciousness after death thus exactly reflects the differences in the attitude toward holotropic states. Ancient and pre-industrial cultures held these states in high esteem, practiced them regularly in socially sanctioned contexts, and spent much time and energy developing safe and effective techniques for inducing them.

These experiences were the main vehicle for their ritual and spiritual life and were a means of direct communication with the archetypal domains of deities and demons, forces of nature, the animal realms, and the cosmos. Additional uses of holotropic states involved diagnosing and healing diseases, cultivating intuition and ESP, and obtaining artistic inspiration, as well as practical purposes, such as following the movement of the game they were hunting and finding lost objects and people. According to British anthropologist Victor Turner, sharing holotropic states in groups also contributes to tribal bonding and tends to create a sense of deep connectedness *(communitas)* (Turner 2005).

Western society pathologizes all forms of holotropic states (with the exception of dreams that are not recurrent or nightmares), spends a lot of time trying to develop effective ways of suppressing them when they occur spontaneously, and tends to outlaw tools and contexts associated with them. Western psychiatry makes no distinction between a mystical experience and a psychotic experience and sees both as manifestations of mental disease. In its rejection of religion, it does not differentiate between primitive folk beliefs or the fundamentalists' literal interpretation of scriptures, and the sophisticated mystical traditions and Eastern spiritual philosophies based on centuries of the systematic introspective exploration of the psyche. This misguided approach has pathologized the entire spiritual history of humanity.

The observations from various fields of consciousness research, however, challenge the materialistic understanding, according to which biological death represents the final end of existence and of conscious activity of any kind. In explorations of this kind, it is important to keep an open mind and focus as much as possible on the facts of observation. An unshakeable *a priori* commitment to the existing paradigm, which characterizes mainstream science in this area, is an attitude that is well known from fundamentalist religions. Unlike scientism of this kind, science in the true sense of the word is open to unbiased investigation of any existing phenomena. With this in mind, we can divide the existing evidence for the possibility of consciousness surviving biological death into two categories:

1) Experiences and observations challenging the traditional understanding of the nature of consciousness and its relationship to matter.

2) Experiences and observations specifically related to the possibility of survival of consciousness after death.

1) Experiences and observations challenging the traditional understanding of consciousness and its relationship to matter.

The work with holotropic states has generated a vast body of evidence that represents a serious challenge for monistic materialistic science and its Newtonian-Cartesian paradigm. Most of these challenging data are related to transpersonal experiences (see pp. 171, Volume I). They suggest an urgent need for a radical revision of our current concepts of the nature of consciousness and its relationship to matter and the brain. Since the materialistic paradigm of Western science has been a major obstacle for any objective evaluation of the data that describes the events at the time of death, the study of transpersonal experiences has an indirect relevance for thanatology.

In transpersonal experiences, it is possible to transcend the usual limitations of the body/ego, three-dimensional space, and linear time. The disappearance of spatial boundaries can lead to authentic and convincing identifications with other people, other animals, plant life, and even inorganic materials and processes. One can also transcend the temporal boundaries and experience episodes from the lives of one's human and animal ancestors, as well as collective, racial, and karmic memories.

Transpersonal experiences can also take us into the archetypal domains of the collective unconscious and mediate encounters with blissful and wrathful deities of various cultures and visits to mythological realms. In all these experiences, it is possible to access entirely new information that by far surpasses anything that we have obtained in this lifetime through the conventional channels. The study of consciousness that can extend beyond the body, William Roll's "theta consciousness" or the "long body" of the Iroquois, is extremely important for the issue of survival, since it is this part of human personalities that would be likely to survive death.

According to materialistic science, any memory requires a material substrate, such as the neuronal network in the brain or the DNA molecules of the genes. However, it is impossible to imagine any material medium for the information conveyed through these various forms of transpersonal experiences as described above. This information clearly has not been acquired during the individual's lifetime through the conventional means and channels, which is to say, by sensory perception. It seems to exist independently of matter in some types of fields that cannot be detected by our scientific instruments or may possibly be contained in the field of consciousness itself.

The observations from the study of transpersonal experiences are supported by evidence that comes from other avenues of research as well. Challenging the basic metaphysical assumptions of Newtonian-Cartesian thinking, scientists like Heinz von Foerster, Rupert Sheldrake, and Ervin Laszlo seriously explore such possibilities as "memory without a material substrate," "morphogenetic fields," and the record of all events in the universe in the subquantum "PSI-field" or "Akashic Holofield" (von Foerster 1965, Sheldrake 1981, Laszlo 1994).

Traditional academic science describes human beings as highly developed animals and biological thinking machines. Experienced and studied in the everyday state of consciousness, we appear to be Newtonian objects made of atoms, molecules, cells, tissues, and organs. However, transpersonal experiences in holotropic states clearly show that each of us can also manifest the properties of a field of consciousness that transcends space, time, and linear causality.

The completely new formula, remotely reminiscent of the wave-particle paradox in modern physics, thus describes humans as paradoxical beings who have two complementary aspects: they can show properties of Newtonian objects and also those of infinite fields of consciousness. The appropriateness of each of these descriptions depends on circumstances and on the state of consciousness in which these observations are made. Physical death seems to terminate one half of this definition, while the other comes into full expression.

2) Experiences and observations specifically related to the possibility of survival of consciousness after death.

A) **Phenomena on the threshold of death.** Researchers have reported a variety of interesting phenomena that occur at the time of death. There have been numerous reports of visions of recently deceased people by their relatives, friends, and acquaintances. Such visions show a statistically significant correlation with that person's death having occurred within a twelve-hour window, even if the person died at a distance (Sidgwick 1889). Reports of unexplained physical events occurring at the time of death also exist, such as watches stopping and starting, bells ringing, paintings or photographs falling off the wall, and others that seem to announce a person's death (Bozzano 1948).

Individuals approaching death often experience encounters with their dead relatives who seem to welcome them to the next world. These deathbed visions are very authentic and convincing; they are often followed by a state of euphoria and seem to ease the transition. A number of cases have been reported in which a dying individual has a vision of a person about whose death he or she did not know; these have been referred to as "peak in Darien" cases.

Near-death experiences (NDEs) that occur in about one-third of the people who encounter various forms of life-threatening situations, such as car accidents, near-drowning, heart attacks, or cardiac arrests during operations are particularly interesting. Raymond Moody, Kenneth Ring, Michael Sabom, Bruce Greyson, and others have done extensive research into this phenomenon and have described a characteristic experiential pattern that typically includes a life-review, passage through a dark tunnel, personal judgment with an ethical evaluation of one's life, an encounter with a radiant divine being, and visits to various transcendental realms. Less frequent are painful, anxiety-provoking, NDEs—experiences of a terrifying void, infernal imagery of ugly landscapes, demonic beings, and frightening animals who make loud, annoying noises (Greyson and Bush 1996).

In our program of psychedelic therapy with terminal cancer patients, conducted at the Maryland Psychiatric Research Center in Baltimore, we were able to obtain some evidence about the similarity of NDEs with experiences induced by psychedelic substances. We observed several patients who first had psychedelic experiences and later an actual NDE when their disease progressed (e.g. a cardiac arrest during an operation). They reported that these situations were very similar and described the psychedelic sessions as invaluable experiential training for dying (Grof 2006b).

The most extraordinary and fascinating aspect of NDEs is the occurrence of "veridical" out-of-body experiences (OBEs), a term used for experiencing disembodied consciousness with accurate extrasensory perception. Thanatological studies have repeatedly confirmed that people who are unconscious or even clinically dead can have OBEs during which they observe their bodies and rescue procedures from above or perceive events in remote locations.

An extensive study conducted by Ken Ring and his colleagues has added a fascinating dimension to these observations: people who are congenitally blind for organic reasons and have never been able to see anything can see the environment when their consciousness is disembodied during emergencies. The veracity of many of these visions has been confirmed by consensual validation (Ring and Valarino 1998, Ring and Cooper 1999). Various aspects of the accurately perceived environment by disembodied consciousness of the blind subjects ranged from details of electrical fixtures on the ceiling of the operating room to the surroundings of the hospital as observed from a bird's eye view.

The occurrence of veridical OBEs is not limited to near-death situations, vital emergencies, and episodes of clinical death. Such experiences can emerge in sessions of powerful experiential psychotherapy, such as primal therapy, rebirthing, or Holotropic Breathwork, and in experiences induced by psychedelics, particularly the dissociative anesthetic Ketalar (ketamine). They can also occur spontaneously, either as isolated episodes in the individual's life or repeatedly as part of a crisis of psychic opening or some other type of spiritual emergency. Robert Monroe, foremost researcher of OBEs, had spontaneous experiences of out-of-body travel himself over a period of many years (Monroe 1971, 1985, 1994). He developed electronic laboratory techniques for inducing OBEs and founded a special institute in Faber, Virginia to conduct systematic studies of them.

Life review, another important aspect of NDEs, is a fast replay or even reliving of one's life in its entirety or as a mosaic of separate events. Life review proceeds with extraordinary speed and can be completed within seconds of clock time. Some of David Rosen's subjects, who had attempted suicide by jumping off the Golden Gate Bridge, experienced complete life review within the three seconds that it takes to fall from the railing of the bridge to the water's surface (Rosen 1975).

The direction of the sequence of events varies. In some instances, the replay begins with birth, follows the actual course of life, and ends in the life-threatening situation. In others, time seems to roll back from the situation of vital threat toward childhood, infancy, and birth. There are even some indications that individuals whose life review unfolds so that it moves away from the accident suffer surprisingly little damage. Yet another possibility is a "panoramic life review," in which one's life appears in its entirety, outside of linear time.

Classical descriptions of OBEs can be found in the spiritual literature and philosophical texts of all ages. Modern thanatological research confirms the descriptions in the *Tibetan Book of the Dead (Bardo Thödol)*, according to which an individual after death assumes a "bardo body" which transcends the limitations of time and space and can freely travel around the earth. OBEs with confirmed ESP of the environment are especially important for the problem of consciousness after death, since they demonstrate the possibility of consciousness operating independently of the body.

According to the Western materialistic worldview, consciousness is a product of the neurophysiological processes in the brain and it is absurd to think that consciousness could detach itself from the body and maintain its sensory capacity. Yet this is precisely what occurs in many well-documented cases of OBEs. Naturally, people who have had them might have come close to death but did not really die. However, it seems reasonable to infer that if consciousness can function independently of the body during one's lifetime, it may be able to do the same after death.

B) Past life experiences. There is a category of transpersonal experiences that has very direct relevance for the problem of survival of consciousness after death. It involves remembering or reliving vivid episodes from other historical periods and from various parts of the world. The historical and geographical universality of these experiences suggests that they represent very important cultural phenomena. They also have critical implications for understanding the nature of consciousness and human beings and for the theory and practice of psychiatry, psychology, and psychotherapy.

For the Hindus, Buddhists, and open-minded and experienced consciousness researchers, reincarnation is not a matter of belief, but an empirical issue, based on a large amount of evidence and research data. According to Christopher Bache, the evidence in this area is so rich and extraordinary that scientists who do not think the problem of reincarnation deserves serious study are "either uninformed or boneheaded" (Bache 1988).

The nature of the existing evidence that one should be familiar with before making any judgments concerning reincarnation is described in mythological language in a passage written by Sholem Asch, a twentieth-century Hassidic scholar:

> *Not the power to remember, but its very opposite, the power to forget, is a necessary condition of our existence. If the lore of the transmigration of souls is a true one, then these souls, between their exchange of bodies, must pass through the sea of forgetfulness.*
>
> *According to the Jewish view, we make the transition under the overlordship of the Angel of Forgetfulness. But it sometimes happens that the Angel of Forgetfulness himself forgets to remove from our memories the records of the former world; and then our senses are*

haunted by fragmentary recollections of another life. They drift like torn clouds above the hills and valleys of the mind, and weave themselves into the incidents of our current existence. (Asch 1967)

Naturally, we need more than a poetic reference to ancient mythology. Careful study of the amassed evidence is absolutely necessary to make any valid conclusions in this area. As we will discuss later, this matter is of great importance, since the beliefs concerning the issue of reincarnation have great ethical impact on human life and possible relevance for not only the situation in the world, but also its future.

C) **Spontaneous past life memories in children.** There are many instances of small children who seem to remember and describe their previous life in another body, another place, and with other people. These memories usually emerge spontaneously shortly after these children begin to talk. They often present various complications in the life of these children and can be even associated with "carry-over pathologies," such as phobias, strange reactions to certain people, or various idiosyncrasies. Cases like this have been described by child psychiatrists. Access to these memories usually disappears between the ages of five and eight.

Ian Stevenson, Professor of Psychology at the University of Virginia in Charlottesville, Virginia, has conducted meticulous studies of more than 3,000 such cases and reported them in his books *Twenty Cases Suggestive of Reincarnation, Unlearned Languages* and *Children Who Remember Previous Lives* (Stevenson 1966, 1984, and 1987). He only reported several hundred of them, because many did not meet the highest research standards. Some of them were eliminated because the family benefitted financially either in terms of social prestige or public attention, and others because Stevenson found a connecting person who could have been the psychic link. Additional reasons were inconsistent testimony, cryptomnesia, witnesses of questionable character, or indications of fraud. Only the strongest cases were included.

The findings of Stevenson's research were quite remarkable. He was able to confirm the stories the children were telling about their previous lives, often with incredible details, through independent investigation. In all the reported cases, he eliminated the possibility that they could have obtained the information through conventional channels. In some cases, he actually took the children into the village that they remembered from their previous life. Although they had never been there in their current lifetime, they were familiar with the topography of the village, were able to find the home they had allegedly lived in, recognized the members of their "family" and the villagers, and knew their names.

To illustrate the nature of Stevenson's material, the following is a condensed version of the story of Parmod Sharma, one of the twenty subjects described in his early publication.

Parmod Sharma was born on October 11, 1944, in Bisauli, India. His father was Professor Bankeybehary Lal Sharma, a Sanskrit scholar at a nearby college. When Parmod was about two-and-a-half-years old, he began telling his mother not to cook meals for him anymore, because he had a wife in Moradabad who could cook. Moradabad was a town about ninety miles northeast of Bisauli. Between the ages of three and four, he began to speak in detail of his life there. He described several businesses he had owned and operated with other members of his family. He particularly spoke of a shop that manufactured and sold biscuits and soda water, calling it "Mohan Brothers." He insisted that he was one of the Mohan brothers and that he also had a business in Saharanpur, a town about a hundred miles north of Moradabad.

Parmod tended not to play with the other children in Bisauli but preferred to play by himself, building models of shops complete with electrical wiring. He especially liked to make mud biscuits, which he served his family with tea or soda water. During this time, he provided many details about his shop, including its size and location in Moradabad, what was sold there, and his activities connected with it, such as his business trips to Delhi. He even complained to his parents about the less prosperous financial situation of their home compared to what he was used to as a successful merchant.

Parmod had a strong distaste for curd, which is quite unusual for an Indian child, and on one occasion even advised his father against eating it, saying that it was dangerous. Parmod said that in his other life he had become seriously ill after eating too much curd one day. He had an equally strong dislike for being submerged in water, which might relate to his report that he had previously "died in a bathtub." Parmod said that he had been married and had five children: four sons and one daughter. He was anxious to see his family again and frequently begged his parents to take him back to Moradabad to visit them. His family always refused the request, though his mother did get him to begin school by promising to take him to Moradabad when he had learned to read.

Parmod's parents never investigated or tried to verify their son's claims, perhaps because of the Indian belief that children who remembered their previous lives died early. News of Parmod's statements, however, eventually reached the ears of a family in Moradabad named Mehra, which fit many of the details of his story. The brothers of this family owned several businesses in Moradabad including a biscuit and soda shop named "Mohan Brothers." The shop had been named after the eldest brother, Mohan Mehra, and had originally been called "Mohan and Brothers." This was later shortened to "Mohan Brothers." This shop had been started and managed by Parmanand Mehra until his untimely death on May 9, 1943, eighteen months before Parmod was born.

Parmanand had gorged himself on curd, one of his favorite foods, at a wedding feast, and had subsequently developed a chronic gastrointestinal illness which was later followed by appendicitis and peritonitis, from which he died. Two or three days before his death, he had insisted, against his family's advice, on eating more curd, saying that he might not have another chance to enjoy it. Parmanand had blamed his illness and impending death on overeating curd. As part of his therapy during his appendicitis, Parmanand had tried a series of naturopathic bath treatments. While he had not in fact died in a bathtub, he had been given a bath immediately prior to his death. Parmanand left behind a widow and five children—four sons and one daughter.

In the summer of 1949, the Mehra family decided to make the trip to Bisauli to meet Parmod, who was a little under five years old at the time. When they arrived, however, Parmod was away and no contact was made. Not long thereafter, Parmod's father took him to Moradabad to explore his son's compelling remembrances firsthand. Among those who met Parmod at the railway station was Parmanand's cousin, Sri Karam Chand Mehra, who had been quite close to Parmanand. Parmod threw his arm around him weeping, calling him "older brother" and saying "I am Parmanand." Parmod had not used the name Parmanand before this meeting. It is common for Indians to call a cousin "brother" if the relationship is a close one, as was the case for Parmanand and Karam.

The intensity and genuineness of the emotions this reunion generated seemed in itself to be as important a piece of evidence as verification and information about external objects and events. Parmod then proceeded to find his way to the "Mohan Brothers" shop on his own, giving instructions to the driver of the carriage which brought them from the station. Entering the shop, he complained that "his" special seat had been changed. In India it is customary for the owner of a business to have an enclosed seat, a *gaddi,* located near the front of the store where he can greet customers and direct business. The location of Parmanand's *gaddi* had in fact been changed some time after his death.

Once inside, Parmod asked: "Who is looking after the bakery and soda water factory?" This had been Parmanand's responsibility. The complicated machine which manufactured the soda water had been secretly disabled in order to test Parmod. When it was shown to him, Parmod knew exactly how it worked. Without any assistance, he located the disconnected hose and gave instructions for its repair.

When Parmanand's mother entered the room, he immediately recognized her as "Mother" before anyone else present was able to say anything. He also correctly identified Parmanand's wife, acting somewhat embarrassed in front of her. She was, after all, a full-grown woman and he was only five, though apparently possessing at least some of the feelings of an adult husband. When they were alone, he said to her: "I have come, but you have not fixed *bindi,*" referring to the red dot worn on the forehead by Hindu wives. He also reproached her for wearing a white *sari,* the appropriate dress for a Hindu widow, instead of the colored *sari* worn by wives.

Parmod correctly recognized Parmanand's daughter and the one son who was at the house when he arrived. When Parmanand's youngest son, who had been at school, showed up later, Parmod correctly identified him as well, using his familiar name, Gordhan. In their conversation, Parmod would not allow the older Gordhan to address him by his first name but insisted that he call him "Father". "I have only become small," he said. During this visit, Parmod also correctly identified one of Parmanand's brothers and a nephew.

Parmod showed a striking knowledge for the details of Parmanand's world. While touring the hotel the Mehra brothers owned in Moradabad, the Victory Hotel, Parmod commented on the new sheds that had been built on the property. The Mehra family confirmed that these had indeed been added after Parmanand's death. Entering the hotel, Parmod pointed to some cupboards and said: "These are the *almirahs* I had constructed in Churchill House." Churchill House was the name of a second hotel the Mehra brothers owned in Saharanpur, a town about a hundred miles north of Moradabad. Shortly after Parmanand's death, the family had in fact decided to move these particular cupboards, which Parmanand had built for Churchill House, to the Victory Hotel.

The reason why children remember their previous life might be the circumstances of death, particularly those involving shock that "can possibly break through the amnesia;" the most vivid memories often involve events leading up to it. Typically, these children do not know anything about events that occurred in the former personality's life after his or her death. This is an important point in deciding if it's possible that they could be unconsciously reconstructing the details of this life by telepathically reading the minds of those who knew the deceased or if they possess these details as genuine memories. Possibly the strongest evidence in support of the reincarnation hypothesis is the incidence of striking birthmarks and various physical defects that reflect injuries and other events from the remembered life. Ian Stevenson described and documented a large number of such cases in his last work, *Where Reincarnation and Biology Intersect* (Stevenson 1997).

In evaluating this evidence, it is important to emphasize that Stevenson's cases were not only from "primitive, exotic" cultures with *a priori* beliefs in reincarnation, but also from Western countries, including Great Britain and the USA. Stevenson's research meets high standards and has received considerable esteem. In 1977, the *Journal of Nervous and Mental Diseases* devoted almost an entire issue to this subject and the work was reviewed in the *JAMA* (Stevenson 1977).

D) Spontaneous past life memories in adults. Spontaneous vivid reliving of past life memories occurs most frequently during spontaneous episodes of holotropic states of consciousness (spiritual emergencies); however, various degrees of remembering can also happen in more or less ordinary states of consciousness in the circumstances of everyday life. Academic psychiatry and current theories of personality are based on the "one-timer view." Traditional professionals are aware of the existence of past life experiences but treat them indiscriminately as indications of serious psychopathology.

E) Evoked past life memories in adults. Past life experiences can be elicited by a wide variety of techniques that mediate access to deep levels of the psyche, such as meditation, hypnosis, psychedelic substances, sensory isolation, bodywork, and various powerful experiential psychotherapies (primal therapy, rebirthing, or Holotropic Breathwork). They often appear unsolicited in sessions with therapists who do not aim for them and do not even believe in reincarnation, catching them completely off guard. Their emergence is also completely independent of the subject's previous philosophical and religious belief system. In addition, past life experiences occur on the same continuum with accurate memories from adolescence, childhood, infancy, birth, and prenatal memories that can be regularly and reliably verified. Sometimes they coexist or alternate with them (Grof 1988, 1992, 2006).

There are specific reasons to assume that past life experiences are authentic phenomena *sui generis* that have important implications for psychology and psychotherapy because of their heuristic and therapeutic potential:

> i) They feel extremely real and authentic and often mediate access to accurate information about historical periods, cultures, and even historical events that the individual could not have acquired through the ordinary channels.
>
> ii) In some instances, the accuracy of these memories can be objectively verified, sometimes with remarkable details.
>
> iii) These experiences are often integral parts of COEX systems underlying various emotional, psychosomatic, and interpersonal problems.
>
> iv) They have a great therapeutic potential, often more powerful than memories from the present lifetime.
>
> v) They are often associated with extraordinary synchronicities (Grof 2006a, 2996b).

It seems to matter little to the psyche whether the pathogenic forces are related to events from ancient Egypt, the French Revolution, Nazi Germany, or prenatal life, birth, infancy or childhood in the individual's present lifetime. The criteria for verification of past life memories are the same as those for determining what happened last year or twenty years ago: we have to identify specific memories as accurately as we can and secure independent evidence for at least some of them.

Naturally, past life memories are more difficult to verify than memories from the present lifetime. They do not always contain specific information that would render itself to a verification procedure. Evidence is harder to come by, since they are much older and often involve foreign countries and cultures. It is important to realize that even memories from our present life cannot always be corroborated; only some of them can. Most evoked memories do not permit the same degree of verification as Stevenson's spontaneous memories, which are typically more recent. However, I have myself observed and published several remarkable cases with highly unusual elements which could later be verified by independent historical research (Grof 2006a, 2006b).

One story that illustrates the remarkable nature of these observations involved Karl, a young American architect who participated in one of our monthlong workshops at the Esalen Institute in Big Sur, California. At an early stage of his self-exploration, when Karl was reliving various aspects of his biological birth, he started experiencing fragments of dramatic scenes that seemed to be happening in another century and in a foreign country. They were associated with powerful emotions and physical feelings and seemed to be related to various aspects of his present life.

Karl had visions of tunnels, underground storage spaces, military barracks, thick walls, and ramparts that all seemed to be parts of a fortress that was situated on a rocky mountain overlooking an ocean shore. This was interspersed with images of soldiers, mostly fighting and killing each other. He felt puzzled, since the soldiers seemed to be Spanish, but the scenery looked more like Scotland or Ireland.

As this process continued, the scenes became more violent and gory; most of them portrayed fierce combat and bloody slaughter. Although all the people in his visions were soldiers, Karl experienced himself as a priest. At one point, he saw his hand holding a Bible and a cross; on his ring finger was a large seal ring. The vision was very clear, and Karl was able to recognize the initials that it bore.

Being a talented artist, he decided to document this strange process. He produced a series of detailed drawings that depicted various parts of the fortress, including places to store food and ammunition, underground passages and tunnels, bedrooms, and the kitchen. Among these pictures was also a drawing of the seal ring with the initials. Karl created very powerful and impulsive finger paintings, featuring scenes of slaughter, including one that showed him being gored by a sword, thrown over the ramparts of the fortress, and dying on the ocean shore.

It was interesting that in this lifetime, Karl's sternum had a very striking deep indention just where his chest might have been penetrated by a sword in the past life memory. This was similar to cases that Ian Stevenson described in his last major work, *Where Reincarnation and Biology Intersect*. These were instances where birthmarks, birth defects, and various other anomalies appeared on parts of the bodies, which were seriously injured in the children's past lives (Stevenson 1997).

As he was recovering bits and pieces of this story, Karl was finding some meaningful connections with his present life. He discovered that many strong feelings and psychosomatic symptoms that he was experiencing at the time were clearly related to his inner process, which involved this mysterious event. A turning point came when Karl suddenly decided to spend his holiday in Western Ireland. After his return, he showed his family the slides that he had taken on the Western coast of Ireland, at which time he realized that he had taken eleven consecutive pictures of the same scenery that did not seem particularly interesting.

He took the map and reconstructed where he stood when he took the photos and in which direction he was facing. He realized that the place which attracted his attention was the ruin of an old fortress called Dún an Óir, or Fort del Oro (Golden Fortress). Suspecting a connection with the experiences from his inner exploration, Karl decided to study the history of Dún an Óir. He discovered that in 1580, at the time of the British-Spanish war, a small invasion force of Spanish soldiers landed in the nearby Smerwick Harbor to assist the Irish in the Desmond Rebellion. After being joined by some Irish soldiers, they numbered about six hundred. They managed to garrison themselves within the defenses of the fort at Dún an Óir before they were surrounded and besieged by a larger English force commanded by Lord Grey.

Sir Walter Raleigh, known as one of the first explorers to bring tobacco from the New World colonies to England, negotiated with the Spaniards and promised them free egress from the fortress if they opened the gate and surrendered to the British. The Spaniards agreed on these conditions, but the British did not keep their promise. Once they were inside the fortress, they mercilessly slaughtered all the Spaniards and threw them over the ramparts to die on the ocean beach.

In spite of this absolutely astonishing confirmation of the story that he had laboriously reconstructed in his sessions, Karl was not satisfied. He continued his library research until he discovered a special document about the battle of Dún an Óir. There he found that a priest accompanied the Spanish soldiers and was killed with them. The initials of the name of the priest were identical with those that Karl saw in his vision of the seal ring and had depicted in one of his drawings.

In this next example is one of the most unusual coincidences that I have encountered during my LSD work; it also shows the complexity of this type of research. The evidence in this case has an ambiguous quality, since the experiences involved have combined characteristics of ancestral and past life memories. It is an episode from the treatment of Renata, a patient suffering from severe cancerphobia. In an advanced stage of her therapy, we encountered an unusual and unprecedented sequence of events. Four of her consecutive LSD sessions had consisted almost exclusively of scenes from a particular period of Czech history.

Renata had a number of experiences in these sessions that took place in Prague in the seventeenth century. This time was a crucial historical period for the Czechs. After the disastrous battle of White Mountain in 1621, which marked the beginning of the Thirty Years' War in Europe, Bohemia ceased to exist as an independent kingdom and came under the hegemony of the Habsburg dynasty, which lasted three hundred years. In an effort to destroy the feelings of national pride and defeat the forces of resistance, the Habsburgs sent out mercenaries to capture the country's most prominent noblemen. Twenty-seven outstanding members of Czech nobility were arrested, brought to Prague, and beheaded in a public execution on scaffolding erected in the Old Town Square in Prague.

Many of Renata's experiences were related to various scenes from the life of a young nobleman, one of the twenty-seven members of the aristocracy beheaded by the Habsburgs. She had an unusual variety of images and insights concerning the architecture of the period, typical armor, weapons and garments, as well as various utensils used in everyday life. She was also able to describe the relationships that existed at that time between the royal family and the vassals. Renata had never specifically studied this period, and I had to consult special books in order to confirm the reported information.

In a dramatic sequence, Renata finally relived, with powerful emotions and in considerable detail, the actual events of the execution, including this nobleman's intense anguish and agony. In all these scenes, Renata experienced full identification with this individual. She was not quite clear how these historical sequences were related to her present personality and did not know what they meant. She finally concluded that these experiences must have been memories from the life of one of her ancestors, although this contradicted her personal beliefs and philosophy.

Being a close witness of this emotional drama, I shared Renata's bewilderment and confusion. Trying to decipher this enigma, I chose two different approaches. On the one hand, I spent a considerable amount of time trying to verify the historical information Renata gave me and was increasingly impressed by its accuracy. On the other hand, I tried use the psychoanalytic approach—asking Renata for free associations for the content of her experiences, hoping that I would be able to understand them as symbolic disguises for her childhood experiences or elements of her present life situation. No matter how hard I tried, the experiential sequences did not make any sense.

I finally gave up on this problem when Renata's LSD experiences moved into new areas. Focusing on other more immediate tasks, I stopped thinking about this peculiar incident. Two years later, when I was in the United States, I received a long letter from Renata with the following unusual introduction: "Dear Dr. Grof, you will probably think that I am absolutely insane when I share with you the results of my recent private search." In the text that followed, Renata described how she happened to meet her father, whom she had not seen since her parents' divorce when she was three years old. After a short discussion, her father invited her to have dinner with him, his second wife, and their children.

After dinner, he told her that he wanted to show her the results of his favorite hobby, which she might find interesting. During World War II, the Nazis had issued a special order that every family in the occupied countries had to present the German authorities with its pedigree demonstrating the absence of persons of Jewish origin for the last five generations. Working on the family genealogy out of necessity, Renata's father became absolutely fascinated by this procedure.

After he had completed the required five-generation pedigree for the authorities, he continued because of his private interest, tracing the history of his family back through the centuries. This was possible thanks to the meticulously kept system of birth records available in the archives of parish houses in European countries. With considerable pride, Renata's father pointed to a large ramified pedigree of their family and showed her that they were descendants of one of the noblemen executed after the battle on White Mountain.

After having described this episode in the letter, Renata wrote how happy she was to have obtained this independent confirmation of her "gut feeling" that her ancestral memory was authentic. She saw this as a proof that emotionally charged memories can be imprinted in the genetic code and transmitted through centuries to future generations. When I got over my initial amazement regarding this most unusual coincidence, I discovered a rather serious logical inconsistency in Renata's account. One of the experiences she had had in her historical LSD sessions was the reliving of the terminal anguish of the nobleman during his own execution. And, naturally, physical death terminates the possibility of further genetic transfer; it destroys the biological hereditary line.

A dead person cannot procreate and "genetically" pass the memory of his terminal anguish to future generations. Before completely discarding the information contained in Renata's letter as supportive evidence for her experiences, several facts deserve serious consideration. None of the remaining Czech patients, who had a total of more than 2,000 sessions, had ever even mentioned this historical period. In Renata's case, four consecutive LSD sessions contained, almost exclusively, historical sequences from this time. It is practically out of the question that something like this is a mere meaningless coincidence. And it is certainly hard to imagine any plausible explanation for this astonishing coincidence that would not violate some basic assumptions of traditional Western science.

Tibetan practices relevant to the problem of reincarnation. Tibetan spiritual literature describes some interesting phenomena suggesting that certain highly developed spiritual masters are able to gain far-reaching knowledge related to the process of reincarnation. This includes the possibility of exerting influence on the time of one's death, predicting or even directing the time and place of one's next incarnation, and maintaining consciousness through the intermediate states *(bardos)* between death and the next incarnation.

Conversely, accomplished Tibetan monks allegedly can, through various clues received in dreams, meditation, and through other channels, locate and identify the child who is the reincarnation of the Dalai Lama, Panchen Lama, Karmapa or another tulku. The child is exposed to a test during which he has to correctly identify, from each of thirteen sets of similar objects, the one that belonged to the deceased. Some aspects of this practice could be subjected to a rather rigorous testing following Western standards. If the reports about this procedure are true, the statistical probability of correctly identifying the right object in all the rows would be astronomically low.

Apparitions of the Dead and Communication with Them

Direct experiences of encounters and communication with deceased persons do not occur only around the time when these people died or as part of the NDEs, but also at a later date, spontaneously or in the context of holotropic states induced by psychedelics, experiential psychotherapies, or meditation. Naturally, the data of this kind have to be evaluated particularly carefully and critically. The simple fact of a private experience of the deceased does not really amount to very much and can easily be dismissed as a wishful fantasy or hallucination. Some additional factors must be present as well before the experiences constitute interesting research material. It is also, of course, important to make a distinction between those apparitions that seem to satisfy some strong need of the percipient and others, where any motivation of this kind cannot be found.

It is important to mention that some of the apparitions have certain characteristics that make them very interesting or even challenging for researchers. There are a number of cases reported that describe apparitions of persons unknown to the percipient, who are later identified through photographs and verbal descriptions. It also is not uncommon that such apparitions are witnessed collectively or by many different individuals over long periods of time, such as in the case of "haunted" houses and castles.

In some instances, the apparitions can have distinct distinguishing bodily marks accrued around the time of death, which is unbeknownst to the percipient. Of particular interest are those cases where the deceased convey some specific and accurate new information that can be verified or is linked with an extraordinary synchronicity. I have myself observed in LSD therapy and in Holotropic Breathwork several amazing instances of the second kind. One example of such is an event that occurred during the LSD therapy of Richard, a young depressed patient who had made repeated suicide attempts.

In one of his LSD sessions, Richard had a very unusual experience involving a strange and uncanny astral realm. This domain had an eerie luminescence and was filled with discarnate beings that were trying to communicate with him in a very urgent and demanding manner. He could not see or hear them; however, he sensed their almost tangible presence and was receiving telepathic messages from them. I wrote down one of these messages that was very specific and could be subjected to subsequent verification. It was a request for Richard to connect with a couple in the Moravian city of Kroměříž and let them know that their son Ladislav was doing all right and was well taken care of.

The message included the couple's name, street address, and telephone number; all of these details were unknown to me and the patient. This experience was extremely puzzling; it seemed to be an alien enclave in Richard's experience, totally unrelated to his problems and the rest of his treatment. After some hesitation and with mixed feelings, I finally decided to do what certainly would have made me the target of my colleagues' jokes had they found out. I went to the telephone, dialed the number in Kroměříž, and asked if I could speak with Ladislav. To my astonishment, the woman on the other side of the line started to cry. When she calmed down, she told me with a broken voice: "Our son is not with us anymore; he passed away. We lost him three weeks ago."

Another example involves a close friend and former colleague of mine,

Walter N. Pahnke, who was a member of our psychedelic research team at the Maryland Psychiatric Research Center in Baltimore, Maryland. He had a deep interest in parapsychology, particularly in the problem of consciousness after death, and worked with many famous mediums and psychics, including his friend Eileen Garrett, president of the American Parapsychological Association. He was also the initiator of our LSD program for patients dying of cancer.

In the summer of 1971, Walter went with his wife Eva and their children for a vacation in their cabin in Maine, situated right on the ocean. One day, he went scuba-diving before lunch, by himself, and did not return. A systematic and extensive search involving the Coast Guard and several famous psychics failed to find his body or any part of his diving gear. Under these circumstances, Eva found it very difficult to accept and integrate his death. Her last memory of Walter when he was leaving the cabin involved him full of energy and in perfect health. It was hard for her to believe that he was not part of her life anymore and she could not start a new chapter of her existence without a sense of closure for the preceding one.

Being a psychologist herself, she qualified for an LSD training session for mental health professionals that was offered through a special program in our institute. She decided to have a psychedelic experience with the hope of getting some insight into this situation and asked me to be her sitter. In the second half of the session, she had a very powerful vision of Walter and carried on a long and meaningful dialogue with him. He gave her specific instructions concerning each of their three children and released her to start a new life of her own, unencumbered and unrestricted by a sense of commitment to his memory. It was a very profound and liberating experience.

Just as Eva was questioning whether the entire episode was just a wishful fabrication of her own mind, Walter appeared once more for a brief period of time and asked Eva to return a book that he had borrowed from a friend of his. He then proceeded to give her the name of the friend, the room where the book was, the name of the book, the shelf, and the sequential order of the book on this shelf. Giving Eva this kind of specific confirmation of the authenticity of their communication was very much in Walter's style. During his life, he had had extensive contact with psychics from different parts of the world and had been fascinated by the attempt of the famous magician Harry Houdini to prove the existence of the Beyond. Following the instructions, Eva was actually able to find and return the book, about the existence of which she had had no previous knowledge.

One of the psychologists participating in our three-year professional training had witnessed a wide variety of his colleagues' transpersonal experiences during our Holotropic Breathwork sessions, and had also had several of them himself. However, he continued to be very skeptical about the authenticity of these phenomena, constantly questioning whether or not they deserved any special attention. Then, after one of his Holotropic Breathwork sessions, he experienced an unusual synchronicity that convinced him that he might have been too skeptical and conservative in his approach to transpersonal experiences and ESP phenomena.

Toward the end of his session, he had a vivid experience of encountering his grandmother, who had been dead for many years. He had been very close to her in his childhood and was deeply moved by the possibility that he might really be communicating with her again. In spite of a deep emotional involvement in the experience, he continued to maintain an attitude of professional skepticism about the encounter. He knew that he had had many real interactions with his grandmother while she was alive and that his mind could have easily fabricated an imaginary encounter using these old memories.

However, this meeting with his dead grandmother was so emotionally profound and convincing that he simply could not dismiss it as a wishful fantasy. He decided to seek proof that the experience was real, not just in his imagination. He asked his grandmother for some form of confirmation and received the following message: "Go to aunt Anna and look for cut roses." Still skeptical, he decided to visit his aunt Anna's home on the following weekend and see what would happen. Upon his arrival, he found his aunt in the garden, surrounded by cut roses. He was astonished. The day of his visit just happened to be the one day of the year that his aunt had decided to do some radical pruning of her roses.

Experiences of this kind are certainly far from being a definitive proof of the existence of astral realms and discarnate beings. However, these astonishing synchronicities clearly suggest that this fascinating area deserves the serious attention of consciousness researchers. Of special interest is the quasi-experimental evidence that is suggestive of the survival of consciousness after death that comes from the highly charged and controversial area of spiritistic seances and mental or trance mediumship, as I examined in Volume I. Although some of the professional mediums were occasionally caught cheating, a number of others—such as Mrs. Piper, Mrs. Leonard, and Mrs. Verrall—successfully passed credible research tests (Grosso 1994).

An interesting innovation in this area is the procedure described in Raymond Moody's book *Reunions* (Moody 1993). Using perceptual ambiguity involved in mirror-gazing, Moody induced in his subjects convincing visionary encounters with deceased loved ones. Some of the spiritistic reports considerably stretch the mind of an average Westerner, let alone a traditionally trained scientist. For example, the extreme form of spiritistic phenomena, the "physical mediumship," includes, among others, telekinesis and materializations, upward levitation of objects and people, projection of objects through the air, the manifestation of ectoplasmic formations, and the appearance of writings or objects without explanation *("apports")*.

In the Brazilian spiritist movement, mediums perform psychic surgeries using their hands or knives, allegedly under the guidance of the spirits of deceased people. These surgeries do not require any anesthesia and the wounds close without sutures. Events of this kind have been repeatedly studied and filmed by Western researchers of the stature of Walter Pahnke, Stanley Krippner, and Andrija Puharich. A relatively recent development in the efforts to communicate with spirits of deceased people is an approach called instrumental transcommunication (ITC), which uses modern electronic technology for this purpose.

This avenue of research began in 1959 when Scandinavian filmmaker Friedrich Jurgensen picked up human voices of allegedly dead persons on an audiotape while recording the sounds of passerine birds in a quiet forest. Inspired by this event, Latvian parapsychologist Konstantin Raudive conducted a systematic study of this phenomenon and recorded more than 100,000 multilingual paranormal voices allegedly communicating messages from the Beyond (Raudive 1971).

More recently, a worldwide network of researchers, including Ernst Senkowski, George Meek, Mark Macy, Scott Rogo, Raymond Bayless, and others have been involved in a group effort to establish "interdimensional transcommunication" (ITC). They claim to have received many paranormal verbal communications and pictures from the deceased through electronic media, including tape recorders, telephones, fax machines, computers, and TV screens. Among the spirits communicating from the Beyond are supposedly some of the former researchers in this field, such as Jurgensen and Raudive (Senkowski 1994).

Individual and Social Implications of the Research on Death and Dying

The research of the psychological, philosophical, and spiritual aspects of death and dying discussed in this chapter has considerable theoretical and practical implications. The experiences and observations I have explored certainly are not an unequivocal "proof" of the survival of consciousness after death, of the existence of astral realms inhabited by discarnate beings, or of reincarnation of the individual unit of consciousness and continuation of its physical existence in another body and lifetime. It is certainly possible to imagine other types of interpretation of the same data, such as extraordinary and amazing paranormal capacities of human consciousness *(superpsi)* or the Hindu concept of the universe as *lila,* the divine play of consciousness of the cosmic creative principle.

However, one thing seems to be clear: none of the interpretations based on careful analysis of these data would be compatible with the Newtonian-Cartesian paradigm of Western materialistic science. The systematic examination and unbiased evaluation of this material would necessarily result in an entirely new understanding of the nature of consciousness, its role in the universal scheme of things, and its relationship to matter and, more specifically, the brain.

Mainstream academic science has been defending, often quite aggressively and authoritatively, its basic metaphysical assumption that human consciousness is the product of neurophysiological processes in the brain and is fully contained inside the skull. This position, inherited from seventeenth-century philosophy and science, has thus far been impervious to modern discoveries, ranging from transpersonal psychology and various areas of consciousness research to quantum-relativistic physics. It can be maintained only through the systematic suppression of a vast amount of data from various disciplines, a basic strategy that is characteristic of fundamentalist religions, but one that should not exist in science.

Besides their theoretical relevance, the issues discussed in this chapter also have great practical significance. I have explored the importance of death for psychiatry, psychology, and psychotherapy at some length in other publications (Grof 1985, 2006b). Our past encounters with death in the form of vital threats during our postnatal history, the trauma of birth, and embryonal existence are deeply imprinted in our unconscious. In addition, the motif of death also plays an important role in the transpersonal domain of the human psyche in connection with powerful archetypal and karmic material. In all these varieties, the theme of death and dying contributes significantly to the development of emotional and psychosomatic disorders.

Conversely, confronting this material and coming to terms with the fear of death is conducive to healing, positive personality transformation, and consciousness evolution. As we discussed in connection with the ancient mysteries of death and rebirth, this "dying before dying" deeply influences the quality of life and the basic strategy of existence. It reduces irrational drives (the "rat race" or "treadmill" type of existence) and increases the ability to live in the present and to enjoy everyday life activities. Another important consequence of freeing oneself from the fear of death is a radical opening to spirituality of a universal and non-denominational type. This tends to occur whether the encounter with death happens during a real brush with death in a NDE, or in a purely psychological way, such as in meditation, experiential therapy, a psychedelic session, or a spontaneous psychospiritual crisis (spiritual emergency).

In conclusion, I would like to mention some of the broadest possible implications of this material. Whether or not we believe in the survival of consciousness after death, reincarnation, and karma has very serious implications for our behavior. The idea that belief in immortality has profound moral implications can already be found in Plato, who in *Laws* has Socrates say that not being concerned for the post mortem consequences of one's deeds would be "a boon to the wicked." Modern authors, such as Alan Harrington and Ernest Becker, have emphasized that the massive denial of death leads to social pathologies that have dangerous consequences for humanity (Harrington 1969, Becker 1973). Modern consciousness research certainly supports this point of view (Grof 1985).

At a time when a combination of unbridled greed, malignant aggression, and the existence of weapons of mass destruction threatens the survival of humanity and possibly life on this planet, we should seriously consider any avenue that offers some hope. While this is not a sufficient reason for uncritically embracing the material suggesting survival of consciousness after death, it should be an additional incentive for reviewing the existing data with an open mind and in the spirit of true science. The same applies to the powerful experiential technologies involving holotropic states of consciousness that make it possible to confront the fear of death and can facilitate deep positive personality transformations and spiritual openings. A radical inner transformation and rise to a new level of consciousness might be the only real hope we have in the current global crisis.

Literature

Alexander, F. 1931. "Buddhist Training As Artificial Catatonia." *Psychoanalyt. Review* 18:129.

Asch, S. 1967. *The Nazarene.* New York: Carroll and Graf.

Bache, C. 1988. *Lifecycles: Reincarnation and the Web of Life.* New York: Paragon House.

Becker, E. 1973. *The Denial of Death.* New York: Simon & Schuster.

Bozzano, E. 1948. *Dei Fenomeni di Telekinesia in Rapporto con Eventi di Morti.* Casa Editrice Europa.

Delacour, J. B. 1974. *Glimpses of the Beyond.* New York: Delacorte Press.

Foerster, H. von. 1965. "Memory Without A Record." In *The Anatomy of Memory* (D.P.Kimble, ed.). Palo Alto: Science and Behavior Books.

Flynn, C. P. 1986. *After the Beyond: Human Transformation and the Near-Death Experience.* Englewood-Cliffs, NJ: Prentice-Hall.

Greyson, B. and Flynn, C. P. (Eds.) 1984. *The Near-Death Experience: Problems, Prospects, Perspectives.* Springfield, IL: Charles C. Thomas.

Grof, S., and Grof, C. 1980. *Beyond Death: Gates of Consciousness.* London: Thames & Hudson.

Grof, S. 1985. *Beyond the Brain: Birth, Death, and Transcendence in Psycho-*

therapy. Albany, NY: State University New York (SUNY) Press.

Grof, S. 1988. *The Adventure of Self-Discovery.* Albany, NY: State University New York (SUNY) Press.

Grof, S. 1992. *The Holotropic Mind.* San Francisco, CA: Harper.

Grof, S. 2006a. *The Ultimate Journey: Consciousness Research and the Mystery of Death.* Santa Cruz, CA: MAPS Publications.

Grof, S. 2006b. *When the Impossible Happens: Adventures in Non-Ordinary Realities.* Louisville, CO: Sounds True.

Grof, S. 1994. *Books of the Dead: Manuals for Living and Dying.* London: Thames and Hudson.

Grosso, M. 1994. "The Status of Survival Research: Evidence, Problems, Paradigms". A paper presented at the Institute of Noetic Sciences Symposium The Survival of Consciousness After Death, Chicago, IL, July.

Harrington, A. 1969. *The Immortalist.* Milbrae, CA: Celestial Arts.

Laszlo, E. 1994. *The Creative Cosmos.* Edinburgh: Floris Books.

Lommel, P. van. 2010. *Consciousness Beyond Life: The Science of the Near-Death Experience.* New York: Harper Collins.

Macy, M. 2005. "The Miraculous Side of Instrumental Transcommunication." A lecture at the Seventh International Conference on Science and Consciousness in La Fonda Hotel, Santa Fe, New Mexico.

Monroe, R. A. 1971. *Journeys Out of the Body.* New York: Doubleday and Co.

Monroe, R. A. 1985. *Far Journeys.* New York: Doubleday and Co.

Monroe, R. A. 1994. *Ultimate Journey.* New York: Doubleday and Co.

Moody, R. A. 1975. *Life After Life.* New York: Bantam Books.

Moody, R. A. 1993. *Reunions.* New York: Villard Books.

Osis, K. 1961. *Deathbed Observations of Physicians and Nurses.* New York: Parapsychology Foundation.

Osis, K. and McCormick, D. 1980. Kinetic Effects at the Ostensible Location of an Out-of-Body Projection During Perceptual Testing. *Journal of the American Society for Psychical Research.* 74:319-24.

Raudive, K. 1971. *Breakthrough.* New York: Lancer Books.

Ring, K. 1982. *Life at Death A Scientific Investigation of the Near-Death Experience.* New York: Quill.

Ring, K. 1985. *Heading Toward Omega: In Search of the Meaning of the Near-Death Experience.* New York: Quill.

Ring, K. and Valarino, E. E. 1998. *Lessons from the Light: What We Can Learn from the Near-Death Experience.* New York: Plenum Press.

Ring, K. and Cooper, S. 1999. *Mindsight: Near-Death and Out-of-Body Experiences in the Blind.* Palo Alto, CA: William James Center for Consciousness Studies.

Rogo, G. S. 1990. *The Return from Silence: A Study of Near-Death Experiences.* New York: Harper and Row.

Sabom, M. 1982. *Recollections of Death: A Medical Investigation.* New York: Harper & Row.

Senkowski, E. 1994. "Instrumental Transcommunication" (ITC). An Institute for Noetic Sciences lecture at the Corte Madera Inn, Corte Madera, CA, July.

Sheldrake, R. 1981. *A New Science of Life.* Los Angeles, CA: J. P. Tarcher.

Sidgwick, H. et al. 1889. "Report on the Census of Hallucinations." *Proc. S.P.R.,* Vol. 10, 245-51.

Stevenson, I. 1966. *Twenty Cases Suggestive of Reincarnation.* Charlottesville, VA: University of Virginia Press.

Stevenson, I. 1984. *Unlearned Languages.* Charlottesville, VA: University of Virginia Press.

Stevenson, I. 1987. *Children Who Remember Previous Lives.* Charlottesville, VA: University of Virginia Press.

Stevenson, I. 1997. *Where Reincarnation and Biology Intersect.* Santa Barbara, CA: Praeger Publications.

Turner, V. 2005. "Rituals and Communitas." *Creative Resistance,* November 26.

Weisse, J. E.: 1972. *The Vestibule.* Port Washington, NY: Ashley Books.

XIV

The Cosmic Game:
Exploration of the Farthest Reaches of Human Consciousness

In this encyclopedia, we have focused primarily on the implications of the research of holotropic states of consciousness for psychiatry, psychology, and psychotherapy. However, this work has also generated many interesting philosophical, metaphysical, and spiritual insights. Irrespective of the initial motivation of the person involved in systematic and disciplined self-exploration using holotropic states, serial sessions sooner or later take the form of a deep philosophical and spiritual quest. On numerous occasions, I have seen people whose initial interest in psychedelic sessions or in Holotropic Breathwork was therapeutic, professional, or artistic, suddenly start asking and answering for themselves the most fundamental questions about existence. This happened when their inner process reached the perinatal and transpersonal levels of the unconscious.

How did our universe come into being? Is the world in which we live merely a product of mechanical processes involving inanimate, inert, and reactive matter? Can material reality be explained solely in terms of its fundamental building blocks and the objective laws that govern their interaction? What is the source of order, form, and meaning in the universe? Is it possible that the creation of a universe like ours and its evolution could have occurred without the participation of a superior cosmic intelligence?

And if there is a supreme creative principle, what is our relationship to it?

How can we come to terms with dilemmas concerning the nature of the universe we live in such as the finiteness of time and space versus eternity and infinity? What is the relationship between life and matter and between consciousness and the brain? How can we explain the existence of evil and its overwhelming presence in the universal scheme of things? Is our existence limited to just one lifetime, spanning the period from conception to death, or does our consciousness survive the biological demise and experience a long series of consecutive incarnations? And what are the practical implications of the answers to the above questions for our everyday life? Who are we, where did we come from, and where are we going?

In the late 1960s, I decided to analyze the records from more than 5,000 psychedelic sessions of my patients and the patients of my colleagues with a specific focus on their metaphysical experiences and insights. I summarized my findings in a paper, "LSD and the Cosmic Game: Outline of Psychedelic Ontology and Cosmology" (Grof 1972). To my surprise, I found far-reaching agreement among my clients and trainees concerning their insights about basic metaphysical issues. The vision of reality that has emerged from this study did not portray the universe as a mechanical Newtonian supermachine, but as an infinitely complex virtual reality created and permeated by superior cosmic intelligence, Absolute Consciousness, Anima mundi, or the Universal Mind.

The metaphysical insights from psychedelic sessions and the answers to the basic ontological and cosmological questions that this work provided were in sharp conflict with the materialistic worldview and the Newtonian-Cartesian paradigm of Western science. However, they showed far-reaching parallels with the great mystical traditions of the world, for which Aldous Huxley used the term *perennial philosophy* (Huxley 1945). They were also surprisingly compatible with the revolutionary advances of modern science that are usually referred to as the *new* or *emerging paradigm* (Grof 1998).

In the following years, as I gained extensive experience with Holotropic Breathwork and with spontaneously occurring episodes of holotropic states ("spiritual emergencies"), I realized that the metaphysical insights described in my paper were not limited to psychedelic experiences but were characteristic for holotropic states in general. In this chapter, I will briefly sketch the basic features of the intriguing vision of reality that has spontaneously emerged in people who have done systematic work with holotropic states of consciousness. A more comprehensive treatment of this subject can be found in my book *The Cosmic Game: Explorations of the Frontiers of Human Consciousness* (Grof 1998).

I have repeatedly heard from my patients and trainees who were involved in self-exploration with serial psychedelic sessions or sessions of Holotropic Breathwork that they saw this process as an ongoing spiritual journey. These statements prompted me to study spiritual experiences in holotropic states of consciousness and find out if any of them gave my clients and trainees the feeling that they had reached the goal of their spiritual journey. In other words, had they found and obtained what they were looking for?

Experience of the Immanent Divine
and of the Ensouled Universe

If we keep our eyes open during a holotropic state of consciousness, this can result in the experience of *the immanent divine,* a profoundly transformed perception of everyday reality. A person having this form of spiritual experience sees people, animals, and inanimate objects in the environment as radiant manifestations of cosmic creative energy and realizes that the boundaries between them are illusory and unreal. This is a direct experience of nature as God, Baruch Spinoza's *Deus sive Natura.* We also discover that underlying the world of separation is a unified, undivided field of cosmic creative energy.

Using the analogy with television, this experience could be likened to a situation where a black-and-white picture suddenly changes into one in vivid, living color. In both situations, many of the old elements of the world remain the same—we can still recognize people, animals, and trees—but the way we perceive them is radically redefined by the addition of a new dimension. In the TV picture this new dimension is color, while in the experience of the immanent divine, it is a sense of *numinosity,* a feeling of sacredness. The word "numinous" is an expression that C. G. Jung borrowed from the German theologian and religious scholar Rudolf Otto.

Jung preferred to use this neutral expression instead of terms like religious, mystical, spiritual, sacred, or magical, which have been used in many different contexts and can be easily misunderstood.

As we saw earlier, in holotropic states we can also have authentic and convincing experiences of conscious identification with animals, plants, and even inorganic materials. Following experiences of the immanent divine, our worldview expands, and we begin to understand the beliefs of animistic cultures, which see the entire universe as being conscious and ensouled. From their perspective, not only all the animals, but also the trees, the rivers, the mountains, the sun, the moon, and the stars appear to be conscious beings. Having this experience, we would not necessarily accept and embrace the worldview of any of these cultures in all its aspects and completely forget and ignore all the findings of Western science.

However, we have to add an important empirical fact to our worldview: everything that we experience in the holotropic state of consciousness as an object has in the holotropic state a subjective experiential counterpart. People who have the experience of the immanent divine and discover that they can experience themselves as other people, animals, and various aspects of the universe, also understand the basic tenet of the great Eastern spiritual philosophies: that everything in the universe is a manifestation of Cosmic Consciousness and the Universal Creative Principle. They simply call it by different names—Brahman, the Tao, or the Buddha.

As far as the search for the Ultimate is concerned, people who have had the experiences described above feel that they have made an important step on the spiritual journey, but do not think that they have reached its final goal. They understand that there is more to discover.

Experience of the Transcendent Divine and of the Archetypal Realm

The experiences of the *transcendent divine* bring into consciousness visions of and encounters with personages and creatures from mythologies of various cultures of the world, complex archetypal sequences, and visits to the abodes of the Beyond as described in these traditions—heavens, paradises, hells and other fantastic mythic sceneries. In this type of spiritual experience, entirely new worlds, which are not part of everyday reality, seem to "unfold" or "explicate" (to borrow terms from David Bohm) from another level or order of reality into our perceptual field (Bohm 1980). If we use the analogy with television as described earlier, this would be like a surprising discovery that different channels exist, each one radically different than the one we have been watching and experiencing every day of our lives.

In this type of experience, we discover that our psyche has access to entire pantheons of mythological figures, as well as the domains that they inhabit. A particularly convincing proof of the authenticity of these experiences is the fact that, like other transpersonal phenomena, they can bring us new and accurate information about the figures and realms involved. The nature, scope, and quality of this information often by far surpasses our previous intellectual knowledge concerning these mythologies. Observations of this kind led C. G. Jung to the assumption that, besides the individual unconscious as described by Sigmund Freud, we also have a collective unconscious that connects us with the entire cultural heritage of humanity. According to Jung, these are manifestations of archetypes, primordial universal patterns that represent intrinsic constituents of the collective unconscious (Jung 1959).

For many people, the first encounter with the sacred dimensions of existence occurs in the context of the death-rebirth process, when the memories of different stages of birth are accompanied by visions of analogous scenes from the archetypal domain of the collective unconscious. However, the full connection with the spiritual realm is made when the process moves to the transpersonal level of the psyche. When that happens, various spiritual experiences appear independently of the fetal sequences in their pure form. In some instances, the holotropic process bypasses the biographical and perinatal levels altogether and provides direct access to the transpersonal realm.

Holotropic states of consciousness can provide deep insights into the worldviews of ancient and native cultures which believe that the cosmos is populated with and governed by various blissful and wrathful deities. The imagery of such experiences is drawn from the collective unconscious and can feature mythological figures and themes from any culture in the entire history of humanity, including those of which we have no intellectual knowledge. If we feel reluctant to confirm and accept the worldview of ancient and native cultures, we might prefer to use modern terminology such as *numinous* instead of *sacred,* and *archetypal figures* instead of *deities* and *demons.* But we can no longer dismiss these experiences as mere hallucinations or fantasies.

Deep personal experiences of this realm help us realize that the images of the cosmos found in pre-industrial societies are not based on ignorance, superstition, primitive "magical thinking," or psychotic visions, but on authentic experiences of alternate realities. To distinguish these phenomena from hallucinatory or imaginary experiences, which do not have any objective basis, Jungian psychologists refer to these transphenomenal realities as "imaginal."

French scholar, philosopher, and mystic Henri Corbin, who first used the term *mundus imaginalis,* was inspired by his study of Islamic mystical literature (Corbin 2000). Islamic theologians call the imaginal world—where everything existing in the sensory world has its analogue—*alam al mithal,* or the "eighth climate," to distinguish it from the "seven climates," regions of traditional Islamic geography. The imaginal world possesses spatial and temporal dimensions, forms and colors, but these are not perceptible to our senses as properties of physical objects. Yet this realm is in every respect as fully ontologically real as the material world that is perceived by our sensory organs, and experiences of it can be verified by consensual validation by other people.

Archetypal experiences have three-dimensional space of their own and unfold in linear time; however, what they miss in comparison with the material world is spatial and temporal cohesion. For example, we can assess the distance between Prague and Baltimore and determine in which direction Prague can be found. We cannot do the same with Shiva's heaven or Valhalla, the resting place built by the god Wotan for Nordic warriors killed in battle. Similarly, we can determine how many years elapsed between the American Civil War and the Russian Bolshevik Revolution. We could not answer the same question if it were asked about the battle of the Titans against the Olympic gods and Ragnarok (Twilight of the Gods), the final battle in Nordic mythology.

Archetypal figures fall into several categories, as we have seen. The first one includes personages embodying various universal roles and principles.

These include the Great Mother Goddess, the Terrible Mother Goddess, the Wise Old Man, the Eternal Youths, the Lovers, Death, the Trickster, the Anima and Animus, and the Shadow. The second major category of archetypal figures involves deities and demons related to a specific culture, geographical area, or historical period. For example, instead of a generalized personification of the Great Mother Goddess, we can experience one of her specific cultural forms, such as the Christian Virgin Mary, Sumerian Inanna, Egyptian Isis, Greek Hera, Hindu Lakshmi or Parvati. It is important to remember that the range of archetypal encounters that individuals in holotropic states can access is not limited by their beliefs, knowledge, or cultural heritage. Resembling something like a laboratory proof of Jung's theory of the collective unconscious, these experiences can be drawn from the mythology of any culture in human history.

For the purpose of our discussion, it is important to distinguish the universal form of spirituality, which emerges spontaneously in holotropic states of consciousness, from religion. Spirituality involves a special kind of relationship between the individual and the cosmos and is, in its essence, a personal and private affair. By comparison, organized religion involves institutionalized group activity that takes place in a designated location and features a system of appointed officials who may or may not have had their own personal experiences of spiritual realities.

The encounters with archetypal figures can be emotionally overwhelming and often bring new and detailed information that is independent of the experiencing persons' racial, cultural, and educational background, as well as previous intellectual knowledge of the respective mythologies. The experiences of blissful and terrifying deities are accompanied by extremely intense emotions, ranging from ecstatic rapture to paralyzing metaphysical terror. People who experience these encounters usually view these archetypal figures with great awe and respect and see them as beings that belong to a superior order, are endowed with extraordinary energies and power, and have the capacity to shape events in our material world. They thus share the attitude of many pre-industrial cultures that believed in the existence of deities and demons.

However, people who have such experiences usually do not confuse the archetypal figures with the supreme principle in the universe, nor do they claim that they have gained the ultimate understanding of existence. They typically experience these deities as creations of a superior power that transcends them. This insight echoes Joseph Campbell's idea that "a useful deity should be transparent to the transcendent." They should point to the Absolute and function as bridges to it, but not be confused with it. When we are involved in systematic self-exploration or spiritual practice, it is important to avoid the pitfall of making a particular deity opaque and seeing it as the supreme cosmic force rather than a window into the Absolute.

Campbell warned that mistaking a specific archetypal image for the ultimate source of creation, or for its only true representation, leads to idolatry, a divisive and dangerous mistake that is widespread in the history of religion. It unites people who share the same belief and are willing to worship in a particular way but sets this group against other ones that have chosen a different representation of the divine. They might then try to convert others or conquer and eliminate them. By contrast, a genuine religion is universal, all-inclusive, and all-encompassing. It has to transcend specific culture-bound archetypal images and focus on the ultimate source of all forms. The most important question in the world of religion is thus the nature of the supreme principle in the universe.

Experience of the Supreme Cosmic Principle

Individuals involved in systematic self-exploration with the use of holotropic states of consciousness repeatedly describe this process as a philosophical and spiritual quest. As mentioned earlier, this inspired me to search the records from psychedelic and Holotropic Breathwork sessions, as well as reports from people who were undergoing spiritual emergency, for experiences which would convey the sense that this quest had reached its final destination. I found out that people whose experience of the Absolute fully satisfied their spiritual longing typically did not see any specific figurative images. When they felt that they had attained the goal of their mystical and philosophical quest, their descriptions of the supreme principle were highly abstract and strikingly similar.

Those who reported such an ultimate revelation were in quite remarkable agreement when describing the experiential characteristics of this state. They reported that the experience of the Supreme involved transcendence of all the limitations of the analytical mind, all rational categories, and all the constraints of ordinary logic. This experience was not bound by the usual limitations of three-dimensional space and linear time as we understand them. It also contained all conceivable polarities in an inseparable amalgam and thus transcended dualities of any kind.

Time after time, my clients and trainees compared the Absolute to a radiant source of light of unimaginable intensity, but they also emphasized that it differed in some significant aspects from any form of light that we know in the material world. To describe the Absolute as light, as much as it seems appropriate in a certain sense, entirely misses some of its essential characteristics. In particular, it misses the fact that it is also an immense and unfathomable field of consciousness that is endowed with infinite intelligence and profound creativity. Another attribute that is regularly mentioned is that it definitely has distinct personal characteristics and an exquisite sense of humor ("cosmic humor").

The supreme cosmic principle can be experienced in two different ways. Sometimes, all personal boundaries dissolve, or are drastically obliterated, and we completely merge with the divine source, becoming indistinguishable from it. Other times, we maintain the sense of separate identity, assuming the role of an astonished observer who is witnessing, as if from outside, the *mysterium tremendum* of existence. We might also assume a filial attitude to the Divine, experiencing it as a Father or Mother. Following the example of St. Teresa of Avila, the bhaktas, or the mystics such as described by the thirteenth-century Persian transcendental poet Rumi, we might also feel the ecstasy of an enraptured lover, experiencing the Divine as the Beloved.

Spiritual literature of all ages abounds in descriptions of both types of experiences of the Divine. A good historical example is the exchange between Sri Ramana Maharshi, Hindu sage and teacher of *Advaita Vedanta,* non-dual meditation, and Sri Ramakrishna, a bhakta worshipper of the goddess Kali. Sri Ramana Maharshi illustrated the non-dual experience through the story of a sugar doll who went for a swim in the ocean because she wanted to experience its depth, and completely dissolved in its water. Sri Ramakrishna countered: "I want to taste sugar, I don't want to be sugar!" Modern consciousness research suggests that both ways of experiencing the Absolute represent major spiritual breakthroughs, leading to positive changes in personality structure, ecstatic feelings of peace and security, and access to higher meaning.

The Cosmic Abyss:
Supracosmic and Metacosmic Void

The encounter with Absolute Consciousness or identification with it is not the only way to experience the supreme creative principle of the Cosmos or the Ultimate Reality. The second type of experience that seems to satisfy those who search for ultimate answers is particularly surprising, since it has no specific content. It is the identification with Cosmic Emptiness and Nothingness as described in mystical literature as the Void. It is important to emphasize that not every experience of emptiness that we can encounter in holotropic states qualifies as the Void. People very often use this term to describe an unpleasant lack of feeling, initiative, content, or meaning. To deserve the name Void, this state has to meet very specific criteria.

When we encounter the Void, we feel that it is a primordial empti- ness of cosmic proportions and relevance. We become pure consciousness aware of this absolute nothingness; however, at the same time, we have a strange paradoxical sense of its essential fullness. This *cosmic vacuum* is also a *plenum,* since nothing seems to be missing in it. While it does not contain anything in a concrete manifest form, it seems to contain all of existence in a potential form. The Void transcends the usual categories of time and space. It is unchangeable, and lies beyond all dichotomies and polarities, such as light and darkness, good and evil, stability and motion, microcosm and macrocosm, agony and ecstasy, singularity and plurality, form and emptiness, and even existence and nonexistence.

Some people call it the Supracosmic and Metacosmic Void, indicating that this primordial emptiness and nothingness appears to be the principle that underlies the phenomenal world as we know it, creates it, and, at the same time, is superordinated to it. This metaphysical vacuum, pregnant with infinite potential, appears to be the cradle of all being, the ultimate source of existence. The Cosmic Abyss has the intelligence, creativity, and immense energy necessary to create universes. The creation of all phenom- enal worlds is then the realization and concretization of its preexisting inherent potentialities. It is impossible to convey in words how experientially convincing and logical these paradoxical answers are to the most basic and profound questions about existence. Full understanding of these extraordinary states requires direct personal experience.

Hungarian-Italian researcher Ervin László, the world's foremost system theorist and philosopher of science, called this mysterious realm beyond space and time the Akashic Holofield. In one of his recent books, *What Is Reality: The New Map of Cosmos, Consciousness, and Existence,* László brings together a rich array of scientific fields, philosophy, and metaphysics, and proposes a brilliant new paradigm (László 2016). László's connectivity hypothesis offers a solution for many paradoxes that plague various disciplines of modern Western science and provides a bridge between science and spirituality (László 2003).

The Beyond Within

In systematic spiritual practice involving holotropic states of consciousness, we can repeatedly transcend the ordinary boundaries of the body-ego. In this process, we also discover that any boundaries in the material universe and in other realities are ultimately arbitrary and negotiable. By shedding the limitations of the rational mind and the straitjacket of common sense and everyday logic, we can break through many separating barriers, expand our consciousness to normally unimaginable dimensions, and eventually experience union and identity with the transcendental source of all being, known in spiritual literature by many different names.

When we reach experiential identification with the Absolute, we realize that our own being is ultimately commensurate with the entire field of cosmic creative energy, with all of existence. The recognition of our own divine nature, our identity with the cosmic source, is the most important discovery we can make during the process of deep self-exploration. This is the essence of the famous answer to the question about our true identity found in the ancient Indian Chandogya Upanishad: *"Tat tvam asi."* The literal translation of this sentence is "Thou are That," meaning "you are of divine nature," or "you are Godhead." It reveals that our everyday identification with the "skin-encapsulated ego," embodied individual consciousness, or "name and form" *(namarupa)* is an illusion and that our true nature is our identity with the entire field of cosmic creative energy (Atman-Brahman).

At the beginning of this encyclopedia, we discussed that the revelation concerning the identity of the individual with the divine is the ultimate secret that lies at the core of all great spiritual traditions. We have illustrated this with many concrete examples from the great religions of the world (pp. 5, Volume I).

Words for the Ineffable

The supreme cosmic principle can be directly experienced in holotropic states of consciousness, but it eludes any attempts at adequate description or explanation. The language that we use to communicate about matters of daily life simply is not adequate for this task. Individuals who have had this experience seem to agree that it is ineffable. Words and the structure of our language are painfully inappropriate tools to describe its nature and dimensions, particularly to those who have not experienced it. Lao-tzu, the legendary Chinese Taoist philosopher, expressed it very succinctly in his classic text Tao-Te-Ching: "The Tao that can be told of is not the eternal Tao; The name that can be named is not the eternal name."

Any attempts at describing transcendental experiences have to rely on the words of the colloquial language that has been developed to communicate about objects and activities as we experience them in the ordinary state of consciousness. For this reason, language proves to be inappropriate and inadequate when we want to talk about the experiences and insights encountered in various holotropic states of consciousness. This is particularly true when our experiences focus on the ultimate problems of existence, such as the Void, Absolute Consciousness, and creation.

Those who are familiar with Eastern spiritual philosophies often resort to words from various Asian languages when describing their spiritual experiences and insights. They use Sanskrit, Tibetan, Chinese, or Japanese terms. These languages were developed in cultures with great sophistication in regard to holotropic states and spiritual experiences. Unlike the Western languages, they contain many technical terms specifically describing nuances of the mystical experiences and related issues, such as *nirvikalpa* and *savikalpa samadhi, sunyata, kenshō, satori, Tao, nirvana, Kundalini, chi* or *ki energy, bardo, anatta, samsāra, maya,* and *avidyā.* Ultimately, though, even these words can be understood only by those who have had the corresponding experiences.

Poetry, although still a highly imperfect tool, seems to be a more adequate and appropriate means for conveying the essence of spiritual experiences and for communicating about transcendental realities. For this reason, many of the great visionaries and religious teachers resorted to poetry while sharing their metaphysical insights. Many people who have experienced transcendental states recall and quote pertinent passages from the work of visionary poets, such as Omar Khayyam, Rumi, Kahlil Gibran, Kabir, princess Mirabai, Sri Aurobindo, William Blake, D. H. Lawrence, Rainer Maria Rilke, Walt Whitman, or William Butler Yeats.

The Process of Creation

People, who in their holotropic states of consciousness experience the cosmic creative principle, often envision the process of creation and become fascinated by its immense scale and grand design. They try to understand the nature of the impulse that moves the Divine to abandon its pristine state and take on the formidable task of creating what seems to be an infinite number of phenomenal worlds. They seem to agree that these worlds are created through an orchestration of experiences, and that they are virtual rather than material. However, the insights concerning why creation happens and what is the "motivation" of the Divine to generate countless phenomenal realities within itself and from itself contain some interesting contradictions.

One important category of these insights emphasizes the fantastic inner richness and inconceivable creative potential of Absolute Consciousness. The cosmic source is so overabundant and overflowing with possibilities that it simply has to give itself expression in the creative act. Another group of insights revealed that Absolute Consciousness also seeks, in the process of creation, something that it lacks and misses in its original pristine state. From an ordinary perspective, these two categories of insights might seem to contradict each other. In holotropic states, this conflict disappears, and the two seeming opposites can easily coexist and actually complement each other.

A biologist participating in our training program was reflecting about the impulse of the Divine to create, as he had experienced it in his LSD session, and found some distant similarity between this process and what he had seen when he observed fertilized eggs. The enormous creative potential of the fertilized egg was at first dormant. Then the seeming inertia of the protoplasm was suddenly interrupted by an impulse, which created ripples and initiated the process of cellular division and embryonic growth. Another of my clients compared the process that leads to cosmic creation with the state of mind of an artist, who experiences inspiration and conceives a great work of art, which then assumes a life of its own.

Other descriptions emphasized the immense desire of the Divine to get to know itself and to discover, explore, and experience its hidden potential. This can only be done by exteriorization and manifestation of all the latent possibilities in the form of a concrete creative act. It requires polarization into subject and object, the experiencer and the experienced, the observer and the observed. A similar idea can be found in medieval kabbalistic scriptures, according to which God's motive for creation is that "Face wants to behold Face" or "Gods wants to see God."

Additional important dimensions of the creative process that have often been emphasized are the playfulness, self-delectation, and cosmic humor of the Creator. These are elements that have been described best in ancient Hindu texts, which talk about the universe and existence as *lila*, or Divine Play. According to this view, creation is an intricate, infinitely complex cosmic game that the godhead, Brahman, creates from itself and within itself.

Creation can also be viewed as a colossal experiment that expresses the immense curiosity of Absolute Consciousness, a passion that is analogous to the infatuation of a scientist who dedicates his or her life to exploration and research. Some people who have experienced insights into the "motives" for creation also point out its aesthetic side, as we saw earlier. From this perspective, the universe we live in and all the experiential realities in other dimensions also appear to be ultimate works of art. The impulse to create them can be likened to the inspiration and creative passion of the supreme artist.

As we also saw, sometimes the insights concerning the forces underlying creation do not reflect overflowing abundance, richness, and mastery of the cosmic creative principle, but rather absence or lack of something important, deficiency, need, or desire. For example, it is possible to discover that, in spite of the immensity and perfection of its state of being, Absolute Consciousness realizes that it is alone. This Loneliness finds its expression in an abysmal yearning for partnership, communication, and sharing, giving and receiving love, a kind of Divine Longing.

Another important motivating force behind the creative process that has occasionally been reported in this category is the divine source's primordial craving for the experiences that characterize the material world. According to these insights, Spirit has a profound desire to experience what is opposite and contrary to its own nature. It wants to explore all the qualities that, in its pristine nature, it does not have and to become everything that it is not. Being eternal, infinite, unlimited, and ethereal, it longs for the ephemeral, impermanent, transient, limited by time and space, solid, tangible, concrete, and corporeal. This aspect of the creative process is beautifully illustrated in the Aztec (Nahuatl) Codex Borgia in a painting showing the dynamic complementary dance of two figures—the Plumed Serpent Quetzalcoatl, representing Spirit, and Tezcatlipoca (Smoking Mirror), representing Matter.

Another important "motive" for creation that is occasionally mentioned is the element of Monotony. However immense and glorious the experience of the Divine might appear from the human perspective, for the divine, it will always be the same and, therefore, monotonous. Creation can then be seen as a titanic effort expressing a transcendental longing for change, action, movement, drama, and surprise. In medieval kabbalistic scriptures, we can read that one of the motives that God has for creation is Divine Boredom.

All those who have been fortunate enough to experience profound insights into the cosmic laboratory of creation seem to agree that anything that they can say about this level of reality cannot possibly do justice to what they have witnessed. The monumental impulse of unimaginable proportions that is responsible for creating the worlds of phenomena seems to contain all the above elements, however paradoxical they might appear to our common sense, and many more. It is clear that, in spite of all our efforts to comprehend and describe creation, the nature of the creative principle and of the process of creation remains shrouded in unfathomable mystery.

It should be mentioned again that the language we are using presents a special problem for expressing what we have experienced in transcendental realms. The best we can do is to find some meek parallels and approximations in feelings that we know from our everyday life. A useful practice developed by psychiatric patients trying to describe their transpersonal experiences is to capitalize the first letters of the words they are choosing in order for them to ward off the banality of their everyday meaning and to indicate the cosmic grandeur of the feelings and states they are describing. I have adopted this practice in this section, when I refer to Divine Loneliness, Love, Longing, Craving, or Boredom.

Besides the revelations concerning the motives or reasons for creation (the "why" of creation), the experiences in holotropic states often bring illuminating insights into the specific dynamics and mechanisms of the creative process (the "how" of creation). These are related to the "technology of consciousness" that generates experiences with different sensory characteristics and, by orchestrating them in a systematic and coherent way, creates virtual realities. Although the descriptions of these insights vary in terms of details, language, and metaphors used to illustrate them, they typically distinguish two interrelated and mutually complementary processes that are involved in creating the worlds of phenomena.

The first of these is the activity that splits the original undifferentiated unity of Absolute Consciousness into infinite numbers of derived units of consciousness. The Divine engages in a creative play that involves complicated sequences of divisions, fragmentations, and differentiations. This results in experiential worlds that contain countless separate entities endowed with specific forms of consciousness which have a convincing sense of self-awareness and autonomy. There seems to be general agreement that these come into being through multiple divisions and subdivisions of the originally undivided field of Cosmic Consciousness. The Divine thus does not create something outside of itself but, through divisions and transformations, creates within the field of its own being.

The second important element in the process of creation is a unique form of partitioning, dissociation, or forgetting, through which the filial conscious entities progressively and increasingly lose contact with their original source and the awareness of their pristine nature. They also develop a sense of individual identity and absolute separateness from each other. In the final stages of this process, intangible but relatively impermeable screens exist between these split-off units and also between each of them and the original undifferentiated pool of Absolute Consciousness.

The relationship between Absolute Consciousness and its parts is unique and complex and cannot be understood in terms of conventional thinking. Aristotelian logic and our common sense tell us that a part cannot simultaneously be the whole and that the whole, being an assembly of its parts, has to be larger than any of its components and cannot be a part. In the universal fabric, separate units of consciousness, in spite of their individuality and specific differences, remain on another level essentially identical with their source and with each other. They have a paradoxical nature, being wholes and parts at the same time.

A quote from the mysterious *Emerald Tablet (Tabula Smaragdina)* of Hermes Trismegistus, "That which is Below corresponds to that which is Above, and that which is Above corresponds to that which is Below, to accomplish the miracles of the One Thing," became the inspiration of many esoteric schools, including hermeticism, alchemy, astrology, Kabbalah, and Tantra. Their basic tenet is that each human being is a microcosm that contains the macrocosm: "As above, so below," and "As without, so within."

A beautiful example of the relationship between Buddha-Nature and all creations can be found in the teachings of Avatamsaka (Hwa Yen) Buddhism about Mutual Interpenetration. Its basic idea is expressed very succinctly in four sentences: "One in One," "One in Many," "Many in Many," and "Many in One." The famous image used to illustrate this situation is the necklace in Indra's heaven in which pearls are arranged in such a way that each of them reflects all the others. The story below is a more elaborate and graphic explanation of this.

Chinese Empress Wu had difficulties understanding the complex teachings of Hwa Yen Buddhism and asked Zen Master Fatsang to explain it to her. Fatsang took her into a hall in which all walls, the ceiling, and the floor were covered with mirrors. He then lit a candle hanging in the middle of the room. In the next moment, they were surrounded by an infinite number of candles. Fatsang commented: "This is how the One is contained in all the creations."

He then reached into his pocket and took out a crystal ball. All these candles were now reflected in a single crystal. "And this is how Many are contained in the One. See, how in the Ultimate Reality the infinitely small contains the infinitely large, and the infinitely large the infinitely small, without obstruction!" He then apologized for using a simple static model to explain what is happening in an infinitely large and complex dynamic system. As we saw in Chapter 8, the basic tenet of esoteric schools regarding the relationship between the microcosm and macrocosm, which in the past seemed absurd and incomprehensible, received unexpected scientific support through the invention of optical holography.

The insights from the research of holotropic states of consciousness portray existence as an astonishing play of the cosmic creative principle that transcends time, space, linear causality, and polarities of any kind. From this perspective, the worlds of phenomena, including the material world, appear to be "virtual realities" generated by a technology of consciousness—by an infinitely complex orchestration of experiences. They exist on many different levels of reality, ranging from the undifferentiated Absolute Consciousness through rich pantheons of archetypal beings to countless humans, animals, and plants existing in the world of matter.

The Ways to Reunion

The process of successive divisions combined with increasing separation and alienation represents only one half of the cosmic cycle. The insights from holotropic states repeatedly reveal another part of this process which consists of events in consciousness that reflect a movement in the opposite direction, from the worlds of plurality and separation toward the increasing dissolution of boundaries and merging into ever larger wholes.

These insights parallel the descriptions and discussions of these two cosmic movements as described in various spiritual and philosophical systems. For example, Plotinus, the founder of Neoplatonism, talked about them as *efflux* and *reflux* (Plotinus 1991). In the East, similar concepts found their most articulate expression in the writings of the Indian mystic and philosopher Sri Aurobindo under the names of *involution* and *evolution* of consciousness (Aurobindo 1965). Modern discussion of the dynamics of *descent* and *ascent* in the cosmic process can be found in the writings of Ken Wilber (Wilber 1980, 1995). I have been using the terms hylotropic (moving toward the world of matter, from the Greek *hyle,* meaning matter and *trepo/trepein,* meaning moving toward) and holotropic (moving toward wholeness).

According to the insights from holotropic states, the universal process offers not only an infinite number of possibilities for becoming a separate individual, but also an equally rich and ingenious range of opportunities for the dissolution of boundaries and fusion that mediate the experiential return to the source. These unitive experiences make it possible for the individual monads of consciousness to overcome their alienation and free

Ken Wilber (1949–), American writer on transpersonal psychology and his own integral theory, a systematic philosophy which suggests the synthesis of all human knowledge and experience.

themselves from the delusion of their separateness. This transcendence of what previously appeared to be absolute boundaries and the resulting progressive merging creates larger and larger experiential units. In its farthest reaches, this process would dissolve all the boundaries, transcend polarities, and bring about a reunion with Absolute Consciousness. The sequences of fusions occurring in many forms and on many different levels complete the overall cyclical pattern of the cosmic dance.

The most frequent trigger of spontaneous unitive experiences is exposure to wonders of nature, such as the Grand Canyon, tropical islands, the aurora borealis, or sunsets over the Pacific Ocean. Exquisite artistic creations of extraordinary beauty can have a similar effect, whether they are musical masterpieces, great paintings and sculptures, or monumental architecture. Additional frequent sources of unitive experiences are rigorous athletic activity, sexual union, and, in women, pregnancy, delivery, and nursing. Their occurrence can be facilitated through a variety of ancient, aboriginal, and modern "technologies of the sacred," which we discussed in the introductory chapter of this encyclopedia.

While unitive experiences are most likely to happen in positive, emotionally charged situations, they can also occur under circumstances which are highly unfavorable, threatening, and critical for the individual. In this case, the ego consciousness is shattered and overwhelmed rather than dissolved and transcended. This happens during severe acute or chronic stress, at the time of intense emotional and physical suffering, or when the integrity or survival of the body are seriously threatened. Many people discover the mystical realms during near-death experiences that occur due to accidents, injuries, dangerous diseases, and operations.

Traditional psychiatrists, who do not recognize the uniqueness of mystical experiences, see unitive experiences as manifestations of psychosis. The credit for demonstrating that this is a serious error belongs to Abraham Maslow, the founder of humanistic and transpersonal psychology. He has shown, in a study of many hundreds of individuals, that these "peak experiences" are supernormal rather than abnormal phenomena. Under favorable circumstances, they can result in superior emotional and physical health and be conducive to what Maslow called "self-realization" or "self-actualization" (Maslow 1964).

The Taboo Against Knowing Who You Are

If it is true that our deepest nature is divine and that we are identical with the creative principle of the universe, how do we account for the intensity of our conviction that we are physical bodies existing in a material world? What is the nature of this fundamental ignorance concerning our true identity, this mysterious veil of forgetting that Alan Watts called "the taboo against knowing who you are" (Watts 1973)? How is it possible that an infinite and timeless spiritual entity creates from itself and within itself a virtual facsimile of a tangible reality populated by sentient beings who experience themselves as separate from their source and from each other? How can the actors in the world drama be deluded into believing in the objective existence of their illusory reality?

The best explanation I have heard from the people with whom I have worked is that the cosmic creative principle traps itself with its own perfection. The creative intention behind the divine play is to call experiential realities into being that would offer the best opportunities for adventures in consciousness, including the illusion of the material world. To meet this requirement, these realities have to be convincing and believable in all details. As an example of this, works of art such as theater plays or movies can occasionally be enacted and performed with such perfection that they make us forget that the events we are witnessing are illusory and react to them as if they were real. Also, a good actor or actress can sometimes lose their true identity and temporarily merge with the character they are portraying.

The world in which we live has many characteristics that the supreme principle in its pure form is missing, such as polarity, multiplicity, density and physicality, change, and impermanence. The project of creating a facsimile of a material reality endowed with these properties is executed with such artistic and scientific perfection that the split-off units of the Universal Mind find it entirely convincing and mistake it for reality. In the extreme expression of its artistry, represented by the atheist, the Divine actually succeeds in bringing forth arguments not only against its involvement in creation, but against its very existence. Sri Aurobindo's definition of an atheist was: "God playing hide and seek with himself."

One of the important ploys that help to create the illusion of an ordinary material reality is the existence of the trivial and ugly. If we were all radiant ethereal beings, drawing our life energy directly from the sun and living in a world where all the landscapes looked like the Himalayas or Grand Canyon, the Arctic aurora borealis, and unspoiled Pacific islands, it would be too obvious that we live in a divine realm. Similarly, if all the buildings in our world looked like Alhambra, Taj Mahal, Xanadu, or the Cathedral in Chartres and we were surrounded by Michelangelo's sculptures and listening to Beethoven's or Bach's music, the divine nature of our world would be easily discernible.

The fact that we have physical bodies with all their secretions, excretions, odors, imperfections, and pathologies, as well as a gastrointestinal system with its repulsive contents is certainly effective in obscuring and confusing the issue of our divinity. Various physiological functions like vomiting, burping, passing gas, defecating, and urinating, together with the final decomposition of the human body, further complicate the picture. Similarly, the existence of unattractive natural sceneries, junkyards, polluted industrial areas, foul-smelling toilets with obscene graffiti, urban ghettoes, and millions of funky houses make it very difficult to realize that our life is a divine play. The existence of evil and the fact that the very nature of life is predatory makes this task almost impossible for an average person. For educated Westerners, the worldview created by materialistic science is an additional serious hurdle.

There is another important reason why it is so difficult to free ourselves from the delusion that we are separate individuals living in a material world. The ways to reunion with the divine source are fraught with many hardships, risks, and challenges. The divine play is not a completely closed system. It offers the protagonists the possibility to discover the true nature of creation, including their own cosmic status. However, the ways leading out of self-deception to enlightenment and to reunion with the source present serious problems, and most of the potential loopholes in creation are carefully covered. This is absolutely necessary for the maintenance of stability and balance in the cosmic scheme. These vicissitudes and pitfalls of the spiritual path represent an important part of the "taboo against knowing who we are."

All the situations that provide opportunities for spiritual opening are typically associated with a variety of strong opposing forces. Some of the obstacles that make the way to liberation and enlightenment extremely difficult and dangerous are intrapsychic in nature. Major breakthroughs, such as psychospiritual death and rebirth, are preceded by terrifying encounters with evil forces, a consuming fear of death, and the specter of insanity. Such experiences can deter less courageous and determined seekers. This situation is very graphically illustrated in the Tōdai-ji Temple in Nara, where before entering the Great Buddha Hall hosting the giant breathtaking sculpture of Buddha Vairochana (Daibutsu), the largest bronze Buddha statue in the world, the visitors must pass through a gate flanked by colossal figures of terrifying temple guardians.

Even more problematic are various interferences and interventions that come from the external world. In the Middle Ages, many people who had spontaneous mystical experiences risked torture, trial, and execution by the Holy Inquisition. In our time, stigmatizing psychiatric labels and drastic therapeutic measures replaced accusations of witchcraft, torture, and *autos-da-fé*. Materialistic scientism of the twentieth century has ridiculed and pathologized any spiritual effort, no matter how well-founded and sophisticated. The authority and prestige that materialistic science had until recently in modern society because of its technological achievements made it difficult to take mysticism seriously and pursue the path of spiritual discovery.

In addition, the dogmas and activities of mainstream religions tend to obscure the fact that the only place where true spirituality can be found is inside the psyche of each of us. At its worst, organized religion can actually function as a grave impediment for any serious spiritual search, rather than an institution that can help people connect with the Divine. By denigrating its members and instilling guilt in them, it makes it difficult for them to believe that they can find the divinity within themselves. It might also cultivate the false belief that regular attendance of formal divine service, prayer, and financial contributions to the church are adequate and sufficient spiritual activities that make a serious spiritual quest unnecessary.

The technologies of the sacred developed by various aboriginal cultures have been dismissed in the West as products of magical thinking and primitive superstitions of uneducated natives. The spiritual potential of sexuality that finds its expression in Tantra is far outweighed by the pitfalls of sex as a powerful animal instinct. The advent of psychedelic medicines that have the capacity to open wide the gates to the transcendental dimension was soon followed by irresponsible secular misuse of these compounds and then threats made toward explorers about bad trips, flashbacks, insanity, alleged chromosomal damage, and draconian legal sanctions.

The Problem of Good and Evil

One of the most challenging tasks of the spiritual journey is to come to terms with the existence of evil. Final understanding and philosophical acceptance of evil always seems to involve the recognition that it has an important or even necessary role in the cosmic process. For example, deep experiential insights into ultimate realities that become available in holotropic states might reveal that cosmic creation has to be symmetrical, since it is *creatio ex nihilo*. Everything that emerges into existence has to be counterbalanced by its opposite. From this perspective, the existence of polarities of all kinds is an absolutely indispensable prerequisite for the creation of phenomenal worlds.

It was also mentioned earlier that one of the motives for creation seems to be the "need" of the creative principle to get to know itself, so that "God can see God" or "Face can behold Face." To the extent to which the Divine creates in order to explore its own inner potential, not expressing the full range of this potential would mean incomplete self-knowledge. If Absolute Consciousness is also the ultimate Artist, Experimenter, and Explorer, it would compromise the richness of creation to leave out some significant options. Artists do not limit their topics to those that are beautiful, ethical, and uplifting. They portray any aspects of life that can render interesting images or promise intriguing stories.

The existence of the shadow side of creation enhances its light aspects by providing contrast and gives extraordinary richness and depth to the universal drama. The conflict between good and evil in all domains and on all levels of existence is an inexhaustible source of inspiration for fascinating stories. A disciple once asked Sri Ramakrishna, the great Indian visionary, saint, and spiritual teacher, "Swamiji, why is evil in the world?" After a short deliberation, Ramakrishna replied succinctly, "To thicken the plot."

This answer might appear cynical in view of the nature and scope of suffering in the world, seen in the concrete form of millions of children dying of starvation or various diseases, the insanity of wars throughout history, countless sacrificed and tortured victims, and the desolation of natural disasters killing thousands of people.

However, when we conduct a mental experiment in which we try to sanitize creation by eliminating all that we consider bad or evil, such as diseases and violence, from the universal scheme, we will get a different picture. Starting with diseases, we quickly realize that such an act of ethical sanitation will also eliminate from the world many aspects of existence that we value and appreciate enormously—healers of all ages, the history of medicine, the invention of medications and surgical interventions that save lives, and all the good Samaritans who have dedicated their lives to alleviate suffering, such as Florence Nightingale and Mother Teresa.

If we imagine a world in which there is no violence or war, we eliminate the triumphs of victory over tyrants, dictators, and oppressive regimes, the heroism of freedom fighters, all the creative intelligence and advances in technology that were developed during the making of weapons and inventing defenses and protection against them—fortresses and fortified castles, the armor of Samurai warriors and medieval knights, colorful pageantry and parades, and all the books, movies, music, paintings, and sculptures inspired by war and the conflicts between good and evil—not to mention the ecstatic ending of wars and efforts to transcend our violent impulses by resolving them internally in deep self-exploration. Would we also eliminate all the animals who live on other animals or attack humans? And what about violent forces of nature, such as earthquakes, volcanic eruptions, storms, and tsunamis? Such a radical purging of the universal shadow would strip creation of its immense depth and richness. Manuals for writing screenplays usually start with a warning: "If you want to create a guaranteed flop at the box office, make a movie about a peaceful village where everybody is happy and nothing bad ever happens." As we can see, the problem of the existence of evil is the most challenging task in any quest to embrace and affirm the Universe.

One important thing has to be considered when we are discussing the problem of good and evil. In the last analysis, all sentient beings are manifestations of the same creative principle, so that all roles in the cosmic play—perpetrators and victims—have the same protagonist. This can be beautifully illustrated by several passages from Thich Nhat Hanh's poem "Call Me by My True Names:"

> The rhythm of my heart is the birth and
> death of all that are alive.
> I am the mayfly metamorphosing on the surface of the river,
> and I am the bird which, when spring comes, arrives in time
> to eat the mayfly.
> …I am the twelve-year-old girl, refugee on a small boat, who
> throws herself into the ocean after being raped by a sea pirate,
> and I am the pirate, my heart not yet capable of seeing and
> loving.
> …Please call me by my true names,
> so I can hear all my cries and laughs at once,
> so I can see that my joy and pain are one.

This way of looking at ethical issues can be very disturbing, in spite of the fact that it is based on very convincing personal experiences in holotropic states. The problems become obvious as we start thinking about the practical consequences that such a perspective has for our life and our everyday conduct. At first sight, seeing the material world as a "virtual reality" and comparing human existence to a movie seems to trivialize life and make light of the depth of human misery. It might appear that such a perspective denies the seriousness of human suffering and fosters an attitude of cynical indifference, where nothing really matters. Similarly, accepting evil as an integral part of creation and seeing its relativity could easily be seen as a justification for suspending any ethical constraints and for the unlimited pursuit of egotistical goals. It might also seem to sabotage any effort to actively combat evil in the world.

Before we can fully appreciate the ethical implications that deep transcendental insights can have for our behavior, we have to take into consideration some additional factors. The experiential exploration that makes such profound insights available typically reveals important biographical, perinatal, and transpersonal sources of violence and greed in our unconscious. Psychological work on this material leads to a significant reduction of aggression and to an increase of tolerance. We also encounter a large spectrum of transpersonal experiences in which we identify with various aspects of creation. This results in a deep reverence for life and empathy with all sentient beings. The same process through which we are discovering the emptiness of forms and the relativity of ethical values thus also significantly reduces our proclivity to immoral and antisocial behavior. It teaches us love and compassion.

We can then develop a new system of values that is not based on conventional norms, precepts, commandments, and fear of punishment, but on our knowledge and understanding of the universal order. We realize that we are an integral part of creation and that by hurting others, we would be hurting ourselves. In addition, deep self-exploration leads to the experiential discovery of reincarnation and the law of karma. This brings us awareness of the possibility of serious experiential repercussions of harmful behaviors, including those that escape societal retributions.

Practical experience also shows that the awareness of the emptiness behind all forms is not at all incompatible with genuine appreciation and love for all creation. Transcendental experiences leading to profound metaphysical insights into the nature of reality actually engender reverence and compassion toward all sentient beings and responsible engagement in the process of life. Our compassion does not require objects that have a material substance. It can just as easily be addressed to sentient beings who are units of consciousness.

Playing the Cosmic Game

For many religions, the strategy for dealing with the hardships of life is to play down the importance of the earthly plane and to focus on the transcendental realms. The religious systems with this orientation portray the material world as an inferior domain that is imperfect, impure, and conducive to suffering and misery. They recommend a shift in attention and emphasis from the material world to other realities. From their point of view, physical reality appears to be a valley of tears and incarnate existence a curse or a quagmire of death and rebirth.

These creeds and their officials offer their dedicated followers the promise of a more desirable domain or a more fulfilling state of consciousness in the Beyond. In more primitive forms of popular beliefs, these are various forms of abodes of the blessed, paradises, or heavens. These become available after death for those who meet the necessary requirements as defined by their respective theology. For more sophisticated and refined systems of this kind, heavens and paradises are only stages of the spiritual journey, and its final destination is dissolution of personal boundaries and union with the divine, reaching the state of a pristine monad uncontaminated by biology, or extinguishing the fire of life and disappearance into Nothingness.

However, other spiritual orientations embrace nature and the material world as containing or embodying the Divine. Using the insights from holotropic states, seekers question what they might actually gain from moving away from life and escaping from the material plane into transcendental realities? And, conversely, what is the value of wholeheartedly embracing the world of everyday reality? Many spiritual systems define the goal of the spiritual journey as the dissolution of personal boundaries and reunion with the Divine. However, those people who have experienced identification with Absolute Consciousness in their inner explorations realize that defining the final goal of the spiritual journey as the experience of oneness with the supreme principle of existence involves a serious problem.

They become aware that the undifferentiated Absolute Consciousness/ Void represents not only the end of the spiritual journey, but also the source and the beginning of creation. The Divine is the principle offering reunion for the separated, but also the agent responsible for the division and separation of the original unity. If this principle were complete and self-fulfilling in its pristine form, there would not be any reason for it to create and the other experiential realms would not exist. Since they do, the tendency of Absolute Consciousness to create clearly expresses a fundamental "need." The worlds of plurality thus represent an important complement to the undifferentiated state of the Divine. In the terminology of the Kabbalah, "people need God and God needs people."

The overall scheme of this cosmic drama involves a dynamic interplay of two fundamental forces, one of which is centrifugal (*hylotropic,* or matter-oriented) and the other centripetal (*holotropic,* or aiming for wholeness)

Gnostic Man. The frontispiece to the first volume of Roberto Fludd's *Uriusque Cosmi* written in 1617.

in relation to the creative principle. The undifferentiated Cosmic Consciousness shows an elemental tendency to create worlds of plurality that contain countless separate beings. We have already discussed some of the possible reasons or motives for this propensity to generate virtual realities as it appears in holotropic states. Conversely, the individualized units of consciousness experience their separation and alienation as painful and manifest a strong need to return to the source and reunite with it. Identification with the embodied self is fraught, among others, with the problems of emotional and physical suffering, spatial and temporal limitations, impermanence, and death.

If it is true that our psyche is governed by these two powerful cosmic forces, hylotropic and holotropic, and that these two are in fundamental conflict with each other, is there an approach to existence that can adequately cope with this situation? Since neither separate existence nor undifferentiated unity is fully satisfactory in and of itself, what is the alternative? Clearly, the solution is not to reject embodied existence as inferior and worthless and try to escape from it. We have seen that phenomenal worlds, including the world of matter, represent not only an important and valuable, but also absolutely necessary, complement to the undifferentiated state of the creative principle. At the same time, our efforts to reach fulfillment and peace of mind will necessarily fail, and possibly backfire, if they involve only objects and goals in the material realm. Any satisfactory solution will thus have to embrace both the earthly and the transcendental dimensions, both the world of forms and the Formless.

The material universe as we know it offers countless possibilities for extraordinary adventures in consciousness. As embodied selves, we can witness the spectacle of the heavens with its billions of galaxies and the natural wonders on earth. Only in the physical form and on the material plane can we fall in love, enjoy the ecstasy of lovemaking, have children, listen to Beethoven's music, or admire Rembrandt's paintings. The opportunities for the explorations of the microworld and the macroworld are virtually unlimited. In addition to the experiences of the present, there is also the adventure of probing the mysterious past, from lost ancient civilizations and the antediluvian world to the events during the first microseconds of the Big Bang.

To participate in the phenomenal world and to be able to experience this rich spectrum of adventures requires a certain degree of identification with the embodied self and acceptance of the world of matter. However, when our identification with the body-ego is absolute and our belief in the material world as the only reality is unshatterable, it is impossible to fully enjoy our participation in creation. The specters of personal insignificance, impermanence, and death can completely overshadow the positive side of life and rob us of its zest. We also have to include the frustration that comes from our attempts to realize our full divine potential while constrained by the limitations of our bodies and of the material world.

To find the solution to this dilemma, we have to turn inside, to a systematic inner quest. As we keep discovering and exploring various hidden dimensions of ourselves and of reality, our identification with the body-ego becomes progressively looser and less compelling. We continue to identify with the "skin-encapsulated ego" for pragmatic purposes, but this orientation becomes increasingly more tentative and playful. If we have sufficient experiential knowledge of the transpersonal dimensions of existence, including our own true identity and cosmic status, everyday life becomes much easier and more rewarding.

As our inner search continues, we also discover, sooner or later, the essential emptiness behind all forms. As the Buddhist teachings suggest, knowledge of the virtual nature of the phenomenal world and its voidness can help us achieve freedom from suffering. This includes the recognition that belief in any separate selves in our life, including our own, is ultimately an illusion. In Buddhist texts, the awareness of the essential emptiness of all forms and the ensuing realization that there are no separate selves is referred to as *anatta (anatman),* literally "no-self."

Awareness of our divine nature and of the essential emptiness of all things, which we discover in our transpersonal experiences, form the foundations of a meta-framework that can be of considerate help to us in coping with the complexity of everyday existence. We can fully embrace the experiences of the material world and enjoy all that it has to offer. However, no matter what we do, life will bring obstacles, challenges, painful experiences, and losses. When things get too difficult and devastating, we can call on the broader cosmic perspective that we have discovered in our inner quest.

The connection with higher realities and the liberating knowledge of *anatta,* and the emptiness behind all forms, makes it possible to tolerate what otherwise might seem unbearable. With the help of this transcendental awareness, we might be able to fully experience the entire spectrum of life, or "the whole catastrophe," as Zorba the Greek called it. The ability to successfully reconcile and integrate the material and spiritual aspects of existence, or the hylotropic and the holotropic dimensions of life, belongs to the loftiest aspirations of the mystical traditions.

A person whose existence is limited to the pedestrian level of everyday consciousness and who has not had experiential access to the transcendental and numinous dimensions of reality will find it very difficult to overcome their deep-seated fear of death and find deeper meaning in life. Under these circumstances, much of the daily behavior is motivated by the needs of the false ego and significant aspects of life are reactive and inauthentic.

For this reason, it is essential to complement our everyday practical activities with some form of systematic spiritual practice that provides experiential access to transcendental realms. In pre-industrial societies, this opportunity existed in the form of various "technologies of the sacred"— shamanic rituals, rites of passage, healing ceremonies, ancient mysteries of death and rebirth, mystical schools, and the meditation practices of the great religions of the world. This important dimension of existence was all but destroyed by the Industrial and Scientific Revolutions with their materialistic philosophy and pragmatic orientation.

In recent decades, the Western world has seen a significant revival of interest in the ancient spiritual practices and in aboriginal consciousness-expanding procedures. In addition, modern depth psychology and experiential psychotherapy have developed effective new approaches that can facilitate spiritual awakening and opening. These tools are available to all those who are interested in psychospiritual transformation and consciousness evolution.

C. G. Jung, the forefather of transpersonal psychology, described a life strategy in his writings that addresses both the secular and cosmic dimensions of ourselves and of existence. He suggested that whatever we do in our everyday life should be complemented by systematic self-exploration, by an inner search reaching into the deepest hidden recesses of our psyche. This makes it possible to connect to a higher aspect of ourselves that Jung called the Self, and to receive its guidance on the way to "individuation."

If we follow Jung's advice, important decisions in our life will be based on a creative synthesis, integrating the pragmatic knowledge of the material world with the wisdom drawn from the collective unconscious. This idea from the great Swiss psychiatrist is in general agreement with the insights and observations from holotropic states of consciousness that have been reported by the people with whom I have had the privilege to work over the last six decades.

It is my personal belief that this strategy of existence would not only greatly enhance the quality of our individual lives but, practiced on a sufficiently large scale, could also significantly improve our chances of overcoming the current global crisis that threatens the survival of life on this planet. It could return a spirituality based on deep personal experience and a sense of meaning in human life, and of the importance of our existence, to the industrial civilization. Over the years, I have witnessed such transformation in many thousands of people. However, whether it can be achieved on a sufficiently large scale and whether we have enough time remains an open question.

I hope that the current renaissance of interest in psychedelic research and in holotropic states of consciousness will continue and make it possible for people living in the industrial civilization to join the rest of humanity in incorporating responsible psychonautics into its social fabric. This would fulfill Albert Hofmann's dream of the New Eleusis, which was born seventy-five years ago. If at least some of you who are already practicing psychonautics and those who are about to embark on this exciting adventure find this encyclopedia to be a useful companion on your inner travels, then it has not been written in vain. I wish you safe, exciting, and productive journeys!

Stanislav Grof, M.D., Ph.D.
Corfu, Greece
July 2018

Literature

Aurobindo, Sri. 1977. *The Life Divine.* New York: India Library Society.

Bohm, D. 1980. *Wholeness and the Implicate Order.* London: Routledge & Kegan Paul.

Corbin, H. 2000. "Mundus Imaginalis, Or the Imaginary and the Imaginal." In: *Working With Images* (B. Sells, ed.). Woodstock, CT: Spring Publications.

Grof, S, 1972. LSD and the Cosmic Game: Outline of Psychedelic Cosmology and Ontology. *Journal for the Study of Consciousness* 5:165, 1972-3.

Grof, S. 1998. *The Cosmic Game: Explorations of the Frontiers of Human Consciousness.* Albany, NY: State University of New York (SUNY) Press.

Jung, C. G. 1959. *The Archetypes and the Collective Unconscious.* Collected Works, Vol. 9,1. Bollingen Series XX, Princeton, NJ: Princeton University Press.

Huxley, A.: 1945. *Perennial Philosophy.* London and New York: Harper and Brothers.

Laszlo, E. 2003. *The Connectivity Hypothesis: Foundations of An Integral Science of Quantum, Cosmos, Life, and Consciousness.* Albany, NY: State University of New York (SUNY) Press.

Laszlo, E. 2016. *What Is Reality: The New Map of Cosmos, Consciousness, and Existence.* New York: Select Books.

Maslow, A. 1962. *Toward A Psychology of Being.* Princeton, NJ: Van Nostrand.

Maslow, A. 1964. *Religions, Values, and Peak Experiences.* Cleveland, OH: Ohio State University.

Plotinus, 1991. *The Enneads.* London: Penguin Books.

Watts, A. 1973. *The Book on the Taboo Against Knowing Who You Are.* London: Sphere Books.

Wilber, K. 1980. *The Atman Project: A Transpersonal View of Human Development.* Wheaton, IL: Theosophical Publishing House.

Wilber, K. 1995. *Sex, Ecology, and Spirituality: The Spirit of Evolution.* Boston, MA: Shambhala Publications.

Epilogue:
Psyche and Cosmos
by Richard Tarnas, Ph.D.

In the following pages, at Stanislav Grof's request, I have briefly outlined the research on which he and I have collaborated over the past four decades. Although during this time we have co-taught many graduate courses and public seminars that presented our ongoing findings, we have not published a basic overview of the research, despite how influential it has been for both of us in understanding the psyche and its transformational processes. With the current reemergence of legalized psychedelic psychotherapy and research, however, it may be appropriate now to introduce here to a wider public at least a brief summation of the evidence and its potential relevance for psychotherapy and self-exploration working with psychedelics and other transformational methods that involve non-ordinary states of consciousness.

Background of Our Research

After his years of practicing psychotherapy using LSD and other psychedelic substances, first in Prague and later in Maryland, Stan moved in the fall of 1973 to Esalen Institute in Big Sur, California, to work on the series of books that would summarize his clinical findings. A few months after he arrived there, I joined him to work under his supervision on my doctoral dissertation on LSD psychotherapy. The move to Esalen turned out to be long-term and pivotal for both of us. During the greater part of the 1970s and 1980s, Stan served as Esalen's Scholar-in-Residence and led many month-long seminars, while I, first as staff member and later as Esalen's director of programs and education, collaborated with him on the research recounted below. In 1993–94, we both joined the faculty of the California Institute of Integral Studies in San Francisco where we would teach for the next twenty years.

At the start of our work together at Esalen, we were interested in the radical variability of psychedelic experiences, a phenomenon widely observed but not well understood. Two individuals of similar clinical status could ingest the same substance, the same number of micrograms, in the same clinical setting, and yet could undergo extremely different experiences. One subject might have an experience of deep spiritual unity and euphoric mystical transcendence, while another who had received the identical substance and dosage might confront a state of sustained metaphysical panic or a condition of bottomless despair that promised never to resolve. Similarly, the same person at different times could have strikingly different psychedelic experiences. The variability also took another form, in which different individuals seemed to be constitutionally prone to encounter certain enduring constellations of related experiences—particular complexes, emotionally charged biographical memories, perinatal matrices, transpersonal encounters—in an evolving way through multiple psychedelic sessions, reflecting specific persistent themes in their life's personal journey. Each individual seemed to have his or her own characteristic set of enduring themes that in the course of time could take variable forms, with either positive or negative inflections at multiple levels of consciousness, often in the same session.

Stan and his colleagues in Prague and Baltimore had long sought a reliable way to predict the nature and outcome of psychedelic sessions, hoping to find tools that would be helpful for anticipating how different individuals might react to psychedelic therapy and whether they would benefit from it. Yet years of research on the problem had been unsuccessful, as none of the standard psychological tests—the MMPI (Minnesota Multiphasic Personality Inventory), POI (Personal Orientation Inventory), TAT (Thematic Apperception Test), Rorschach Test, Wechsler Adult Intelligence Scale, and others—proved to have any predictive value for this purpose. Such an outcome was in a sense understandable for at least the second form of variability, involving the same person taking the same substance at different times, because retesting individuals with standard psychological tests typically does not change the results. If one tests today and tests again a month from today, the results will not significantly change, whereas if a subject takes LSD today and then takes the same dose next month, the session could be altogether different. Yet given the intensity of psychedelic experiences, the possibility of being able to anticipate how different individuals might respond to such therapy, perhaps even how the same individual might respond at different times, impelled the hope that a useful method might someday be found.

While we were not fully aware of it at the time, several decades earlier C. G. Jung had opened up another possible approach to this variability in psychological experience. On the basis of lengthy studies of various esoteric systems, he came to regard astrology as providing an extraordinary window for understanding the qualitative dimension of time, and specifically the archetypal dynamics at work at any particular time, including that of birth. He posited that time was not merely quantitative, an ongoing neutral or homogeneous continuum, but rather possessed an intrinsically qualitative dimension. More surprisingly, he came to believe that the qualitative dimension of time was intrinsically connected in some undetermined manner to the positions of the Sun, Moon, and planets relative to the Earth. As he wrote in *Memories, Dreams, Reflections,* "Our psyche is set up in accord with the structure of the universe, and what happens in the macrocosm likewise happens in the infinitesimal and most subjective reaches of the psyche."[i] In his later years Jung came to employ the analysis of birth charts as a regular aspect of his analytical work with patients. Yet given the intellectual climate of his time, and indeed of our own time, one can well appreciate his reluctance to make more public the extent of his

---

[i] Jung, C. G., *Memories, Dreams, Reflections* (New York: Pantheon, 1963; Vintage, 1989), p. 335.

use of astrology. He had already pushed the envelope of twentieth-century intellectual discourse about as far as could be sustained.

During the years of Stan's and my residence there, Esalen Institute was well known as an educational center where an unusually diverse range of perspectives and transformational practices was explored—Eastern and Western, ancient and contemporary, psychological, somatic, philosophical, scientific, shamanic, mystical, esoteric. Of all those perspectives and practices, astrology was perhaps the last one that either of us would have imagined seriously investigating. In contemporary intellectual culture, astrology has served as a kind of gold standard of superstition, that to which one compares something if one wants to emphasize how ludicrous it is and beneath serious discussion. Nevertheless, in early 1976, prompted by a suggestion from an Esalen seminar participant who had extensively studied astrology, we decided we should at least examine the evidence for possible correlations. The participant, an artist named Arne Trettevik, was especially focused on the study of planetary "transits," the ongoing movements of the planets from day to day, year to year, as they move into specific geometrical alignments with respect to an individual's birth chart. He studied the ways in which transits seemed to correspond with the variable kinds of experiences people undergo in the course of life— periods especially marked by personal happiness or failure, for example, or falling in love, entering a new phase of life, and so forth. After hearing Stan's lectures, he had suggested that planetary transits might be similarly relevant for understanding the kinds of experiences people would have in the powerful states of consciousness catalyzed by psychedelic substances.

Stan in turn mentioned the idea to me, and subsequently Trettevik showed us how to calculate birth charts as well as transits, using the necessary reference works such as a planetary ephemeris, a world atlas with time-zone references, and the required mathematical tables. This was still in the years before personal computers were available, so each birth chart and transit calculation had to be done by hand. We also secured several standard interpretive reference works that set out the characteristic meanings for various planetary combinations and their alignments as measured in celestial longitude along the ecliptic (for example, Saturn opposite the Sun, or Jupiter conjoining the Moon)[ii]. Because Stan and I both had records for our own LSD sessions over the years, including dates and major themes, we were able to compare retrospectively our actual experiences with the descriptions in the astrological texts of what kinds of events and experiences were supposedly likely to take place during the concurrent transits.

Initial Correlations

Much to our astonishment, we were highly impressed by both the quality of the correlations and their consistency. What we had experienced in our sessions during those transits seemed to be archetypally intensified versions of the more common life experiences that were generically described in the astrological texts. For example, based on the specific planets and alignment involved, the text might indicate that the period of a particular planetary transit was potentially an appropriate time for expanding one's intellectual horizons, learning new perspectives, or traveling to a distant country and discovering a new culture. It might indicate a period of potentially increased spiritual insight, or by contrast, increased tensions and frustrations within one's career, or the emergence of problematic family issues. One transit might be described as coinciding with greater accident proneness and risk-taking impulses, while another might be characterized as indicating a greater potential for heightened anger or aggressiveness, depression, or generalized anxiety. These astrological text descriptions of more common circumstances and emotions proved helpful for us in gaining a sense for what underlying archetypal energies might be at work in each case. In fact, I was very much struck by how the underlying archetypal nature of the astrological paradigm was apparent even in the many astrological texts that did not use a Jungian vocabulary or reflect a conscious relationship with the Platonic tradition or with its own deeper esoteric roots in which some form of the archetypal perspective was central. Each planet was understood as bearing an underlying cosmic association with a particular archetypal principle, which could express itself multivalently in diverse inflections and

---

[ii] We began our research using Reinhold Ebertin's *Transits* and the individual planets' transit booklets by Frances Sakoian and Louis Acker, followed soon after in those early months by the just-published *Planets in Transit* by Robert Hand, Ebertin's *The Combinations of Stellar Influences,* Charles Carter's *Principles of Astrology,* Sakoian and Acker's *Handbook of Astrology,* and several pioneering works by Dane Rudhyar.

in different dimensions of life—psychologically, circumstantially, interpersonally, physically, and so forth—but always with a clear connection to the essential nature of that archetypal complex. The correlations were not concretely predictive, but rather archetypally predictive.

Based on our records of experiences during such transits, it seemed that LSD sessions typically catalyzed more intense, often perinatal or transpersonal versions of the more common states and themes, the ordinary ups and downs of life, described in the standard astrological texts. During the psychedelic session one might experience a sudden opening of consciousness to a much vaster view of reality, deep insight into another culture's religion or mythology, mystical awakening, spiritual rebirth, or conversely, powerful states of cosmic aloneness, a sudden confrontation with the ruthless inevitability of human mortality, or an eruption of collective aggression and fear such as that activated in an entire nation at war. One factor that made the correlations much easier to recognize than expected was the fact that in psychedelic states, the archetypal qualities constellated during the session tended to be unmistakable because of their relative intensity—for example, not only feeling constrained or oppressed by one's particular life circumstances but undergoing a deep experiential identification with all people who have ever been imprisoned or enslaved. And in turn, most surprisingly, those qualities were intelligibly correlated with the individual's natal chart and current transits. On occasion, the experiential intensity within the psychedelic session could take the form of a direct experience of the archetypal dimension that underlay both the more ordinary conditions and the collective transpersonal experiences, with the particular mythic figures or archetypal powers encountered closely matching the specific archetypal principles that the astrological tradition associated with the relevant natal and transiting planets.

After this initial examination of our own sessions, we turned our attention to a larger range of individuals and their experiences, beginning with the fifty or sixty long-term members of the Esalen community who requested to have their transits calculated and interpreted, then expanding the research to include the many seminar participants who came to Esalen week after week. The institute was in fact an ideal laboratory for such research as thousands of people traveled there each year with the specific intention of pursuing deep self-exploration and potentially transformative experiences. Esalen was at that time a kind of epicenter of psychospiritual experiment and consciousness research. We therefore had available a substantial and continually growing database to work with. In addition to these current cases, we had access to case histories, session dates, and birth dates of a number of Stan's patients and subjects from previous years.

I should mention that, despite our initial impression that the evidence showed remarkable correlations, our understanding of the nature of those correlations arrived in halting stages that produced significant revisions in our first tentative conclusions. Over time, our grasp of the evidence underwent a definite evolution. We initially noticed a very general division in which transits involving certain planets and alignments seemed to coincide with easier, more smoothly resolved sessions while other transits seemed to coincide with more difficult sessions that ended without resolution. Then more specific observations emerged concerning sessions that brought dramatic psychological and spiritual breakthroughs in comparison with others that remained stuck in agonizing "no-exit" situations. Eventually, through much trial and error, it became apparent that these simple binary patterns masked a far more complex interplay of multiple transiting and natal factors that were involved in the fuller range of psychedelic experiences in their extraordinary diversity.

Correlations with Perinatal Experiences

An especially surprising finding from the early period of research concerned a remarkably robust correlation between the four basic perinatal matrices (BPMs) and the four outer-planet archetypes as described in the standard astrological texts. On the one hand, the complex phenomenology of each BPM had first been extracted from psychedelic session reports and described by Stan in the mid-1960s, by which point he had recognized the connection between these four dynamic constellations of experience and the successive stages of biological birth. On the other hand, working within a completely distinct tradition of research and interpretation going back many centuries, astrologers had gradually arrived at a strong consensus about the meanings of Saturn (the outermost planet known to the ancients), and over the past two centuries, Uranus, Neptune, and Pluto (discovered by telescope in the modern era). Fairly early in the research I had noticed an apparent one-to-one general correspondence between experiences reflecting the four perinatal matrices and coinciding transits involving the four slower-moving outer planets.[iii] To our amazement, upon closer reading of the astrological texts, it became apparent that every single feature of the four BPMs closely fit the widely accepted astrological meanings of the four outer planets. Because the perinatal category of correlations is typical of the kinds of archetypal correspondences we subsequently found involving the wider range of psychedelic experiences we researched, I will take a moment here to indicate the correspondences involved, comparing the phenomenology for each matrix as set forth in Stan's work with the standard planetary meanings delineated in the astrological literature. I will begin with BPM IV, the first perinatal matrix for which I noted this pattern.

The fourth perinatal matrix is associated both biologically and archetypally with the emergence from the birth canal and the moment of birth. It is reflected in experiences of sudden breakthrough, unexpected liberation, release from constriction and imprisonment, brilliance of vision and understanding, awakening to a sense of deeper meaning and purpose in life, being flooded by intensely bright light, sudden intellectual and spiritual illumination, the feeling of being reborn after a long and dangerous passage, and so forth. In its negative aspect, when activated but uncompleted, BPM IV can take the form of manic inflation, restless impatience, eccentric ideation accompanied by a sense of unprecedented personal brilliance, insatiable craving for excitement, and compulsive hyperactivity.

Having observed a correlation between BPM IV experiences and major transits of Uranus, I was very much struck by how fully the set of symbolic meanings universally attributed to Uranus by contemporary astrologers coincides with the phenomenology of BPM IV. The astrological Uranus is typically described as the principle of sudden change, of unexpected openings and awakenings, creative breakthroughs and inventiveness, brilliance of inspiration and achievement, sudden illumination and flashes of

---

[iii] For the sake of simplicity and brevity, I will include Pluto here as a "planet." The correlations we consistently observed with respect to Pluto did not seem to reflect any tangible difference in archetypal importance compared with correlations involving Neptune, Uranus, Saturn, and the other traditional planets.

insight. It is also associated with the impulse toward freedom, rebellion against constraints and the status quo, tendencies towards eccentric or erratic behavior, instability, restless unpredictability, the drive towards novelty and the new, the unexpected, the disruptive, the exciting and liberating.

By contrast, the second perinatal matrix is associated with the difficult perinatal stage of uterine contractions when the cervix is still closed. BPM II is typically expressed in experiences of claustrophobic constriction, images of imprisonment and hell, physical and emotional pain, helpless suffering and victimization, fear of dying, states of intense shame and guilt, depression and despair, feelings of "no exit" in Sartre's sense, existential alienation and meaninglessness, being trapped in a perspective in which all that exists is mortal life in a disenchanted material world with no deeper meaning or purpose.

In this case, I noticed how often the planet Saturn was involved in transits that coincided with BPM II states. And again, the set of symbolic meanings long attributed by the astrological tradition to the planet Saturn closely matched the BPM II phenomenology: constraint, limitation, contraction, necessity, hard materiality, the pressures of time, the weight of the past, strict or oppressive authority, aging, death, the endings of things; judgment, guilt, trials, punishment; the tendency to restrict, hold back, burden, separate, negate and oppose, to experience difficulty, problems, decline, deprivation, defeat, loss; the labor of life, the workings of fate, karma, the consequences of past action, pessimism, melancholy; the dark, cold, heavy, dense, dry, old, slow.

However, whereas in the three other cases, both positive and negative sides of the astrological principle involved seemed to be expressed in the large range of potential experiences related to each perinatal matrix, in the case of BPM II, only the negative and problematic features of the Saturn archetype were evident. Subjects under the sway of the second perinatal matrix seem to experience everything through an encompassingly negative filter that allows no positive or redeeming dimension of life. Only in retrospect, after the perinatal process has unfolded and been at least to some extent resolved and integrated, does the experience of BPM II become seen in a different light with new meaning. Then the positive dimension of contraction, separation, loss, suffering, the encounter with death, and so forth becomes altogether evident in the concrete manifestation of biological birth or spiritual rebirth, in the experience of having joined the realm of the "grateful dead" because one is now happily reborn. The crushing defeat of the old identity or structure of reality is seen as making possible an enduring wisdom that has known both sides of life, and that can embrace pain and loss as necessary for a deeper mode of being. The realities of aging and of mortality itself are seen in a new way, permitting the emergence of the positive qualities that are also traditionally associated with the Saturn archetype.

Stan and I were especially struck by the uncannily similar, indeed virtually identical, sets of meanings correlating BPM III with the astrological Pluto. The phenomenology of the third perinatal matrix is unusually diverse and brings together a unique constellation of extremely intense experiences. In terms of the stages of biological birth, it is associated with the propulsion of the baby through the birth canal with the cervix fully dilated. Experientially, one finds a powerful convergence of experiences involving titanic elemental energy of volcanic proportions, intense arousal of sexual libido and aggression, enormous discharge of pent-up energies, dramatic experiences involving violent struggle, life-and-death danger, bloody biology, war, scenes of immense destruction, descent to the underworld, demonic evil, sadomasochism, pornographic sexuality, degradation and defilement, scatology, sewers and decay, purifying fire or pyrocatharsis, elemental transformation, ritual sacrifice, orgiastic bacchanalia, and the paradoxical merging of agony into ecstasy. In general, BPM III represents overwhelmingly intense elemental energies within a cathartic, transformational crucible that culminates in the experience of death and rebirth.

Given these several distinctive themes converging within one perinatal matrix, we found the consistent coincidence of BPM III experiences with transits of Pluto especially extraordinary, for the descriptions of the many-sided principle of Pluto by contemporary astrologers encompassed precisely the same convergence of diverse themes: elemental intensity, depth, and power; that which compels, empowers, and intensifies whatever it touches, sometimes to overwhelming and catastrophic extremes; a dominant concern with survival, sexuality, or power, the lower chakras; the primordial instincts both libidinal and aggressive, destructive and regenerative; the volcanic, cathartic, eliminative, transformative, ever-evolving; the biological processes of birth, sex, and death, the cycles of death and rebirth; breakdown, decay, and fertilization; violent purging of repressed energies; situations of life-and-death extremes, power struggles, all that is titanic, potent, and massive, the powerful forces of nature emerging from its chthonic depths both within and without, the intense, fiery underworld and underground in many senses (geological, psychological, sexual, urban, political, criminal, demonic, mythological); Freud's primordial id, "the broiling cauldron of the instincts," Darwin's ever-evolving nature and the biological struggle for existence.

As with the other perinatal matrices, subjects often had direct experience of specific mythic deities when reaching the deeper dimensions of that matrix. In the case of BPM III, the mythic figures encountered tended to be the same as those brought up in astrological texts describing the nature of the Pluto archetype: deities of destruction and regeneration, descent and transformation, death and rebirth such as Dionysus, Hades and Persephone, Pan, Priapus, Medusa, Lilith, Inanna, the volcano goddess Pele, Quetzalcoatl, Kundalini activation and the Serpent power, Shiva, Shakti, Kali.

Finally, a similar set of parallels was apparent in examining the coincidence of the very different range of BPM I experiences with transits of Neptune. The first perinatal matrix is associated with the prenatal condition immediately prior to the beginning of the birth process: experiences of the amniotic universe, floating oceanic sensations, the melting of boundaries, a porous relationship to the environment, lack of differentiation between inner and outer, embryonic experiences multidimensionally blended with aquatic, interstellar, galactic, and cosmic experiences. Here also are found experiences of mystical unity, spiritual transcendence, the dissolution of material reality and of the separative ego, a sense of merging with the womb, with the mother, with other persons or beings, with all life, with the divine, access to other ontological dimensions beyond consensus reality, transcendence of time and space. Experiences of idyllic nature such as tropical islands or childhood play in beautiful meadows or on seashores can merge into experiences of cosmic unity, oceanic ecstasy, and images of Paradise. In its negative aspect, BPM I is associated with experiences that involve a disorienting loss of boundaries, the dissolving of a stable identity or reality structure, susceptibility to delusional thinking, feeling enveloped by a threatening atmosphere filled with invisible dangers and subtly infecting influences, and experiences of a toxic womb merging into experiences of drug poisoning, psychic contamination, or oceanic pollution.

Remarkably, astrologers symbolically associate the planet Neptune with experiences having a spiritual, transcendent, or mystical character; with the subtle and intangible, the unitive, timeless, immaterial, and infinite; all that transcends the limited world of matter, time, and concretely empirical reality. Neptune is connected with states of psychological fusion, physical and psychological permeability, and the longing for the beyond. It has a symbolic association with water, the sea, streams and rivers, mist and fog, with liquidity and dissolution of any kind, and with what Freud termed "the oceanic feeling." Negatively, it is seen in tendencies towards illusion and delusion, *maya,* deception and self-deception, disorganization, escapism, intoxication, addiction, perceptual and cognitive distortions, projection, inability to distinguish the inner world from the outer, and vulnerability to toxic drug reactions, infections, and contamination.

With respect to all four perinatal matrices, what especially struck us was the two-fold nature of the correlations: On the level of the comparative study of symbol systems, the fact that two entirely distinct interpretive traditions, psychology and astrology, could have independently formulated four fundamental sets of qualities and meanings which so closely corresponded to each other—point for point, matrix to archetype—was certainly surprising on its own terms. But apart from these clear parallels of meaning, the fact that the timing of subjects' experiences of each perinatal matrix in psychedelic sessions actually coincided so consistently with transits involving the very planet that bore the matching astrological character seemed to us astounding.

These perinatal correspondences that emerged into view early in our research became greatly complexified as time passed and we gained a greater understanding of how the major geometrical alignments involving two or more planets (the major planetary "aspects" such as conjunction, opposition, and square), played out in natal charts and transits. For example, Neptune transiting a person's natal Sun seemed to play out differently than if it transited the Moon, even though there were common "Neptunian" features in both instances. In the case of Neptune transits to Saturn, the coinciding experiences tended to be in certain respects virtually opposite those of Neptune transits to Jupiter, though again they had essential underlying features in common that reflected in different ways the archetype associated with Neptune. The differences in each case were directly related to the archetypal qualities associated with the second planet involved in the transit.

Each planetary combination seemed to involve a mutual activation of the two archetypal principles involved, with each archetype infusing and inflecting its specific nature through the other, with each archetype thereby shaping the expression of the other and creating a live compound of the two. Moreover, different individuals seemed to experience the same transit of a specific planet to a natal planet differently depending on how that natal planet was situated relative to the other planets in the birth chart, or depending on what other transits were going on simultaneously. Nothing happened in a vacuum. Everything was always situated in and shaped by a unique context, whether biographical and circumstantial, cultural and historical, or archetypal.

As another example of these complexities, in full-fledged BPM II experiences a specifically perinatal level of content in psychedelic sessions generally seemed to involve the presence of Saturn in alignment with one of the three outer planets Pluto, Neptune, or Uranus. A Saturn transit on its own, for example, in alignment with the Sun, Moon, or one of the inner planets, tended to coincide with more common life experiences reflecting the various themes associated with the Saturn archetype. By contrast, experiences of BPM II were more likely during Saturn transits that involved Pluto or Neptune, each bringing out specific inflections of the second matrix reflecting the relevant archetype: Saturn with Pluto, for example, being more likely to coincide with experiences of helpless suffering in the face of extreme cruelty or titanically intense contractions with no release, while Saturn with Neptune was found more in the case of confrontations with the meaninglessness of mortal life, the dark night of the soul, loss of spiritual meaning, suicidal despair, or fears of insanity. Transits involving Saturn together with Uranus were more associated with experiences involving the sudden confrontation with death, unexpected fall from grace, or the sudden collapse of previously secure structures, whether of identity or of reality itself. Uranus, Neptune, and Pluto all seemed to have a more emphatically transpersonal character, while Saturn represented more of a symbolic threshold between the personal and transpersonal, and between life and death.

Moreover, all of the above combinations of planets in transit could unfold in ways that moved through the perinatal depths into very different healing inflections of the same archetypal principles: Stan's dictum that the full affective and somatic experience of a difficult emotion is "the funeral pyre of that emotion"[iv] was relevant to understanding how a given archetypal complex could evolve from its most challenging forms to highly positive expressions. Thus after the integration of traumatic or otherwise problematic unconscious material, including BPM II experiences of hellish torment, Saturn-Pluto transits were observed in connection with a new capacity for unflinching courage in the face of death and danger, a new willingness to engage life's gravest realities and bear great burdens, to mobilize immense energy with sustained effort and determination for prolonged periods of time, as in the titanic hard labor of birth. Similarly, experiences during Saturn-Neptune transits could unfold into heightened compassion for the suffering of others and sustained practical efforts to alleviate that suffering, a new capacity for sacrifice and renunciation of personal attachments in the service of one's spiritual aspirations, or bringing spiritual ideals into concrete manifestation in a practical, focused, and disciplined way.

Such complexities reflected the intrinsic multivalence of archetypes, their carrying a far greater range of interconnected meanings than a simplistic grid could ever convey. It also gradually became clear that the archetypes that we observed in perinatal experiences and that corresponded with the specific transiting and natal planets seemed to exist at a supraordinate level with respect to the perinatal dimension of the psyche. This supraordinate status became apparent when we noticed a remarkable category of correlations involving the COEX systems, which informed not only the biographical level of the unconscious but also the transpersonal, with the perinatal level often serving as an experiential gateway between the two realms.

Correlations with COEX Systems

In the course of his early work in the 1960s using psycholytic therapy, before he had recognized the perinatal matrices, Stan observed the existence

---

[iv] Personal communication, Esalen Institute, March 1974.

of certain dynamic constellations of emotionally charged memories that shared similar affective and somatic qualities: the COEX systems, or systems of condensed experience. In serial sessions involving low to medium doses of LSD, these COEX systems gradually emerged as various memories from different periods of life that were thematically related came to the surface, eventually often converging in a cluster and becoming condensed into a powerful multidimensional experience. Such retrieved memories in earlier sessions were typically based on more recent events and experiences, while in later sessions they reached deeper into the unconscious to early childhood and infantile experiences that were thematically related to the more recent memories.

Different individuals tended to carry their own particular sets of COEX systems, both negative ones such as various experiences of abandonment, shame, or claustrophobic constriction, and positive ones such as diverse experiences of nourishing love, joyful triumph, or expansive awakening. Careful analysis of individuals' birth charts and transits in the course of their lives suggested that these COEX systems corresponded in striking ways with major planetary alignments in the natal chart whose archetypal meanings were directly relevant to the themes of the emerging COEX. Even more striking was the fact that the timing of the major events that contributed to the COEX system in the course of life, such as the death of a parent, a numinous childhood experience, or a romantic awakening, consistently coincided with major transits crossing the specific planetary configurations in the natal chart related to that COEX. In turn, the emergence into consciousness and integration of such a COEX during a psychedelic session tended to take place when the relevant natal configuration was again undergoing a major transit. The evidence suggested that such transits of a particular COEX-related natal configuration could be experienced either as a further magnification of the unconscious COEX system, thus increasing its psychological power, or as an opportunity to bring it to consciousness and, in the case of negative COEXes, release the jammed energies and painful emotions associated with the original traumas.

As Stan has discussed in the current work and elsewhere, the COEX systems associated with various biographical experiences turned out to be more deeply rooted in the unconscious in one of the four perinatal matrices, whose rich and complex phenomenology contained in prototypical form the elementary themes of virtually all COEX systems. Biographical experiences of abandonment such as the tragic loss of a parent during childhood, a devastating romantic rejection, or a wrenching divorce were all thematically connected with each other but also had common roots in the perinatal experience of the primordial loss of the maternal womb. By contrast, later experiences of unexpected personal success at school or sports in one's youth, of major professional success in one's career during one's adult years, or more generally of sudden joy after overcoming great obstacles found deeper roots in the experience of sudden successful emergence from the constricting birth canal.

Yet over time in more advanced stages of therapy and self-exploration, the COEX systems proved to be rooted at even deeper levels of the unconscious than the perinatal, such as ancestral, historical, collective, karmic, and phylogenetic experiences. What in earlier sessions might have seemed to be an acutely personal psychological issue or biographical theme specific to the individual could be discovered to be grounded in underlying familial patterns stretching back across many generations, or in vivid experiences connected to an earlier historical era, to an entire culture, or to another species of life. In the case of negative COEX systems, integration of these deeper transpersonal levels of a COEX system was often necessary for deep healing and release from the traumatic syndrome to occur. In the case of positive COEX systems, connecting with their deeper transpersonal sources such as mystical unity with the Godhead or the all-nourishing embrace of the Great Mother Goddess could provide an especially powerful healing experience. At the core of each such COEX system we consistently found a particular archetypal principle or complex whose thematic character informed and interconnected the biographical, perinatal, and transpersonal dimensions of the COEX.

This finding closely resembled Jung's understanding of the archetype as constituting the core of every psychological complex, but the COEX system added a dynamic temporal dimension in which major events and experiences from different periods of life, from the stages of birth, and from various prenatal, historical, and other transpersonal levels of the psyche can accumulate and constellate into an integrated system that can be experientially accessed in non-ordinary states of consciousness. The concept of the archetypal complex developed in Jungian and archetypal psychology provided us with a nuanced understanding of the various archetypal principles with their rich array of mythological and esoteric meanings and interrelationships.[v] In turn, Stan's concept of the COEX system offered a more precisely delineated view of the multilayered dynamic constellations of memories and events lodged in the deep psyche, rooted in biographical, perinatal, fetal, ancestral, karmic, historical, phylogenetic and other transpersonal levels. Over time these COEX systems seem to accumulate greater and greater psychic and somatic charge, like a snowball going downhill, drawing into themselves more events and experiences that magnify the inherited psychosomatic structures and impulses until they are made conscious and integrated. The overall picture that emerged from this synthesis is depicted in the diagram below.

Systems of Condensed Experience (COEX) and Levels of Consciousness

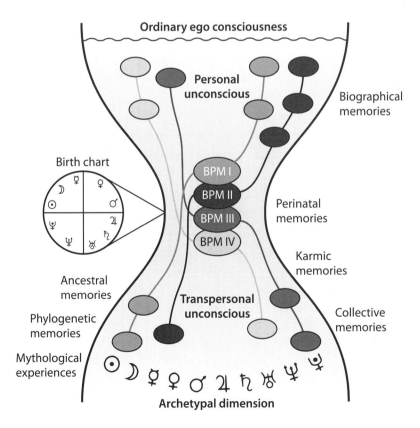

Two important implications of our research findings can be mentioned here, both of which are suggested in the above diagram. One is the supra-ordinate role of the archetypes in relation to all three levels of consciousness—biographical, perinatal, and transpersonal—informing the differentiated dynamic constellations and matrices of experience at each level, and thematically unifying them within the multivalent complexes of meaning carried by each archetype or combination of archetypes. The archetypal forms seem to serve as general organizing principles of the deep psyche, much as described in Jungian and archetypal psychology, but within the more differentiated architecture of psychodynamics that emerged from transpersonal consciousness research, psychedelic therapy, and other holotropic experiences.

The second implication worth noting here is the unexpected correspondence between Stan's finding of the crucial psychological importance of birth and astrology's focus on the planetary positions at birth. One might say that both birth and the birth chart in some sense mediate access to archetypal and transpersonal dimensions. More specifically, the careful study of the birth chart and the reliving of birth in perinatal experiences of death and rebirth both appear to provide powerful ways for individuals to access more directly and consciously the deeper archetypal and transpersonal dimensions that inform their lives and influence their present state of consciousness. Both the perinatal level of the psyche and the astrological natal chart seem to represent a gateway, a *via regia* opening up consciousness to the depths of the unconscious.

The above diagram can in fact be read in both directions, from the top down and from the bottom up: In long-term serial sessions of experiential psychotherapy and self-exploration, a characteristic sequence is for an individual to move from more recent experiences that share certain underlying qualities to successively earlier and earlier experiences of a similar emo-

---

v Besides the *Collected Works of Carl Gustav Jung* (trans. R. F. C. Hull, ed. H. Read, M. Fordham, G. Adler, W. McGuire, Bollingen Series XX [Princeton, N.J.: Princeton University Press, 1953–79]), especially valuable have been the writings and lectures of James Hillman, including his manifesto of archetypal psychology, *Re-Visioning Psychology* (New York: Harper, 1975) and his remarkable early essay "On Senex Consciousness" (first published in *Spring 1970*, now available in *Puer and Senex, Uniform Edition of the Writings of James Hillman,* vol. 3 [Thompson, Conn: Spring, 2015]).

tional or somatic character from youth, childhood, and the pre-oedipal and infantile periods of life; then a significant deepening to the perinatal level and the death-rebirth complex of experiences; with this in turn connecting with and opening up to a vast range of transpersonal experiences in the collective unconscious. Beyond and in a sense surrounding and informing all the above is the archetypal realm, in some manner associated with the vast cosmos and starry sky. The revelation of this domain, captured in Plato's Myth of the Cave, was eloquently anticipated in a passage from the early twentieth-century Polish writer Bruno Schulz:

> So it comes to pass that, when we pursue an inquiry beyond a certain depth, we step out of the field of psychological categories and enter the sphere of the ultimate mysteries of life. The floorboards of the soul, to which we try to penetrate, fan open and reveal the starry firmament.[vi]

Reading the diagram in the other direction: After experiencing the larger spectrum of experiences across these many levels, the individual often gains insight into how various factors from the larger transpersonal domain—ancestral, karmic, historical, and so forth—seem to have translated themselves into specific powerful aspects of the birth experience. Here the vector of the diagram can be seen as moving upward from the transpersonal to the personal. For example, an experience of death by hanging in a previous life can morph into a birth this lifetime in which the umbilical cord is wrapped around the neck causing near-asphyxiation, which in turn can be experienced as unfolding within the postnatal life in various forms such as suffering severe difficulty in breathing during an episode of infantile diphtheria or whooping cough, or being aggressively choked as a child by an older sibling or a bully in a fight. In both directions, the perinatal can be seen as the point of convergence between the transpersonal and personal.

Over the years of research, with further analysis and the wider range of data that emerged during the 1980s, 1990s, and 2000s, we gained a

---

[vi] *Letters and Drawings of Bruno Schulz, with Selected Prose,* ed. J. Ficowski, trans. W. Arndt with V. Nelson. New York: Harper & Row, 1988; quoted in John Updike, "The Visionary of Brohobycz," *The New York Times Book Review,* Oct. 30, 1988.

somewhat different understanding of the role of the perinatal in relation to the rest of the unconscious in therapeutic and transformational work. Rather than serving as a mandatory threshold through which all individuals inevitably pass in the course of their journeys into the deep psyche, we found that a person could potentially undergo a powerful transpersonal experience, such as a deep identification with Gaia or the entire Earth community, or what seemed to be an event from another historical era or a memory from a past life, without necessarily having undergone the biographical-perinatal-transpersonal sequence observed by Stan in many patients and subjects during the 1960s and early 1970s. Instead, an individual may access any level at any time, depending on the catalyzing method (psychedelic session, breathwork, kundalini yoga, gestalt therapy, spiritual emergency, etc.), the setting, the stage of therapy or self-exploration, the specific psychedelic medicine used and dosage level, and perhaps other less knowable factors such as the spontaneous unfolding of the individual's inner healing intelligence, the *telos* of individuation in Jung's sense or the holotropic movement towards wholeness in Stan's sense, or perhaps even karma or grace. What proved to be key across these variables, however, was the archetypal character of the experience, which consistently tended to be correlated with specific natal and transiting planetary alignments, and which could express itself at any level whether biographical, perinatal, or transpersonal. The dominant qualities of any particular psychedelic session, holotropic experience, spiritual emergency/emergence, or therapeutic turning point could be discerned in archetypal terms and correlated with the natal chart and transits.

World Transits

I have so far been discussing correlations involving individuals' birth charts and personal transits. After the initial years of research in which I focused on the lives and experiences of individuals involved in deep self-exploration, psychotherapy, psychedelic experimentation, and various other transformational practices, I increasingly turned my attention to the study of major cultural and historical figures. I was curious, for example, what transits Freud had when on July 24, 1895, "The secret of dreams was revealed" to him, as he put it, and he grasped how the unconscious symbolically expressed itself through the dream; or what convergence of transits Jung had during the crucial 1913–18 period of his life when he underwent a powerful descent into his own unconscious that brought forth the principal images and ideas with which he would work for the rest of his career. I was curious what transits were taking place when Galileo first turned his telescope to the heavens in 1609–10 and glimpsed the new Copernican universe that he would help open up to modern understanding. Or what transits Rosa Parks had in December 1955 when she refused to get up from her seat on the segregated bus in Montgomery, Alabama and catalyzed the U.S. civil rights movement. Or what transits Beethoven had when he wrote the *Eroica* Symphony and revolutionized classical European music—or, by contrast, what he had when he first came to the tragic realization that he was becoming incurably deaf, unable to hear his own music. With each of these major biographical and cultural turning points, and hundreds more like them, I discovered the same consistency and archetypal precision of the planetary correlations as we had been finding in the psychotherapeutic and psychedelic research.

Gradually, however, another level of understanding opened up that recontextualized the findings so far considered. As the five slower-moving outer planets, from Jupiter through Pluto, orbit around the Sun along with the Earth, they gradually move into and then out of major alignments with each other—conjunctions, oppositions, and so forth—relative to the Earth in ongoing cycles. Depending on the planets and orbital speeds involved, some of these periods of cyclical alignments last longer and happen more rarely, such as the Uranus-Pluto conjunction that encompassed the entire period of the 1960s and early 1970s, while others are shorter in duration and happen more frequently, such as the Jupiter-Uranus cycle whose conjunctions and oppositions each last about fourteen months and happen approximately every seven years. I found that the periods encompassed by these world transits were consistently marked by a convergence of major historical events, cultural movements, and public figures in many countries and areas of human activity, all of which reflected a shared zeitgeist whose archetypal character corresponded with the planets aligned during that time with the Earth.

These historical patterns were both synchronic and diachronic in nature, a dual form of archetypal patterning that was strikingly consistent throughout the larger body of historical evidence. The *synchronic* patterns took the form of many events of the same archetypal character occurring simultaneously in different cultures and individual lives in coincidence with the same planetary alignment—simultaneous revolutionary movements or major waves of artistic creativity occurring independently in separate countries and continents, or multiple scientific breakthroughs achieved at the same time by different scientists working entirely independently of each other. The *diachronic* patterns reflected the fact that events taking place during one planetary alignment had a close archetypal and often historically causal association with the events that occurred during preceding and subsequent alignments of the same two planets in a manner that suggested a distinct unfolding cycle. The relevant periods were thus linked to each other not only because they shared the same archetypal character but also by virtue of their sequential continuity and unfolding historical and causal connections from one cycle to the next. The associated historical trends and cultural movements seemed to undergo a sharply intensified or accelerated development during each successive period in what appeared to be a continuously unfolding but cyclically "punctuated" spiralic evolution.

Because I have already published an extensive account of such historical correlations between planetary cycles and archetypal patterns in my book *Cosmos and Psyche*,[vii] I will not discuss them further here except as they proved relevant for understanding individual experiences in therapeutic, psychedelic, and holotropic contexts. For as I deepened my analysis of individual transformational experiences over the decades, I became aware that the overarching archetypal dynamics reflected in the world transits appeared to provide a kind of meta-context that encompassed and informed the specific archetypal dynamics reflected in an individual's personal transits. For example, the Uranus-Pluto conjunction of the 1960s and early 1970s with its characteristic quality of intensified elemental energy and revolutionary transformation seems to have provided the archetypal context for the powerful emergence of perinatal experiences that Stan observed and formulated at that time. The entire collective field had

---

[vii] *Cosmos and Psyche: Intimations of a New World View* (New York: Random House, 2006).

a perinatal intensity that expressed itself in the LSD sessions in a manner that seemed to come directly from a larger archetypal source.

By contrast, the long Uranus-Neptune conjunction from the mid-1980s through the end of the millennium provided a different archetypal context, reflected in such archetypally relevant phenomena as the widespread use of MDMA or Ecstasy with its characteristic stimulation of numinous merging experiences in group settings like the countless raves occurring throughout the world beginning in the late 1980s; the increasing participation in ayahuasca rituals not only in indigenous South American settings but in North American and European societies, which was part of a more general widespread engagement with the sacred ritual use of vision plants; and the rapid spread of holotropic and other forms of breathwork and deep meditation techniques. Reports from many psychedelic and holotropic experiences at this time made clear that individuals were accessing various transpersonal dimensions without necessarily first passing through the titanic upheavals and breakthroughs of the perinatal domain. Similarly appropriate in archetypal terms during this time of increasing globalization and internet connectivity was the increasing dissolution of boundaries between different cultural and religious traditions. This dissolving of boundaries occurred not only at the collective level of multicultural interaction and a resulting creative religious syncretism, but also at an entirely interior individual level whereby subjects in non-ordinary states of consciousness reported having spontaneous religious and mythological experiences and insights from cultural traditions entirely outside of their previous knowledge, suggesting that the collective psyche was undergoing an unprecedented internal globalizing process apart from the more literal one happening in the external world.

In addition, other major world transits of briefer duration during these decades, such as the several Saturn-Neptune or Jupiter-Uranus alignments, coincided with still other major archetypal tendencies in individual experiences and non-ordinary states of consciousness. Moreover, it became clear that with both world transits and personal transits, faster-moving inner-planet transits seemed to synchronistically "trigger" or catalyze the specific timing of events and experiences associated with the longer, more powerful transits of the slower-moving outer planets. Finally, there was the important ongoing issue of multiple transits happening simultaneously that were often of very different archetypal quality, and on occasion virtually polar opposite in nature. Only gradually did we gain a sense for how to synthesize and weigh the relative importance of these multiple transiting and natal factors as they were expressed in psychedelic and holotropic sessions, and in individual lives more generally.

The Issue of Causality

From our first encounter with the evidence of potential planetary correlations, Stan and I were confronted with the theoretical difficulty of imagining how the physical planets, at widely varying distances from the Earth, could exert an influence on not only external events in human history and biography but the interior realities of private human experience. It was difficult to imagine any physical factor, at least as conventionally understood, that could serve as a plausible source or medium of the observed correlations. Very early in our research, Stan suggested that a more likely explanation for what we were seeing is that the universe has woven into its very fabric a meaningful coherence between the macrocosm and the microcosm. Instead of a Cartesian-Newtonian form of linear causality involving some kind of physical emanations, like electromagnetic radiation, the nature of the correspondences suggested more of an intrinsic synchronistic orchestration between planetary movements in the heavens and archetypal patterns in human experience. As we learned later, the concept of synchronicity had indeed been invoked by Jung on several occasions as a possible explanation for why astrology worked in spite of modern assumptions that it should not.[viii]

After these several decades of research, I believe that the range of correspondences between planetary positions and human existence is too vast and multidimensional—too clearly ordered by structures of meaning rather than physically measurable forces, too suggestive of creative intelligence, too pervasively informed by aesthetic patterning, too symbolically multivalent, too experientially complex and nuanced, and not least, too

---

[viii] I have discussed Jung's concept of synchronicity and its relationship to the astrological correlations in greater depth in *Cosmos and Psyche,* pp. 50–79.

responsive to human participatory inflection—to be explained by straight-forward material factors alone. A more plausible and comprehensive explanation of the available evidence points to a conception of the universe as a fundamentally interconnected whole, informed by creative intelligence and pervaded by patterns of meaning and order that extend through every level. This would represent, as Jung suggested, a cosmic expression of the principle of synchronicity. It also parallels the Hermetic axiom, "As above, so below." In this perspective, the planets do not "cause" specific events any more than the hands on a clock "cause" a specific time. Instead, the planetary positions seem to be *indicative* of the cosmic state of archetypal dynamics at that time. The Neoplatonic philosopher Plotinus expressed a world conception along this line in the *Enneads:*

> The stars are like letters which inscribe themselves at every moment in the sky…. Everything in the world is full of signs…. All events are coordinated…. All things depend on each other; as has been said, "Everything breathes together."[ix]

There is, however, a sense in which causality does appear relevant in this context, and this is in the sense of *archetypal* causation, comparable to Aristotle's concept of formal and final causation. While the movements of the physical planets may bear a synchronistic rather than mechanistically causal connection with a given human experience, one could say that the experience is in some sense being constellated—variously affected, impelled, drawn forth, patterned—by the relevant archetypes, and in this sense it may be appropriate to speak, for example, of Saturn (as archetype) as "influencing" one in a specific way, as "governing" certain kinds of experience, and so forth. But while the archetype may be *a* cause, I would not consider it *the* cause, as archetypal factors are always acting in complex recursive relationship with human agency, level of consciousness, cultural context, concrete circumstance, interpersonal field, genetic inheritance, past actions, and many other possible factors.

[ix] Plotinus, *Enneads,* II, 3, 7, "Are the Stars Causes?" (c. 268), quoted in Eugenio Garin, *Astrology in the Renaissance,* trans. C. Jackson and J. Allen, rev. C. Robertson (London: Arkana, 1983), p. 117.

The Nature of Archetypes

The evidence of planetary correlations with human experience centers on the multidimensional principle of archetypes. When Jung, influenced by both Kant's critical philosophy and Freud's instinct theory, brought the idea of archetypes into contemporary discourse in his recognition of certain universal constants that structure the deep levels of the human psyche, he was using a term and a concept drawn from the Platonic philosophical tradition. In the background of both the Jungian and Platonic perspectives was the ancient mythological experience of gods and goddesses, essentially personified expressions of the equally numinous Platonic Forms and Jungian archetypes. To simplify a complex historical development, in the course of which the cultural focus evolved from myth to philosophy to psychology, one could say that the Platonic tradition gave philosophical articulation to the primordial mythic vision of powerful essences or beings that both informed and transcended human life. In turn, while Plato understood the transcendent Forms or Ideas to be the fundamental structuring principles of an ensouled cosmos, Jung understood the archetypes to be the fundamental structuring principles of the human psyche. These important distinctions reflected the long epistemological and cosmological evolution that took place in Western thought during the past twenty-five hundred years, gradually differentiating psyche from cosmos and leading to the modern disenchantment of the world within which depth psychology emerged over a century ago.

On the basis of his long study of synchronicities, however, Jung came to the conclusion that the archetypes could not justifiably be localized within human subjectivity but instead seemed to inform both psyche and world, serving as an underlying unitive principle. In this sense, the later development of Jung's archetypal theory more closely approached the Platonic view, though with a greater psychological emphasis and a fuller recognition of both the multivalence and the shadow dimension of the archetypes. Jung's later thinking is also consistent with the many archetypal experiences reported in the psychedelic literature, which suggest that archetypes can fluidly express themselves as psychological forms, as cosmic principles, or as mythic beings.

Contrary to the disenchanted modern world view, the evidence of systematic planetary correlations with the archetypal patterns of human experience suggests that the cosmos is a living, ever-evolving matrix of being and meaning within which the human psyche is embedded as a co-creative participant. In Jungian terms, the research points to the possibility that the collective unconscious is in some way embedded in the universe itself, whereby the planetary motions reflect at a macrocosmic level the unfolding archetypal dynamics of human experience. In Platonic terms, the evidence seems to reflect the existence of an *anima mundi* informing the cosmos, a world soul in which the human psyche participates as a microcosm of the whole. In Homeric mythic terms, the evidence indicates a continuity with the world views of the great archaic civilizations, such as ancient Mesopotamia and Egypt, with their awareness of an intimate connection between the gods and the heavens that both inspired and structured their religious and social life, astronomical observations, and monumental architecture.

In retrospect, humanity's long evolution of consciousness and world views seems to have been accompanied by an evolution in how the archetypal domain has been perceived and theorized, as well as how it was eventually negated and then rediscovered in new forms. In the course of that evolution, including its modern disenchanting stages in particular, there occurred a decisive differentiation of an autonomous self and a strengthening of human agency. In a further dialectical unfolding, more recent developments in archetypal theory and experience have emphasized the participatory and multivalent nature of the archetypes. This emerging perspective both recognizes the underlying power of archetypes while giving the human being a greater co-creative as well as co-responsible role in their expression. This has led to the possibility of a new form of human relationship to the *anima mundi* that permits and even thrives on the simultaneous existence of autonomy and embeddedness. Yet paradoxically, the disenchantment of the universe and radical separation of human consciousness from the whole may have been the precondition for both the alienation that helped precipitate the crisis of modern consciousness and the forging of a modern identity capable of reengaging the *anima mundi* in a newly participatory manner. The journey of depth psychology from the 1880s to the present, from Freud to Grof, so to speak, would have been neither possible nor necessary without the long cosmological and existential evolution that preceded it.[x]

Returning to the planetary correlations with psychedelic experiences: Only as I came to fully recognize the multidimensional and multivalent nature of archetypes—their formal coherence and consistency that could nevertheless give rise to a plurality of meanings and possible expressions—did the extraordinary elegance of the planetary correlations become discernible. Any particular manifestation of a given archetype can be "positive" or "negative," creative or destructive, admirable or base, profound or trivial. The archetypes associated with specific planetary alignments are equally apt to express themselves in the interior life of the psyche as in the external world of concrete events, and often both at once. Closely linked yet entirely opposite polarities contained in the same archetypal complex can be expressed in coincidence with the same planetary configuration. A person undergoing a particular transit can be on either the acting or the receiving end of the relevant archetypal gestalt, with altogether different consequences. Of these many related possibilities, which mode actually occurs does not seem to be observable in the birth chart or planetary alignments per se. Instead, the archetypal principles at work in these correlations appear to be dynamic but radically indeterminate in their multivalent nature. Though they represent enduring forms or essences of complex meaning, and are clearly discernible underlying the flux and diversity of the observed phenomena, they are also both fundamentally shaped by many relevant circumstantial factors and co-creatively modulated and enacted through human will and intelligence.

Because of this combination of dynamic multivalence and sensitivity

---

[x] *The Passion of the Western Mind* (New York: Ballantine, 1991, 1993) sets out a narrative history of the Western world view in which the evolution of the archetypal perspective plays a central role, from Plato and the ancient Greeks to Jung and the postmodern. *Cosmos and Psyche* provides a summary overview of the archetypal perspective and the ontologically fluid, multivalent nature of planetary archetypes before going on to examine the evidence of planetary correlations with the archetypal patterns and cycles of history. Finally, my "Notes on Archetypal Dynamics and Complex Causality," originally written in 2002 and published in three parts in *Archai: The Journal of Archetypal Cosmology*, Issues 4, 5, and 6 (2012, 2016, 2017), represents a more systematic effort to understand and articulate the unique features of archetypal dynamics observed in planetary correlations and in human experience more generally.

to particular conditions and human participation, I believe that, contrary to its traditional reputation and employment, such an astrology is best regarded, as mentioned before, not as concretely predictive but as archetypally predictive. Compared with, for example, some forms of intuitive divination with which astrology in earlier eras was often systematically conjoined, the focus of an archetypal astrology reflective of the evidence we have studied is not the prediction of specific outcomes but rather the precise discernment of archetypal dynamics and their complex unfolding in time. I believe that such an understanding shines a light on numerous long-standing issues surrounding astrology, such as the question of fate versus free will, the problem of identical planetary configurations coinciding with concretely different though archetypally parallel phenomena, and the fundamental inadequacy of statistical tests for detecting most astrological correlations.

The planetary correlations may offer a uniquely valuable form of insight into the dynamic activity of archetypes in human experience—indicating which ones are most operative in a specific instance, in what combinations, during which periods of time, and as part of what larger patterns. In providing such a perspective, archetypal astrology can be seen as essentially continuing and deepening the depth psychology project: to make conscious the unconscious, to help free the conscious self from being a puppet of unconscious forces (as in acting out, inflated identification, projection, self-sabotage, drawing towards one as "fate" what is repressed or unconscious, and so forth). Its study can mediate a heightened quality of communication and coordination between consciousness and the unconscious, with "the unconscious" now suggestive of considerably larger dimensions than originally conceived—less exclusively personal, less subjective, more cosmically embedded. It provides this mediation, however, not by spelling things out in a literal, concretely predictive manner, but rather by disclosing intelligible patterns of meaning whose very nature and complexity—multivalence, indeterminacy, sensitivity to context and participation, and a seemingly improvisatory creativity—are precisely what make possible a dynamically co-creative role for human agency in participatory interaction with the archetypal forces and principles involved.

Final notes

An unexpected consequence of pursuing astrological research in the area of psychedelic exploration was that the latter brings forth profound encounters with the deep psyche that can often include direct experiences of the archetypes in various forms. Such encounters gave us a more vivid experiential ground for understanding astrological factors and opened up to us a better grasp of the multivalent character of the archetypal principles. Psychedelic and holotropic experiences also tend to bring about a deep change in epistemological outlook, what might be called a dissolution of the Cartesian-Kantian double-bind of modern consciousness that experiences itself as evolved from and contextualized by a universe that is unconscious, purposeless, and ultimately unknowable. This shift of vision can lead to a recognition of the universe as ensouled, and help mediate a spiritual-moral awakening—a shift of heart not just of mind—that is necessary for entering into such an astrological perspective: strengthening a mature hermeneutics of trust to balance and integrate with our already robust postmodern hermeneutics of suspicion. Such experiences can result in a new openness to the possibility of a cosmic intelligence that is coherent with and responsive to our own.

Using archetypal astrological analysis in close examination of our own and others' psychedelic experiences, we were also able to assess with greater experimental precision which astrological factors tended to be most significant in this area, and what were the orbs (the range of degrees before and after exact alignment) within which planetary alignments seemed to be archetypally operative. We found that by far the most important factors in understanding these experiences were the planetary archetypes and the major aspects of the planets in natal charts, personal transits, and world transits. So too the planetary positions relative to the horizontal and vertical axes, the Ascendant-Descendant and Midheaven-Imum Coeli. The approach we found most helpful was similar to that of the astronomer Johannes Kepler, with his Pythagorean emphasis on the planetary aspects as the dominant astrological indicators, within an unfolding cosmic geometry of archetypal meaning centered on the moving Earth.[xi]

Our evidence also suggested the importance of recognizing larger orbs than have generally been used in traditional astrology. We came to see aspects not as acting like isolated on-and-off light switches within a narrow orb, but rather as indicating archetypal wave forms that enter into the individual or collective psychic field and interact with the larger complex whole of archetypal dynamics cumulatively operative in the field. These are then shaped and inflected by the specific circumstances and creative responses of the individuals and communities in question, and expressed as concrete events and experiences.

I am acutely conscious of a number of important issues that remain to be discussed in this context, but that space does not permit at this time. One issue is certainly the potential misuses and dangers of using astrology in this area. In general, one must maintain a constant epistemological discipline and self-awareness to avoid the projection of fears or wishes, the drawing of definite conclusions on the basis of limited data, and the urge to control life rather than participate in it. On the practical side, the setting out of strategies for timing psychedelic sessions will require a separate publication. So too the different operative orbs for the different forms of correspondence (natal charts, personal transits, and world transits); the differences between the hard or dynamic aspects (conjunction, opposition, square) and the soft or confluent aspects (trine, sextile); and the differential importance to be attributed to each of the multiple planets involved in transits at any given time.

Over the decades, Stan and I have discussed an enormous number of individuals' psychedelic and holotropic experiences that have come our way and examined the relevant birth charts and transits. In all cases where we had adequate data, the correlations consistently proved of great interest, instructive, and even after these many years, striking in their combination of precise archetypal correlation and seemingly infinite creative diversity.

---

xi While the major aspects between the planets were the most important factors for this research, other factors such as planetary midpoints, minor aspects, progressions, and lunations were often helpful. Of less discernible importance in this context were many factors that are usually focused on in traditional astrology such as the signs, houses, rulerships, and related matters. It was far more important to know that Pluto was transiting in conjunction to the natal Moon than to know whether this happened in Virgo or Libra. The correlations we found of most consequence were thus unrelated to such issues and controversies as the precession of the equinoxes affecting the placement of the zodiacal signs, the two zodiacs (tropical and sidereal), or the multiplicity of potential house systems and rulership systems.

While in some ways extraordinarily elegant in its simplicity, the archetypal astrological perspective revealed such an intricate orchestration of cosmic movements and psychological patterns as to leave both of us at times shaking our heads in sheer admiration and awe at the universe's unimaginably powerful intelligence and creative artistry.

As Stan has often remarked, the great irony of our quest for understanding the variability of psychedelic experience was that when we finally found a method that illuminated the character and timing of people's psychedelic experiences, it was as controversial as psychedelics themselves. It seems that the greatest treasures are sometimes hidden in the most scorned and humble places. Jung often spoke of the stone the builders rejected that turns out to be the keystone. Archetypal astrology does indeed seem to be, as Stan has described it, a kind of Rosetta Stone, allowing us to connect the symbolic language of the psyche with the symbolic language of the cosmos. Just as the expanded cartography of the psyche that emerged from psychedelic research has been immensely clarifying and even liberating as a comprehensive map of the realms of consciousness, we have found that the archetypal correlations with planetary movements have provided us with both an orienting compass and a detailed weather report, at once psychological and cosmic, that can be invaluable aids for the explorer of deep realms.

Beyond its usefulness for the individual, what is perhaps especially thought-provoking and timely about this body of evidence is that just when our Earth community as a whole faces a great perinatal crisis of its own, we discover that the archetypal symbolism of the outermost planets of the solar system—the "ambassadors of the galaxy," as Dane Rudhyar called them—points with such vivid precision toward the perinatal threshold and the death-rebirth mystery.

I am grateful to Stanislav Grof as well as Renn Butler, Max DeArmon, Lilly Falconer, Chad Harris, William Keepin, Becca Tarnas, and Yvonne Smith Tarnas for their helpful comments.

Richard Tarnas, Ph.D.

May 2019

© Copyright 2019 by Richard Tarnas

Afterword
by Brigitte Grof

The idea for this encyclopedia was born out of a series of teleseminars that Stan did for the Shift Network in 2017. He was giving lectures via Zoom about many areas of transpersonal psychology, consciousness research, psychedelic experiences, and the ancient spiritual wisdom of the world. The deep knowledge that he has gained through his own inner travels, as well as by accompanying thousands of people in holotropic states of consciousness, is a treasure that should be shared with the world.

As a passionate psychonaut, I have read Stan's books and heard his lectures many times over the last thirty years. For me, they represent deep and true perennial knowledge. Stan and I have also known and worked with each other for over three decades. However, since we got married and began sharing our inner and outer travels, and working side by side, it feels like I am getting access to a new, deeper level of understanding and appreciation for his vast and profound knowledge about the psyche and the universe.

I feel very blessed to be loved by this wonderful man, whose other outstanding qualities, besides his wisdom, are his free spirit, outrageous humor and his big, warm, loving heart and compassion for all beings and all of existence. With his limitless curiosity and courage, Stan began his research about sixty years ago into the hidden worlds of the psyche, many of which had not been mapped by psychology at that time. He added the perinatal and transpersonal domains to the model of the unconscious and finally completed his discoveries by finding deep spiritual insights that have been known for thousands of years by the mystics of all spiritual traditions.

The wisdom of the mystics comes from a deep and personal experience of holotropic states. It is not just theoretical knowledge, but a path of direct experiential knowing. This kind of information is very important for others embarking on inner travel. This encyclopedia offers detailed information about many subjects important for psychonauts, such as spiritual emergency, synchronicity, archetypes, the cosmic game, higher creativity, mysteries of death and rebirth, and many others. Embarking on that journey of adventure, it is a great gift to be able to learn from an experienced traveler like Stan what kind of inner territories one might access.

Although his observations have been confirmed and validated by thousands of people undergoing inner exploration with psychedelics, Holotropic Breathwork, or during spiritual emergency, many of his paradigm-breaking insights have not yet been accepted by mainstream psychology and psychiatry, even to this day. I believe this encyclopedia will become a treasured source of knowledge for every dedicated psychonaut. When we encounter challenging places on our inner journeys, the experience might be unusual or difficult to put into words, but it can be very helpful and make a difference to know: "Oh, this is what Stan has been talking about in his book!"

Wishing you safe and happy Journeys!

Brigitte Grof
Mill Valley, California, March 2018

Index

A

Abraham a Sancta Clara 224
abreaction 10
Absolute Consciousness. *See* divinity
Abu Ghraib prison, abuse of prisoners
    at 176
Abyss, Cosmic 264–322
acausal connecting principle. *See* syn-
    chronicity
acetylcholine, discovery of 112
Adams, Samuel 196
adults, past life memories in
    evoked 238–243
        Karl (patient) 239–241
        Renata (patient) 241–243
    spontaneous 237
Advaita Vedanta 263
aggregate psychedelic therapy 11–13
aggression. *See also* violence
    evolutionary and psychosocial
        theories of 174–322
    global crisis of 173–322
    perinatal roots of 176–322
        birth trauma 193–194
        Communism 201–202
        concentration camps 202–204
        intrauterine disturbances 193

    sociopolitical implications
        195–322
    survival, psychology of 210–322
    transpersonal roots of 205–322
Ahriman 205
Ahura Mazda 205
Akashic Holofield 228, 265
alam al mithal 260
alchemy 115, 271
alcoholism, LSD for treatment of
    5–9
Aldrin, Buzz 212
Alexander, Franz 219
Alighieri, Dante 153, 208
Allah 129, 209
Allan, Frances 68
Allan, John 69
Alpert, Richard 17
Alpher, Ralph 72
alternating current
    invention of 123
    Tesla's support for 125–322
American Parapsychological Associa-
    tion 246
American Revolution 196
amplification, Jung's method of 75

of greed 206–322
Birth of Tragedy, The (Nietzsche) 150
birth trauma. *See* Basic Perinatal
   Matrices (BPMs)
Blake, William 267
Blewett, Duncan 17
bodywork 21, 24
Bohm, David 259
Bohr, Niels 36, 112–113
Bojaxhiu, Mary Teresa (Mother
   Teresa) 279
Bolshevik Revolution 201
Bonaparte, Marie 68–322
Book of Revelation 45
Books of the Dead 145
Boredom, Divine 269
BPM. *See* Basic Perinatal Matrices
   (BPMs)
Brahman 209, 258
Brahms, Johannes 136
Brazilian spiritist movement 248
Breuer, Joseph 10
Brugmansia 45
Buchenwald 204. *See also* concentra-
   tion camps, perinatal roots of
Buckman, John 14
Buddha 149, 209, 219, 258, 271, 277
Buddhism. *See also* reincarnation; *See*
   also Buddha
   anatta 267, 285
   archetypal iconography in 145
   Avatamsaka (Hwa Yen) 271–272
   Mutual Interpenetration 271
   Tibetan 222
"Buddhist Training as Artificial
   Catatonia" (Alexander) 219
Bufo alvarius 22
buried alive motif 71
Burkhardt, Jacob 151
Bush, George W. 206

C

California Institute of Integral Studies
   (CIIS) 61
"Call Me by My True Names" (Hanh)
   280
Campbell, Joseph
   archetypes and 157, 163
   Eranos meetings and 30
   "Hero's Journey" 153
   new planetary myth, search for
     160–322
   on dieties 262–322
   on unfulfilling pursuit of goals
     208
   synchronicity, experience with
     41–43
   Viking ritual recreated by 49–50
cancer patients, psychedelic therapy
   with 17, 20, 230, 246
Capra, Fritjof 113
cardiac arrhythmia, as contraindiction
   for psychedelic therapy 20
Cardinal, Roger 76
Cartesian worldview
   Bell's theorem 36
   death and dying in 249
   evidence suppressed by 225
   Jung influenced by 40
   paradox of 113–322
   psychedelic research as challenge to
     227–322, 256
Case of the Midwife Toad, The (Koestler) 31
"Cask of Amontillado, The" (Poe) 71
causality, alternatives to 39. *See*
   also synchronicity
cave paintings, shaman archetype in
   144
cawa plant 45
Centaur 146

tion
  ancient and pre-industrial attitudes
    toward 221–224
  consciousness, survival after
    biological death
      past life experiences 232–322
      phenomena on threshold of
        death 229–232
      transpersonal experiences
        227–322
  deceased persons
    apparitions of 244–322
    communication with 244–322
  "dying before dying" 222, 224,
    250
  near-death experiences (NDEs)
    229–232
  research implications 249–322
  Western attitude toward 217–221
Death archetype 156, 261
de Beauvoir, Simone 78
deceased persons. See also reincarnation
  apparitions of 244–322
  communication with 244–322
defense intellectuals (DIs) 197
Delacour, Jean-Baptiste 220
Delacroix, Eugène 19
delirium tremens 5
"delusions of reference" 30
"delusions of reference" 41
Demokritos 109, 157
Denial of Death, The (Becker) 217
depression, LSD therapy for 4
depth psychology 150
Descartes, René 107, 113, 116–322
descent 273
"Descent into the Maelstrom, A"
  (Poe) 70
Deschamps, Émile 32

destructiveness. See violence
Deus sive Natura (Spinoza) 257
"Devil's Trill" (Tartini) 135–136
direct current, Edison's promotion
  of 125
Discourse on the Method (Descartes)
  113, 116
Ditman, K.S. 5
Divine Comedy (Dante) 153
divine inspiration. See higher creativity
Divine Play. See lila
divinity. See also archetypes
  creation, process of 267–322
  experiential identification with
    265–322
  good and evil, problem of 278–
    322
  immanent divine 257–322
  inadequacy of language for
    266–322
  supreme cosmic principle 262–
    322
  taboo against knowing who you are
    275–322
  transcendent divine 258–322
  unitive experiences 272–322
Dollard, J. 175
dominants of the collective unconscious. See archetypes
Doomsday Machine, The (Ellsberg)
  197
dosages, microdosing 18–322, 137
Dostál, Tomáš 51–52
"Dostoevsky and Parricide" (Freud)
  67
Dostoevsky, Fyodor Mikhailovich 67
Driesch, Hans 41, 149
Duino Elegies (Rilke) 134
Dumas, Alexandre 19

329

Dún an Óir 240
Durckheim, Karlfried Graf 163
"dying before dying" 222, 224, 250

E
Ecce Homo (Nietzsche) 109–322
Edison, Thomas A. 125
efflux 272
ego 285
eidos 146
"eighth climate" 260
Einstein, Albert 36, 37, 71, 107, 118–322
Einstein-Podolsky-Rosen (EPR) experiment 36
élan vital 75
electric generator, invention of 123
electric motor, invention of 123
electrons, Einstein-Podolsky-Rosen (EPR) experiment 36
electroshock therapy 4
"elevator in empty space" (thought experiment) 119–120
Eliade, Mircea 31, 163
Ellsberg, Daniel 197
Elysian Fields 146
embodied existance, gaining appreciation of 281–322
Emerald Tablet (Trismegistus) 271
emerging paradigm 256
endogenous psychoses 153
endorphins 210
Engelbart, Douglas 138
enlightened intellect 146
Enola Gay 197
entelechy 75, 149
entheos 116
environment for sessions 23–24
epilepsy, Dostoevsky diagnosed with 67

Eranos meetings 30
Erdman, Jean 42
Eros 150
Esalen Institute 42, 44–48, 61, 153
Eternal Youths archetype 156, 261
Eureka (Poe) 71–73
evil, problem of 278–322
evoked past life memories 238–243
  Karl (patient) 239–241
  Renata (patient) 241–243
evolutionary theories of violence 174–322
evolution of consciousness 273
Existentialists 208
eyeshades 16, 23
Ezekiel (prophet) 129

F
Faces of the Enemy, The (Keen) 198
facilitators 23
Fadiman, James 17, 18, 137
"Fall of the House of Usher, The" (Poe) 71
Father Sky 50
"Fat Man" (atomic bomb) 197
Fatsang (Zen Master) 271–322
Feynman, Richard 198
Fibonacci series 148
First International Transpersonal Conference 49
Flammarion, Camille 32
Flournoy, Theodore 75
Fludd, Robert 128
Flynn, Charles 224
Foerster, Heinz von 228
Fontgibu, Monsieur de 32
Fordham, Michael 57
Forest Lawn Memorial Park and Mortuaries 221
Forgetfulness, Angel of 232

Native American Church, psychedelic rituals in 13

Nazi Germany, Freud's escape from 68

Nazism 176, 202–204

near-death experiences (NDEs) 229–232

Near Death Experience, The (Greyson and Flynn) 224

Neitzsche, Friedrich 108

neo-Platonism 39, 272

Nerval, Gérard de 19

Neumann, Erich 30, 66

New Eleusis 287

Newman, Max 128

new paradigm 256

Newtonian-Cartesian paradigm 113

Newton, Isaac 107, 113, 113–322

nibbio (kite) 64, 65

Nietzsche, Friedrich 109–322, 150

nirvana 267

nirvikalpa 267

No Exit (Sartre) 80

Nominalists 150, 154

non-dual experience 263

nootropic effect 18, 138

Number and Time (Franz) 147

numinosity 257–322, 260

O

OBEs. *See* out-of-body experiences (OBEs)

Odent, Michael 210

Oedipal complex, representations in art

  da Vinci 64–67

  Dostoevsky 67

  Oedipus Rex 62, 150

  Poe 68–322

  Shakespeare 63

Oedipus Rex (Sophocles) 62, 150

Olatunji, Babatunde 54

olymerase Chain Reaction (PCR), development of 138

On Divination and Synchronicity (Franz) 37

ontology 255–322

  creation, process of 267–322

  embodied existance, appreciation of 281–322

  experiential identification with the divine 265–322

  good and evil, problem of 278–322

  immanent divine 257–322

  inadequacy of language for 266–322, 270

  Supracosmic and Metacosmic Void 264–322

  supreme cosmic principle 262–322

  taboo against knowing who you are 275–322

  transcendent divine 258–322

  unitive experiences 272–322

opium 136

Oppenheimer, Robert 206

"Oppenheimer's baby" (atomic bomb) 198

"orbiting sun in space-time" thought experiment) 120

orishas 153

Osis, Karlis 220

Osmond, Humphry 5, 6, 17

Other Side of the Moon, The (Lemle) 212

Otto, Rudolf 30, 257

Ouroboros 35, 110

out-of-body experiences (OBEs) 230–232

"Premature Burial" (Poe) 71
pre-session interviews 22
Presocratics 146
Près, Terrence des 203
primordial images. *See* archetypes
Prinzhorn, Hans 76
prolactin 210
PSI-field 228
psilocybin-containing mushrooms 12, 13, 22
psychedelic-assisted psychotherapy. *See* therapeutic uses of psychedelics
"Psychedelic Experience, The" (Stolaroff, Harman, and Hubbard) 8
psychedelic rituals 13–14
psychedelic therapy. *See also* therapeutic uses of psychedelics
  components of 16–17
  early development of 5–8
"psychoid" quality of archetypes 41
psychological principles, archetypes as 144, 151–322
psycholytic therapy 5, 14–16
psychonautics, history of
  art analysis and 76–322
  therapeutic uses 3–322
    abreaction 10
    aggregate psychedelic therapy 11–13
    alcoholism, treatment of 5–9
    antidepressant studies 4
    as adjunct to psychotherapy 9
    fusion therapy 10–11
    hypnodelic therapy 9
    psychedelic rituals 13–14
    psychedelic therapy 5–8, 16–17
    psycholytic therapy 5, 14–16
    shock therapy 4–5
    Stoll's paper 3
psychosocial theories of violence 174–322
psychosynthesis 11–13
psychotherapy, psychedelic-assisted. *See* therapeutic uses of psychedelics
Puccini, Giacomo 108, 136
Puella Aeterna 156
Puer Aeternus 156
Puharich, Andreija 248
pulsating universe, theory of 73
Pythagoras 146, 147

Q

Quadrature of the Circle 35
quantum-relativistic physics, synchronicity in 35–36
Quetzalcoatl 269
Qur'an 129

R

radically nonlocal nature of universe 36
Radium Corporation, Hubbard Energy Transformer purchased by 5
Ragnarok 205, 260
rainbow archetype 50
rajas 72
Raleigh, Walter 241
Ramakrishna 219, 278
Ramanujan, Srinivasi 126–322
Rangda 156
Rank, Otto 74–322
Rao, Ramachandra 126
Raudive, Konstantin 248–322
Reagan, Ronald 206
Realists 150, 154
"realm beyond heaven," archetypes inhabiting 146
Realms of the Human Unconscious (Grof) 16, 52, 194

Esalen workshop experience
44–48
in Hinduism 39
Jung's observations of 30–35,
36–37, 49
mainstream psychiatry's dismissal
of 29, 41
Pocket Range retreat experience
48–49
in primal worldview 38
in quantum-relativistic physics
35–36
seriality 31–32
"Synchronicity: An Acausal Connecting Principle" (Jung) 30

T
taboo against knowing who you are
275–322
Tabula Smaragdina (Trismegistus)
271
Tales of the Father (Bonaparte) 68
Tales of the Mother (Bonaparte) 68
tamas 72
Tantra 145, 271, 277
Tao 209, 258, 267
Taoism 222, 266
Tao of Physics (Capra) 113
Tao-Te-Ching (Lao-tzu) 266
Tarnas, Richard 61, 144, 161, 200
Tarot 37
Tartaros 146
Tartini, Giuseppe 135
Tate, Sharon 176
"technologies of the sacred" 222,
274, 286
Teller, Edward 198
"Teller's baby" (atomic bomb) 198
Teresa of Avila (saint) 130, 219, 263
Terrible Love of War, A (Hillman) 205

Terrible Mother Goddess archetype
75, 156, 261
"territorial imperative" theory 174
Tesla, Nikola 107, 122–322
Tezcatlipoca 269
Thales 146
thanatology. *See also* reincarnation
ancient and pre-industrial attitudes
toward 221–224
consciousness, survival after biological death 229–232
past life experiences 232–322
phenomena on threshold of
death 229–322
transpersonal experiences
227–322
deceased persons
apparitions of 244–322
communication with 244–322
"dying before dying" 222, 224,
250
near-death experiences (NDEs)
229–232
past life experiences 232–322
research implications 249–322
Western worldview 217–221
Thanatos 150
thangkas 145
theory of relativity 36, 119–322
therapeutic uses of psychedelics
contraindications 20–21
guidelines for productive sessions
19–322
history of 3–322
abreaction 10
aggregate psychedelic therapy
11–13
alcoholism, treatment of 5–9
antidepressant studies 4
fusion therapy 10–11

Y
yantras 145
Yeats, William Butler 267

Z
Zeff, Leo 164
Zeus 146
Zimmer, Heinrich 30
Zorba the Greek 286

About the Publisher

Founded in 1986, the Multidisciplinary Association for Psychedelic Studies (MAPS) is a 501(c)(3) non-profit research and educational organization that develops medical, legal, and cultural contexts for people to benefit from the careful uses of psychedelics and marijuana. **Learn more about our work at maps.org.**

MAPS furthers its mission by:

- Developing psychedelics and marijuana into prescription medicines

- Training therapists and establishing a network of treatment centers

- Supporting scientific research into spirituality, creativity, and neuroscience

- Educating the public honestly about the risks and benefits of psychedelics and marijuana.

Why Give?
maps.org/donate

Your donation will help create a world where psychedelics and marijuana are available by prescription for medical uses, and where they can safely and legally be used for personal growth, creativity, and spirituality. Donations are tax-deductible as allowed by law, and may be made by credit card, or by personal check made out to MAPS. Gifts of stock are also welcome, and we encourage supporters to include MAPS in their will or estate plans (**maps.org/bequests**).

MAPS takes your privacy seriously. The MAPS email list is strictly confidential and will not be shared with other organizations. The *MAPS Bulletin* is mailed in a plain white envelope.

Sign up for our monthly email newsletter at **maps.org**.

MAPS
PO Box 8423, Santa Cruz CA 95061 USA
Phone: 831-429-MDMA (6362) • Fax: 831-429-6370
E-mail: **askmaps@maps.org**
Web: **maps.org | psychedelicscience.org**

MAPS-Published Books
maps.org/store

Ayahuasca Religions: A Comprehensive Bibliography & Critical Essays by Beatriz Caiuby Labate, Isabel Santana de Rose, and Rafael Guimarães dos Santos, translated by Matthew Meyer
ISBN: 978-0-9798622-1-2 $11.95

Drawing it Out by Sherana Harriet Francis
ISBN: 0-9669919-5-8 $19.95

Healing with Entactogens: Therapist and Patient Perspectives on MDMA-Assisted Group Psychotherapy by Torsten Passie, M.D.; foreword by Ralph Metzner, Ph.D.
ISBN: 0-9798622-7-2 $12.95

Honor Thy Daughter by Marilyn Howell, Ed.D.
ISBN: 0-9798622-6-4 $16.95

LSD: My Problem Child by Albert Hofmann, Ph.D. (4th English edition, paperback)
ISBN: 978-0-9798622-2-9 $15.95

LSD Psychotherapy by Stanislav Grof, M.D. (4th Edition, Paperback)
ISBN: 0-9798622-0-5 $19.95

Modern Consciousness Research and the Understanding of Art; including the Visionary World of H.R. Giger by Stanislav Grof, M.D.
ISBN: 0-9798622-9-9 $29.95

The Ketamine Papers: Science, Therapy, and Transformation edited by Phil Wolfson, M.D., and Glenn Hartelius, Ph.D.
ISBN: 0-9982765-0-2 $24.95

The Manual of Psychedelic Support: A Practical Guide to Establishing and Facilitating Care Services at Music Festivals and Other Events edited by Annie Oak, Jon Hanna, Kaya, Svea Nielsen, Twilight, and Zevic Mishor, Ph.D.
ISBN: 978-0998276519 $19.95

The Secret Chief Revealed by Myron Stolaroff
ISBN: 0-9660019-6-6 $12.95

The Ultimate Journey: Consciousness and the Mystery of Death by Stanislav Grof, M.D., Ph.D. (2nd edition)
ISBN: 0-9660019-9-0 $19.95

Shipping and Handling

Shipping varies by weight of books.

Bulk orders are welcome. Please contact MAPS for details.

Books can be purchased online by visiting **maps.org** (credit card or Paypal), over the phone by calling +1 831-429-MDMA (6362), or through your favorite local bookstore.

You may also send orders by mail to:

MAPS

P.O. Box 8423

Santa Cruz, CA, 95061

Phone: +1 831-429-MDMA (6362)

Fax: +1 831-429-6370

E-mail: **orders@maps.org**

Web: **maps.org**

About the Author

Stanislav Grof, M.D., Ph.D., is a psychiatrist with over sixty years of experience researching non-ordinary states of consciousness, and one of the founders and chief theoreticians of transpersonal psychology. He was born in Prague, Czechoslovakia, where he also received his scientific training, including his M.D. from the Charles University School of Medicine and his Ph.D. (Doctor of Philosophy in Medicine) from the Czechoslovakian Academy of Sciences. He was also granted honorary doctoral degrees from the University of Vermont in Burlington, Vermont, the Institute of Transpersonal Psychology in Palo Alto, California, the California Institute of Integral Studies (CIIS) in San Francisco, and the World Buddhist University in Bangkok, Thailand.

He conducted his early research at the Psychiatric Research Institute in Prague, where he was principal investigator of a program exploring the heuristic and therapeutic potential of LSD and other psychedelic substances. In 1967, he received a scholarship from the Foundations Fund for Research in Psychiatry in New Haven, Connecticut, and was invited to serve as Clinical and Research Fellow at Johns Hopkins University and the research unit of Spring Grove Hospital in Baltimore, Maryland.

In 1969, he became Assistant Professor of Psychiatry at Johns Hopkins University, and continued his research as Chief of Psychiatric Research at the Maryland Psychiatric Research Center in Catonsville, Maryland. In 1973, he was invited as Scholar-in-Residence to the Esalen Institute in Big Sur, California, where he developed, with his late wife Christina, Holotropic Breathwork, an innovative form of experiential psychotherapy that is now being used worldwide.

Dr. Grof was the founder of the International Transpersonal Association (ITA) and for several decades served as its president. In 1993, he received an Honorary Award from the Association for Transpersonal Psychology (ATP) for major contributions to and development of the field of transpersonal psychology, given at the occasion of the 25th Anniversary Convocation held in Asilomar, California. In 2007, he received the prestigious Vison 97 lifetime achievement award from the Foundation of Dagmar and Václav Havel in Prague, Czechoslovakia. In 2010, he received the Thomas R. Verny Award from the Association for Pre- and Perinatal Psychology and Health (APPPAH) for his pivotal contributions to the field. He was also invited as consultant for special effects in the science fiction films *Brainstorm* (MGM) and *Millenium* (20th Century Fox).

Among Dr. Grof's publications are over 160 articles in professional journals and many books, including *Realms of the Human Unconscious,* republished as *LSD: Gateway to the Numinous* (2009); *Beyond the Brain* (1985); *LSD Psychotherapy* (1978); *The Cosmic Game* (1990); *Psychology of the Future* (2000); *The Ultimate Journey* (2006); *When the Impossible Happens* (2006); *Books of the Dead* (1994); *Healing Our Deepest Wounds* (2012); *Modern Consciousness Research and the Understanding of Art* (2015); *The Call of the Jaguar* (2002); *Beyond Death* (1980); *The Stormy Search for the Self* (1990); *Spiritual Emergency* (1989); and *Holotropic Breathwork* (2010) (the last four with Christina Grof).

These books have been translated into twenty-two languages, including German, French, Italian, Spanish, Portuguese, Dutch, Swedish, Danish, Russian, Ukrainian, Slovenian, Romanian, Czech, Polish, Bulgarian, Hungarian, Latvian, Greek, Turkish, Korean, Japanese, and Chinese.

Since April 2016, he has been happily married to Brigitte Grof. They live together in Germany and California and travel the inner and outer worlds in tandem, conducting seminars and Holotropic Breathwork workshops worldwide.

His website is **stanislavgrof.com.**

Stanislav Grof, M.D., Ph.D.

The Way of the Psychonaut is a treasure trove of insights distilled from Stanislav Grof's long and distinguished career in psychedelic therapy and Holotropic Breathwork. This is a rich and comprehensive statement from a master clinician who has forever changed our understanding of our mind and the mind of the universe. Essential and wonderful reading.
—**Chris Bache, Ph.D.,** author of *Dark Night, Early Dawn; Lifecycles;* and *Living Classroom*

Future historians will describe the emergence of psychedelic compounds and plants in the mid-1960s as an event that radically changed psychology, psychiatry, and psychotherapy. It also sent shockwaves through Western culture, transforming lifestyles, worldviews, the arts, theoretical physics, technology, and the computer industry. If you think this is an exaggeration, read *The Way of the Psychonaut,* Stanislav Grof's well-crafted and beautifully written account of an era that may save humanity in spite of itself.
—**Stanley Krippner, Ph.D.,** Alan Watts Professor of Psychology, Saybrook University, Oakland, California

Stanislav Grof's *Way of the Psychonaut* is an odyssey through time, mind, consciousness, culture, psyche, politics, society, and cosmos that leaves one amazed—how can one man in one lifetime experience so much depth, delve into mysteries so passionately, and emerge so transformed and so clear about how to express the universalities of his experience to other seekers on the Path? Stan is a world treasure, his journey that of the new humanity.
—**Jim Garrison, Ph.D.,** founder of Ubiquity University

I consider Stanislav Grof to be a far out eclectic involved in transpersonal psychology, psychedelics, and scientific psychiatry as well as a very dear friend who has made significant contributions with his work.
—**Ram Dass**

Stanislav Grof is one of the great pioneers of consciousness research whose far-reaching explorations and wide-ranging syntheses have significantly expanded our view of the psyche and its potentials. You may not agree with all of his conclusions, but you certainly want to be aware of his work, which he skillfully summarizes in these volumes.
—**Roger Walsh, M.D., Ph.D.,** University of California, Irvine

Stanislav Grof has generated overwhelming evidence that the so-called impossible happens, and because it does, the world is different from what the dominant paradigm claims. Really different!
—**Robert McDermott,** President Emeritus, California Institute of Integral Studies (CIIS)